Journeys into Darkness

Studies in Supernatural Literature
Series Editor: S. T. Joshi

Titles in the Series

Journeys into Darkness

Critical Essays on Gothic Horror

James Goho

ROWMAN & LITTLEFIELD
Lanham • Boulder • New York • Toronto • Plymouth, UK

Published by Rowman & Littlefield
4501 Forbes Boulevard, Suite 200, Lanham, Maryland 20706
www.rowman.com

10 Thornbury Road, Plymouth PL6 7PP, United Kingdom

Copyright © 2014 by Rowman & Littlefield

British Library Cataloguing in Publication Information Available

Library of Congress Cataloging-in-Publication Data
Goho, James, 1946- author.
Journeys into darkness : critical essays on gothic horror / James Goho.
pages cm. -- (Studies in Supernatural Literature)
Includes bibliographical references and index.
ISBN 978-1-4422-3145-0 (cloth : alk. paper) -- ISBN 978-1-4422-3146-7 (electronic)
1. Horror tales, American--History and criticism. 2. Horror tales, English--History and criticism. 3. Gothic fiction (Literary genre), American--History and criticism. 4. Gothic fiction (Literary genre), English--History and criticism. I. Title.
PS374.H67G64 2014
813'.0873809--dc23
2013043655

∞ ™ The paper used in this publication meets the minimum requirements of American National Standard for Information Sciences Permanence of Paper for Printed Library Materials, ANSI/NISO Z39.48-1992.

Printed in the United States of America

For Pam

"Who ever lov'd, that lov'd not at first sight?"
Christopher Marlowe, *Hero and Leander*, 176

Contents

Acknowledgments

I want to thank the people who generously gave their time or counsel on this book. S. T. Joshi encouraged me to prepare the manuscript. He is a continuing source of wisdom on Gothic matters. I cannot say thanks enough to him. Several of the chapters in this book are revised from articles published in journals edited by Mr. Joshi. I also want to thank Jason V. Brock for his kind comments on and publishing of one of the essays. Thanks also to Jared Waters, of the wonderful Centipede Press, for publishing two of the essays. And thanks to Derrek Hussey of Hippocampus Press for publishing my essays on H. P. Lovecraft. The Winnipeg Millennium Library was instrumental in obtaining copies of difficult-to-access references through interlibrary loans. Jill Pascoe and Shaun Goho read the manuscript and provided valuable suggestions. Special thanks to both for their contributions. It is a much better book due to their help. Any errors or flaws in the book are mine alone. Of course, the real source of any inspiration there may be in this book is the Gothic authors; they are the creative source. And deepest thanks to Pam, who is always magical, for her countless hours helping on this book.

The publishing history of the original essays follows:

"The Haunted Wood: Algernon Blackwood's Canadian Stories." *Weird Fiction Review* no. 4 (2013).

"'The Outsider': A Sequel to 'The Fall of the House of Usher'?" *Nameless Digest* 1, no. 1 (2012): 99–115.

"Suffering and Evil in the Short Fiction of Arthur Machen." *Weird Fiction Review* no. 3 (2013): 57–84.

"The Aboriginal in the Works of H. P. Lovecraft." *Lovecraft Annual* no. 6 (2012): 54–75.

"What Is 'the Unnamable'? H. P. Lovecraft and the Problem of Evil." *Lovecraft Annual* no. 3 (2009): 10–52.

"The Sickness unto Death in H. P. Lovecraft's 'The Hound.'" *Lovecraft Annual* no. 2 (2008): 88–103.

Introduction

Literature tells the stories of a people, but Gothic literature tells the hidden stories of a people. Hidden because they tell darkly of dark things.[1] They look underneath beds, go into attics, wander through graveyards, and go deep down into cellars and caves. There is darkness in Gothic tales, the darkness of a forest, or a city, or in our houses, and in our heads. We are all afraid of the dark. The Gothic tells what terrifies people.

This book explores Gothic horror through the lenses of recognized masters in that literary genre. Charles Brockden Brown is the earliest American Gothic writer. His novels carved out a unique American Gothic and his themes and images are still found in recent horror fiction and film. There is something startlingly new in Brown; he unearths lasting American Gothic archetypes: the dark forest, a city ravaged by disease, the indigenous peoples as Gothic monsters, and the violence found in ordinary home settings. Edgar Allan Poe is the foremost Gothic short story artist. His stories repeatedly broke new ground and initiated new narrative readings. In this book, Poe's "The Fall of the House of Usher," the greatest of all haunted house stories, is hypothesized to be the precursor of one of H. P. Lovecraft's signature stories, "The Outsider." It seems that horror does breed its own offspring. Lovecraft is the twentieth century's Gothic master. He is the inspiration for so many horror writers. This book studies Lovecraft's "The Hound" in depth from the perspective of Søren Kierkegaard's *The Sickness unto Death*. As well, Lovecraft's use of the image of the aboriginal is traced across his fiction to reveal the centrality of it in his body of work. A third chapter on Lovecraft focuses on his keystone story, "The Unnamable." It is a fictionalized treatise on the art of horror narrative. But more so, it contains clues to guide us deep into the caverns of Lovecraft's ruminations on the problem of evil. In the Arthur Machen chapter, suffering and evil is the guiding principle in my review of

1

four of his greatest stories, written in the 1890s. The stories reveal the darkness shrouding the *fin de siècle* of the nineteenth century in England.

The forest is a dark place, but one also of solace for Algernon Blackwood. Here his Canadian stories are surveyed to understand their influence on his fiction writing and how the wood can be seen as both dangerous and full of awe. Many of Ambrose Bierce's stories take place in a forest. His American Civil War stories often show armies and individuals in woods, separated by an open field. Bierce is a keystone author within the Gothic horror tradition and a master of the short story form. He is the foremost writer about war and its effects on individuals. But he writes of the agony of individuals in crisis and chaos both in war and in peace.

The original Gothic arose as a sort of scream against the ruling order. It was a critique of a decadent society, reigned over by despotic royals, and lorded over by a hypocritical clergy. The prisons and hideous tortures of the Inquisition were real; the ravine between the rich and poor was unbridgeable. The traditional European Gothic can be thought of as an expression of rebellion against perverse power. It illuminated a decadent social edifice for what it really was: violent in enforcing a rigid social order, and oppressive against the poor, women, and outsiders. And more, there is a deep dread in the Gothic, a terror in the soul, as Poe would say, of an ultimate void. No name can be given to real dread. Great Gothic gives readers an experience of an unexplainable dread.

The American Gothic is different from the European in its topography, with the wilderness and frontier as Gothic spaces, and the indigenous peoples of America transformed into Gothic monsters. Slavery as well is part of the darkness at the heart of the American Gothic. Another recurring image is the witch, rising up from the 1692 Salem horror. The penultimate chapter traces the witch archetype from Salem through recent American films. The book concludes with a survey of Fritz Leiber's urban Gothic. He reanimated the Gothic by taking horror into ordinary settings, especially the modern city, which seems to spawn its own terror. A city not only will break your heart; a city will cut your throat. His works are also a sociological critique of aspects of modern life in a mechanized and marketing-focused society. But underneath it all, Leiber writes about the fragility of humans in a cosmos of indifference at best and perhaps of fierce hostility. Not only does Leiber speak to urban social anxieties and despairs, he triggers our fundamental dread.

There are several themes woven throughout the essays. One is the urban Gothic, starting with Brown, seen in Machen and Lovecraft, and realized in Leiber; another is the wilderness as a dangerous Gothic space in Brown, Lovecraft, and Algernon Blackwood. A third theme is understanding Gothic literature, in part, as a manifestation of economic, social, and political anxieties and conflicts, which is found in Brown, Bierce, and Leiber most explicitly. A fourth notion is Gothic horror as giving a voice to those who suffer, those who experience evil. This stands out in Brown's *Wieland* and *Arthur Mervyn*, and Bierce's short fiction takes place in a realm of suffering. The suffering and sacrifice of women is told in Machen's four stories and also in the chapter on witchcraft. A common theme in the chapters is that Gothic horror narrative is about dread, about a primal fear and an ontological unease in the world. It expresses an ineluctable encounter with the invisible. Every Gothic writer goes into that darkness, especially Poe. But the Gothic is not escapism. It liberates what is hidden.

NOTE

1. See Judith Wilt, *Ghosts of the Gothic: Austen, Eliot and Lawrence* (Princeton, NJ: Princeton University Press, 1980), 6.

Chapter One

Dark Beginnings

*Fear and Trembling in the Novels of
Charles Brockden Brown*

The film *World War Z* (2013) opens with Gerry Lane (Brad Pitt) making breakfast for his wife and two daughters. It is a domestic, happy scene—in harsh contrast to the coming horrors on the streets of Philadelphia. In the city, Gerry stops the family Volvo in a traffic-clogged street. There are sirens and police, an explosion, people running in panic, and then the speed demon zombies crash through car windshields to get at the occupants. Gerry finds a way out of the mayhem. Philadelphia is a city in chaos, rampant with the zombie epidemic. The population is fleeing the city, all the streets are night-mares, people fight for food and water, and they attack each other. They try to barricade themselves away from the disease, mostly to no avail.[1]

Charles Brockden Brown's (1771–1810) novel *Arthur Mervyn*[2] (1799–1800) also depicts Philadelphia as a city in chaos, ravaged by disease, bodies on the streets, people fleeing the city and those left behind afraid of everyone and everything. It is a nightmare city. Yellow fever is the cause.[3] The protagonist of the novel, Arthur Mervyn, goes into the cursed city. The fever has transformed Philadelphia into a city of chaos, near barbarity, and revulsion. The "malady was malignant, and unsparing" and "terror had exter-minated all sentiments"[4] among residents. Corpses were everywhere. Mer-vyn is horrified by the devastation; at one point he is nearly crated up in a coffin as if dead. He sees the wealthy fleeing while the poor try to survive not only the disease, but also hunger, and the growing hostility of all.

J. H. Powell says *Arthur Mervyn* and Brown's *Ormond* (1799) are the "greatest of all literary monuments to the plague of 1793."[5] They are not historical accounts but depict "the plague in all its grim and fantastic sense-

5

lessness."[6] Brown uses the incident of the actual plague for his novel, but *Arthur Mervyn* is a Gothic fiction of what happens in a city assailed by an unknown and senseless assailant. It is horror in an urban setting. Jeffrey Andrew Weinstock argues that Brockden Brown "pioneered the Urban Gothic."[7] In *Arthur Mervyn*, yellow fever is a fulcrum for Gothic fiction. The novel portrays what happens to people and their interrelationships in the face of a horrid pestilence. Seemingly there is no cure and no end. For many there is no escape. Leslie Fiedler suggests that Brown's archetype for human fate is a city under the plight of plague.[8] This is also the theme of Daniel Dafoe's *A Journal of the Plague Year* (1722). But the city as a zone of horror is just one theme in Brown's novels.

Not only did Brown create the American Urban Gothic, but he created the American Gothic as a whole. It is a dark fiction. Richard Chase argues that Brown's novels forecast much that is worthy in Poe, Hawthorne, Melville, Faulkner, and Henry James.[9] In Brown's novels, characters experience the extremes of fear and trembling. Here, three of Brown's novels are explored: *Wieland*[10] (1798), *Arthur Mervyn*, and *Edgar Huntly* (1799). The intent is to capture the nature of his Gothic vision. Fred Botting suggests that in *Wieland* Brown drew "a new and different darkness" arising from the "delusion inspired by religion."[11] With *Edgar Huntly*, Brown shifts the Gothic from European manor houses and evil aristocrats to the wilderness of Pennsylvania and the deep fear of the indigenous peoples. Brown's novels are diverse. With them, he creates the key American Gothic figures, themes, and landscapes. There is the dangerous wilderness. Cities are breeding grounds for disease, despair, and death. Houses seem always haunted but perhaps because the mind itself is a haunted space. Brown did start the American Gothic, but there are some American sources for his Gothic vision, and traces of his dark vision are found in the later American Gothic.

Reading Brown, one feels that there is something new in the writing, as if Brown has caught the spirit of a place. He originated iconic American Gothic figures, themes, and landscapes that keep reappearing in the American Gothic. Eric Savoy contends that one of Brown's lasting achievements was to center American Gothic in a pathology of a present that "witnesses the unfolding and fulfillment of terrible destinies incipient in the American past."[12] The plague in Philadelphia mirrors the epidemics that ravaged indigenous populations.[13]

Brown writes about the darkness and forbidding nature of the new lands for Europeans. He writes how the beliefs and actions of the newcomers interacted with their new environment and the indigenous population. In part, Brown sets the landscape as a source of terror. In *Edgar Huntly*, the shape of darkness is in the dark wood. The wilderness seems to be a character in itself and nearly sentient, at least in how it influences the acts of Brown's characters. Yet houses, as in *Wieland*, are also sets for terror either within a family, or fired by plague as in *Arthur Mervyn*, or the intrusion of the seemingly alien American Indians in *Edgar Huntly*. Moreover, the symbol of civilization, the city, degenerates to barbarity in *Arthur Mervyn*. There is no escape.

Charles Brockden Brown was born in Philadelphia, Pennsylvania, in 1771 into a Quaker family. At that time Philadelphia was the thirteen colonies' main political and intellectual center.[14] He grew up in a time of revolution and upheaval in America. His father, although sympathetic to the revolution, was a pacifist and was jailed for a brief period. In 1787 Brown began a law apprenticeship in Philadelphia. From an early age, he was interested in literature and writing. He often traveled between New York City and Philadelphia. He moved to New York in 1798 but returned to Philadelphia in 1800 to work in the family business. Brown wrote his four Gothic novels in eighteen months in 1798 and 1799—a rush of creativity. Fiedler points outs that although the novels were critically acclaimed, they did not sell.[15] Back in Philadelphia, he wrote two prosaic novels, *Clara Howard* and *Jane Talbot*, in 1801. Brown died in 1810 of tuberculosis.[16]

Brown's fiction is linked to European models such as William Godwin's *Caleb Williams* (1794),[17] but differs in images, themes, and topography.[18] His novels depict family disintegration and individual disintegration through collisions with the uncanny. The novels are violent, full of personality disorders, and redolent with nightmare scenes where the characters drift away from rationality to madness. He draws a hallucinatory Gothic landscape, which subsequent writers roamed. Edgar Allan Poe expressed his admiration for Brown.[19] Donald A. Ringe finds that Nathaniel Hawthorne admired Brown, as did others, such as James Fenimore Cooper, John Greenleaf Whittier, and Margaret Fuller.[20] H. P. Lovecraft extolls the importance of Brown's novels for the development of the American Gothic.[21]

WIELAND, OR THE LOSS OF UTOPIA

Peter Kafer boldly asserts that at "the age of twenty-seven Charles Brockden Brown invented the American Gothic novel"[22] with *Wieland*. Kafer also traces parallels between *Wieland* and Stephen King's *The Shining* (1977). Both take place in a wilderness setting. In each, the protagonist transforms from family man to killer after hearing voices telling him to kill. As well, both novels have an innocent woman as victim, and both have internal premonitions of the horrors to come later.[23] Brown's influence was long lived. Alan Axelrod says Brown "has long haunted American literature as a ghostly presence."[24] Kafer suggests that Brown's influence, in part, is due to his unique "Gothic imagination to sense the dark histories already weighing down the American republic."[25]

Similar to *Arthur Mervyn*, *Wieland* is founded in part on reality, but again Brown transforms the reality into high American Gothic. Axelrod identifies the reality as James Yates's slaughter of his wife and four children in 1781 in Tomhannock, New York. Yates claimed a good angel enjoined him to destroy all idols. He killed his two sons in his house. In a fury, he chased down his daughter, wife, and baby, who had fled. He smashed the baby against a log. He trailed his wife and daughter back to his homestead, where he killed his wife ferociously and chopped his daughter's head in two with a hatchet.[26] This was a gruesome and highly publicized case in the late eighteenth and early nineteenth centuries. Brown notes this in his "Advertisement" to *Wieland*: "most readers will probably recollect an authentic case, remarkably similar to that of Wieland."[27] This might have been Brown's source for the critical event, but his novel is more than a retelling of a frightful crime.

In the novel, religious fanaticism seems to conjure voices, voices that direct domestic violence and murder. Although Brown grew up as a Quaker, *Wieland* seems suffused with Puritan paranoia. In this Gothic tale, religion breeds horror the way castles and dungeons did in the traditional European Gothic.

Clara Wieland, whose father was a religious fanatic, narrates the book. The elder Wieland immigrated to America to "convert the savage tribes" (12) to his unique brand of religion. This religion is reified in his garden temple of worship, later converted into a summerhouse. The elder Wieland fails in his conversion mission and fails his god. One night there is a burst of flame in the temple as the elder Wieland prays. It may be self-combustion or perhaps divine intervention.

After his death, his son, Theodore, and daughter, Clara, inherit the Mettingen estate in Pennsylvania. Theodore marries Catherine Pleyel and they have four children. He and Clara have separate houses on the estate. The Mettingen estate is a sort of utopia, for a spell, where the Wielands and the Pleyels (including Catherine's brother Henry, whom Clara secretly loves) discuss philosophy within an insular familiarity filled with happiness and ease. Their houses are sanctuaries of rationality until Francis Carwin, the ventriloquist, intrudes. He is the mystery behind many of the disembodied voices in the novel, although he claims never to have told Theodore to kill. In the novel, the utopia disintegrates and Mettingen becomes a scene of terror.

Early in *Wieland*, Theodore says he has heard Catherine's voice from the former temple while she was really at home. It is an omen of dread. When Clara hears her brother tell this, she is spooked. She muses on her fear about her brother's experience:

> I could not bear to think that his senses should be the victims of such delusion.
> It argued a diseased condition of his frame, which might show itself hereafter
> in more dangerous symptoms. The will is the tool of the understanding, which

must fashion its conclusions on the notices of sense. If the senses be depraved, it is impossible to calculate the evils that may flow from the consequent deductions of the understanding. (33)

Clara fears depravity is creeping into their happy enclave. She grasps hesitantly that rationality may be crumbling around her, that her world of reason and order is about to be overturned. Underneath it all is a savagery; reason is not able to overcome the dread creeping into the ordinary. Brown's characters act in an unknown space, a Gothic space.

Clara's house is not safe. It becomes a haunted place, ringing with disembodied voices. She broods "darkness suited the color of my thoughts" (147) while plagued by intangible voices. She "is tormented by phantoms" (69). Her "fears" were imaged in part as a "hand invisible and of preternatural strength" (70–71). She hears a shriek, and it acts on her "nerves like an edge of steel" (71). She is in terror at the voices in her room; she is "overpowered by horror" (75). There is someone hiding in her closet. When the door finally swings open, the person inside "was shrouded in darkness" (73). It turns out to be Carwin, whom she fears intends to rape her. But Carwin departs, believing he has heard a voice protecting Clara. During the entire ninth chapter, Clara repeatedly expresses her fear, anguish, and terror at the voices. She vividly imagines their source and what will happen to her in the room. As Clive Bloom says, the Gothic portrays "the passions of fear and torment."[28]

Theodore Wieland is pictured at first as an upstanding family man. But, as if inheriting his father's mania, he is transformed by "voices" into a killer, who slaughters his wife and children and their ward, Louisa Conway, believing he has been divinely commanded. His house becomes a scene of death. He also breaks out of jail three times and tries to kill Clara. Clara is overwhelmed by fear and trembling in her brother's house when he tries to kill her, but Carwin uses a voice to stop him.[29] When he realizes his delusion, Wieland takes up a knife, plunging "it to the hilt in his neck; and his life instantly escaped with the stream that gushed from the wound" (173). It is as if another had overtaken him and now he had to kill that thing. Clara anguishes: "The world of men was shrouded in misery and blood, and constituted a loathsome spectacle" (140).

After Theodore kills himself, Clara retreats to her house for safety. This proves an illusion. There, she is tormented by visions of being "swallowed up by whirlpools, or caught up in the air by half-seen and gigantic forms and thrown upon pointed rocks" (177). She stands upon a "dark abyss" (177). She imagines she is at the edge of a volcano with its "fiery torrents and its pillars of smoke" (177). Then she realizes her house is ablaze but she cannot move, she is trapped, "scorched by heat and nearly choaked by the accumulating vapours" (177). No house is safe. Is she to replay her father's fiery death? No, Clara is rescued as the house burns to the ground.

The darkness in this novel is cast by a deformed religious delusion. It is a tale of the breakdown of utopia. It is an account of the derangement of a family. The elder Wieland seems to hover ominously over the novel. Into the peaceable kingdom of Mettingen comes the voice-stealing Carwin, who is the spark for the Gothic contagion. He unleashes the evil that hides in the lush landscape. This is the heritage of isolation, guilt, violence, and repression, which is the darkness at the heart of American Gothic. There is no safety, no utopia. No reasoning will overcome the madness latent in the Wielands, and no safety is to be found in their homes. All homes are haunted.

But more so it seems the minds of Theodore and Clara are haunted. Nicolas Abraham elaborates a theory of "the phantom," as a sort of intergenerational haunting. It is the return of a family's repressed secret to subsequent generations. It is a secret buried in the tomb of the unconscious that passes from a parent's unconscious into a child's. Abraham writes, the "phantom's periodic and compulsive return . . . works like a ventriloquist, like a stranger within the subject's own mental topography."[30] This seems an apt description of what transpires in *Wieland*.

The voices whispering to Theodore and Clara speak from their own heads. They reenact, sometimes in a distorted manner, past events in their family's history, with an unknowing awareness of a family secret. The secret is, why did their maternal grandfather fling himself off a cliff; what had he done? In her fear, Clara repeats his standing on an abyss, but she does not leap, even in her reverie. This novel is about a phantom haunting a family; as Abraham posits, "what haunts are not the dead, but the gaps left within us by the secrets of others."[31]

ARTHUR MERVYN, OR THE DEPRAVED CITY

Houses also breed disease and corruption in *Arthur Mervyn*. Brown transforms a real event, the yellow fever epidemic in 1793, into the Gothic. The disease is a terror and it seems to augur the collapse of society and a moral regression of the populace. As Weinstock argues, Brown was the first writer who "Gothicizes the city experience."[32] In *Arthur Mervyn*, the yellow fever stalks every house and everyone. On the streets, Mervyn sees only a few people and they "were ghost-like, wrapt in cloaks, from behind which they cast upon me glances of wonder and suspicion; and, as I approached, changed their course, to avoid touching me" (356).

Death threatens all, and as nearly happens to Arthur Mervyn, one could be collected as dead and sealed up in a coffin alive. An unnerving scene occurs when Mervyn is searching a house for a friend. He looks into a mirror

and believes he sees an apparition nearing. He turns and is knocked uncon-
scious. Coming to, he finds two men about to nail him in a coffin. Two
themes that resound throughout the American Gothic appear here. The first,
premature burial, appears in Edgar Allan Poe's "The Fall of the House of
Usher" (1839) and "The Cask of Amontillado" (1846), and, more recently, in
Ramsey Campbell's "Digging Deep" (2007). Mirrors also appear in the
Gothic, for example, Hawthorne's "Monsieur du Miroir" (1837), Lovecraft's
"The Outsider" (1921), and Fritz Leiber's "Midnight in the Mirror World"
(1964).

In the yellow fever–ravaged city, death is near for everyone. Even the
living appear dead. Mervyn sees "an apparition of the dead." It was "yellow-
ish and livid; bones, uncovered with flesh; eyes, ghastly, hollow, woe-
begone . . . and locks, matted and negligent" (380). It seems a zombie, the
walking dead.

The hospital at Bushhill is not a place of solace for the sick but a house of
horrors. The hospital ward is filled with stinking beds: "Each sustained a
wretch, whose groans and distortions, bespoke the desperateness of his condition. The atmosphere was loaded by mortal stenches" (386). The afflicted
are soon to join the dead. The sick "in this scene of horrors [hear] the sound
of laughter. . . . While the upper rooms of this building, are filled with the
sick and the dying, the lower apartments are the scene of carrousals and
mirth" (386). The caregivers who were paid to comfort the sick were "bloat-
ed with malignity and drunkenness" (386).

The hospital is a scene of horror, and the "misery was more frightful,
because it was seen to flow from the depravity of the attendants" (387). A
coffin is thrown down and a "wretch, whose heart still quivered, was seized
by rude hands, and dragged along the floor into the passage" (387). Brown
writes that to avoid this "wickedness so enormous" many crawl away "to die
in garrets and cellars and stables, unvisited and unknown" (387).

There is a "train of horrors" (363) deadening the city. The city itself is
dying. Brown's novel *Ormond* also depicts Philadelphia in its death throes:
"Every day added to the devastations and confusions of the city. The most
populous streets were deserted and silent. . . . No carriage but the hearse was
seen."[33] The only sounds were the "shrieks and laments of survivors, who
could not be prevented from attending the remains of a husband or child to
the place of interment . . . [and] urged by a furious delirium, the sick would
break from their attendants, rush into the streets, and expire on the pavement,
amidst frantic outcries and gestures" (82). But then the fear may be so great
that one struggles for "shrieks, but [is] incapable of uttering a sound" (212).
Brown depicts the cityscape of Philadelphia as transforming into a space of
deception and deceit among the inhabitants and a deepening depravity as the
fever gnaws at the sense of community or fellow-feeling in the city.

There is more than one contagion in the city. It is a city where homes are chalked with death symbols. It is a city of smoky streets nearly all deserted except for hungry, orphaned children wailing for dead parents. As the death toll rises, hysteria grows, leading to suicide. Death carts roll toward mass graves. In this mayhem, thieves lurk in the shadows and charlatans hawk fake cures. In this poisonous city, people are depraved. Philadelphia becomes a city of death and looting.

The scenes of desolated streets and people barricaded in their homes are still common images in post-apocalyptic films, for example, *28 Days Later* (2002), which depicts a plague-desolated London. A man-made virus "rage" has infected the populace, turning them into red-eyed killers. The zombies in this movie are on fast-forward.[34]

Brown himself experienced plague. He nearly died in New York City in 1798.

In this novel, the disease is like a malignant thing overwhelming the populace and changing the city from a place of safety to one of peril, from rationality to madness, from community to lawlessness. It is a city in ruin, dangerous to its inhabitants. This becomes the theme for modern urban horror writers, such as Fritz Leiber and Ramsey Campbell.

EDGAR HUNTLY, OR THE AMERICAN INDIAN AS GOTHIC MONSTER

The American landscape is a source of terror in *Edgar Huntly*. The shape of darkness in this novel comes from the wilderness of Pennsylvania. With this novel, Weinstock claims, Brown established the "haunted American wilderness as an archetype of American Gothic."[35] Brown was clearly separating the American Gothic from the traditional European Gothic of Walpole and Radcliffe. Brown's purpose in the novel was "to exhibit a series of adventures, growing out of the condition of the country."[36] In *Edgar Huntly*, Brown states the break in his "Note to the Public," insisting Americans should not use "puerile superstition and exploded manners, Gothic castles and chimeras" but rather "the incidents of Indian hostility, and the perils of the Western wilderness" (4). Indeed, the novel enacts the break with the European Gothic in its structure. Its first twelve chapters center on Clithero, with much of the action in Ireland, while the final twelve chapters focus on Huntly in the wilderness and his conflict with the Lenni Lenape, or Delawares. The Gothic monster in this book is not a monk or a count but the American Indian, *The Demon of the Continent*, as is the title of a recent book by Joshua David Bellin. He argues the conflict between American Indians and European invaders is at the core of American literature.[37]

In the Norwalk wilds of Pennsylvania, the Delawares are portrayed as "brawny and terrific figures" (115), "savage" (119), with "gigantic form and fantastic ornaments" (117). They are Gothic monsters. The Delawares are said to raid and massacre white settlements, sometimes carrying off young women, who would face "a fate worse than death; to gratify the innate and insatiable cruelty of savages by suffering all the torments their invention can suggest" (155), a common theme in the American nightmare. Part of this narrative is that Huntly's parents had been killed in an Indian assault. His encounter with the Delawares in the wilds is nearly a revenge tale.

Early Puritan accounts depicted the indigenous peoples as brutes and savages. An example is found in *Of Plymouth Plantation*, the journal of William Bradford (1590–1657), a leader and governor of the Plymouth colony. He kept the journal from 1630 to about 1650.[38] Bradford writes that the land where the pilgrims settled was "some of those vast and unpeopled countries of America, which are fruitful and fit for habitation, being devoid of all civil inhabitants, where there are only savages and brutish men, which range up and down, little otherwise then the wild beasts of the same."[39] Another example prior to Brown's novel is Mary Rowlandson's 1682 account of a raid on Lancaster, Massachusetts, in 1675, during the so-called King Philip's War. She was captured and eventually escaped. She describes American Indians brutally killing people in the town. She calls her captors "a company of hell-hounds, roaring, singing, ranting,"[40] as if they are demons. In 1702, Cotton Mather also contributed to the American tradition of white women's captivity stories in "A Notable Exploit: wherein, Dux Faemina Facti." He tells of the capture of Hannah Dustan in 1697 and her subsequent escape from and slaying of the Abenaki "Salvages," "furious Tawnies," "raging Dragons."[41] Mather uses a string of racist terms. Dustan scalped the "Ten Wretches" and earned "Fifty Pounds."[42] William S. Simmons suggests the Puritans' belief that the indigenous people were in league with the devil gave them "a rationale for destruction or enslavement of entire populations in war."[43]

After an episode of sleepwalking (of which Huntly is unaware until later in the novel), he finds himself in a cavern in total darkness, a pit.[44] His "thoughts were wildering and mazy" (107). It seems the spirit of the wilderness captures him. His mind mirrors the labyrinthine system of caves where he finds himself. Trapped underground in "utter darkness" (108), Huntly muses: "Sometimes I imagined myself buried alive" (109). He is terrified in the darkness, not knowing where he is or how he got there. In his struggle to escape he moves to a higher cave where "the darkness was no less intense than in the pit below, and yet two objects were distinctly seen. They resembled a fixed and obscure flame. They were motionless. . . . These were the eyes of a panther" (111). He kills the panther, drinks its blood, and eats it raw, very much like an initiation rite into barbarism.

Searching for a way out of the pit, he comes upon a cave in which Delawares are holding captive a young white woman. Most are asleep. After killing the guard, Huntly manages to release the young woman and they flee to an old cabin. The remaining Delawares appear at the cabin and Huntly, who at first bore no weapons, ends up killing all three, leaving a "field of blood" (129). After the battle, Huntly passes out. Awakening, Huntly cannot find the young woman. He leaves the scene, abandoning the bodies unburied in the forest. In the forest, he encounters yet another Delaware and wounds him with a shot. Then, with supposed sympathy, Huntly bayonets him, taking away a prize, the slain Delaware's "Tom-hawk" (134). The mighty Euro-American overcomes the demons of the wood. In the novel, Huntly's killings are on-stage while those attributed to the Delawares are off-stage. The Indians are all inarticulate brutes, seemingly, like the panther. Huntly turns out to be an apt name; he is able to "cut the sinews of a cat-o'mountain, at the distance of sixty feet" with a "Tom-hawk" (84). He has incredible mastery of the "Indians' ways" of killing and hunting, so much so that he overpowers them. This prowess comes from his rebirth journey through the dark cave. Huntly is perhaps the first frontier hero rescuing a maiden from Indians and avenging Indian massacres.

If a Euro-American ventures into the forest wilderness, he becomes feral. This is part of the danger of the wilderness. J. Hector St. John de Crèvecoeur, in *Letters from an American Farmer* (1782), sees the wilderness, the frontier, as dangerous. He suggests the dark wood changes those who live in it; "they grow up a mongrel breed, half civilized, half savage."[45] This is echoed in Roderick Frazier Nash's study of the effects of the wilderness on early settlers. It is true that the forest was a source of terror, but it was also a source of freedom, a freedom "for men to behave in a savage or bestial manner."[46] Roger B. Salomon says the frontier in America is the "place for an encounter with some terrible Other."[47] In Brown's novel, it is the American Indian.

The episodes in the wilds are told virtually as a modern thriller with hair's-breadth escapes. The character Clithero in the novel is the double to Huntly. Both are sleepwalkers, both killers, and both go into the wilderness. Brown's novel deploys not only the Gothic theme of the double, but also the journey through a wild land and being trapped in dark constricted spaces. In *Edgar Huntly*, caves are Clithero's and Huntly's haunts, natural Gothic spaces of darkness. As well, the houses in this novel are not safe. In one scene a Delaware passes, like a ghost, through Huntly's room, as he lies on the bed, and then leaps out the window back into the wilderness. Here, the fear of the wilderness is portrayed as invading one's safest, most private places. Clara, the narrator of *Wieland*, is also haunted in her bedroom. Houses and settlements on the frontier were isolated and vulnerable so near the wilderness.

Salomon writes: "Americans have always had the wilderness that lurked beyond the settlements."[48] Brown wrote first about the dangers lurking in that wilderness, but its horrors continue to be evoked. For example, in M. Night Shyamalan's *The Village* (2004), a dense forest encircles the village of Covington. In the opening credits the trees are shown black and stark against a gray sky. They are dark bones of tall skeletal sentinels, keeping the villagers out. It defines the limits of the world for the villagers. The forest is the territory of monsters: "those we do not speak of."[49] At first the villagers seem to be living in the late nineteenth century, but it turns out that it is a modern hideout for people trying to escape urban violence, as if anyone can escape into the past, a haunt of the Gothic. The elders control the other villagers by using the deep fear of the forest and what may lurk in it. But there are no real monsters here. Ivy, who is blind and the heroine of the film, is told this in the "old shed not to be used." What are out there are elders dressed as forest monsters. They don red cloaks and bony claws, as if distorted American Indians, inciting another deep-seated fear. There is even a sense of Puritan fundamentalism in the movie mixed with the back-to-the-earth movement. The elders set up the village to escape their personal horrors in the city. The village is in the heart of a nature reserve. They want to protect innocence, but the village falls prey to internal violence, not an intrusion from the wood. Teresa A. Goddu argues that the American Gothic exposes the American myth of New World innocence. She says that the Gothic tells of historical horrors, such as "the violent origins of the nation in Indian massacre,"[50] in fictionalized form. Brown's *Edgar Huntly* was the first. Charles L. Crow argues that the Gothic "patrols the line between . . . living and dead."[51] This is part of the meaning of frontier. American literature is a literature at the frontier. In *Edgar Huntly*, Brown illuminates the darkness at the heart of America, largely ignored or overwritten; the real frontier in America was a killing field.

CHARLES BROCKDEN BROWN'S AMERICAN GOTHIC

H. P. Lovecraft praised Charles Brockden Brown's "uncanny atmospheric power" and his ability to describe "some memorably frightful scenes."[52] Brown's fiction paints a hellish world of sleepwalkers, commanding voices, violence in the wilderness, insanity, and disease. In *Edgar Huntly*, Brown sets the source of terror, the shape of darkness, in the dark forest. The wilderness, almost sentient, seems to orchestrate the actions of Huntly, as he transforms into a savage. The wilderness is a Gothic space, shrouded in darkness, booby-trapped with pits and cliffs, and home to Gothic monsters.[53] In *Wieland*, the Gothic ascends from religious fanaticism. It leads to madness and horror in peaceable estates and murder in homes, all passed down from a temple of a fire deity. Eventually the Gothic is found within the self. Weinstock suggests Brown was the first to develop the psychological Gothic. In *Wieland*, Clara is depicted as if she has a haunted mind. Much of the narration is like a strange film playing in her head. She lives in a mindscape of fear and trembling. In *Arthur Mervyn*, the city is transformed into a nightmare. What Brown unearthed was horror in a city under the sway of disease and corruption. It descends into madness, violence, and death, nearly as if the cityscape itself is the cause. Later, the city as the source of horror is most explicitly advanced in Fritz Leiber, for example in *Our Lady of Darkness*, or in many of Ramsey Campbell's stories.

Brown's novels are diverse. He created iconic American Gothic figures, themes, and landscapes. This new world of America is full of horrors. In the wilds there are savage indigenous peoples and wild animals. Yet in the face of these external horrors, the city, the home, the family, and even the self are not safe havens. *Edgar Huntly* most directly addresses those external fears, while *Arthur Mervyn* addresses the city, *Wieland* the home and family, and *Edgar Huntly* then returns to the self. If a Euro-American goes into the forest, he becomes nearly feral, as happens to Edgar Huntly. Religion, as in *Wieland*, calls forth punishment and death such as that delivered by Theodore Wieland to his wife and children—"as a sacrifice,"[54] notes Lovecraft. In *Arthur Mervyn*, the urban landscape is pested by yellow fever into a wasteland of horror. Philadelphia seems inhabited by the dead. The living are on borrowed time, and the coffins are outside the door, or rolling by in the streets. Arthur's experience in the city is one of a Gothic city of "phantoms and pestilence,"[55] as Goddu says. There is no safe place.

Brown defined the spaces and themes of the American Gothic. There is the wilderness, there is the haunted built environment, be it houses or cities, and there is the mind itself as a deranged and haunted space. Brown developed archetypes of fear: fear of the primitive (or what is deemed to be the primitive), and fear of the forest. In a city, one fears contagion from others, as if they are alien. In *Wieland*, fear is everywhere, of one's own family and perhaps of oneself.

Brown's novels (especially *Arthur Mervyn*) present a near incoherence in style and plot, which Goddu claims is a hallmark of the Gothic as a distorting picture of reality. Crow also sees Brown, "America's first Gothic master," as experimenting with "ambiguity and narrative unreliability."[56] Ringe uses nearly the same language, claiming that Brown "retains an aura of ambiguity and uncertainty right to the end."[57] Beverly Lyon Clark thinks that Brown's ambiguity "anticipates . . . contemporary writers like Pynchon [in] *Gravity's Rainbow*."[58] In *Wieland*, some of the events are never clearly defined, perhaps because they are viewed through Clara's mind. Arthur Mervyn says his "behaviour . . . was ambiguous and hazardous" (522). Arthur Mervyn is a strange hero, sometimes portrayed, at least by himself, as an innocent in a world of deceivers, but then it seems that he always manages to survive while others may not. In addition, *Arthur Mervyn*, as a book, is written in a manner that illustrates the plague distorting the narration, as if it spreads, so to speak, from character to author to reader. Some of the explorations of Mervyn in the city are nearly hallucinogenic, and very confusing to read.

The American darkness is different from that in traditional European Gothic. The dark past comes from the unique circumstances of America. Europeans colonized it with a fierce and stern religion. The colonies revolted against European domination. The settlers dominated and virtually exterminated the indigenous people, continuously moving the frontier across the country. They created a slave society and fought a civil war to end it. And America built an empire. Reading American Gothic literature is akin to reading the buried history of America. It is a literature that unearths what society wants to keep buried, hidden in attics, locked in cellars, or killed in forests. American Gothic is clearly founded on a tradition of fear of the wild land, the vanquished peoples, and the corrupting influence of cities. Crow argues that the American Gothic "has given voice to suppressed groups"[59] —groups who may have been denied a voice. Brown started this.

Charles Brockden Brown made the major themes of the American Gothic from the very history of the nation, but perhaps for one. Toni Morrison argues that slavery shaped American literature and is the source of the "darkness from which our early literature seemed unable to extricate itself."[60] An early example is found in Crèvecoeur's *Letters from an American Farmer*, where James makes a gruesome discovery in the forest. There "a Negro [was] suspended in a cage and left there to expire! . . . the birds had already picked out his eyes . . . from the edges of the hollow sockets and from the lacerations with which he was disfigured, the blood slowly dropped."[61] Albert E. Stones, in his introduction to *Letters from an American Farmer*, claims that "American literature, as the voice of our national consciousness,"[62] started with this book, originally published in 1782. Literature is the voice of a nation's consciousness and spirit. The Gothic in America gives voice, often in a disfigured and threatening fashion, to those displaced by the nation, to the anxieties of the nation, and to the fears of the nation. Charles Brockden Brown founded this tradition.

NOTES

1. *World War Z*, film, directed by Marc Forster (Hollywood, CA: Paramount, 2013).
2. The complete title of the novel is *Arthur Mervyn; or, Memoirs of the Year 1793*.
3. Philadelphia suffered a real yellow fever epidemic in 1793. This was the first major American yellow fever epidemic and it devastated the city. Five thousand out of a population of 55,000 died. It is estimated that another 17,000 fled the city. See J. J. Powell, *Bring Out Your Dead: The Great Plague of Yellow Fever in Philadelphia in 1793* (Philadelphia: University of Philadelphia Press, 1993), x and xviii.

4. Charles Brockden Brown, *Arthur Mervyn; or Memoirs of the Year 1793*, in *Three Gothic Novels* (New York: Library of America, 1998), 346. Hereafter cited in the text.

5. Powell, *Bring Out Your Dead*, 283.

6. Powell, *Bring Out Your Dead*, 284. "Panic was as contagious as sickness," according to Powell, *Bring Out Your Dead*, 103.

7. Jeffrey Andrew Weinstock, *Charles Brockden Brown* (Cardiff: University of Wales Press, 2011), 54.

8. Leslie Fiedler, *Love and Death in the American Novel* (New York: Criterion, 1960), 133.

9. Richard Chase, *The American Novel and Its Tradition* (Baltimore: John Hopkins University Press, 1980), 37.

10. The complete title is *Wieland; or, The Transformation*.

11. Fred Botting, *Gothic* (London: Routledge, 1996), 116.

12. Eric Savoy, "The Rise of American Gothic," in *The Cambridge Guide to Gothic Fiction*, ed. Jerrold E. Hogle (Cambridge: Cambridge University Press, 2002), 174.

13. The epidemic of 1616–1618 took "seventy-five percent of the coastal Algonquin population" in southern New England, according to Daniel K. Richter, *Facing East from Indian Country* (Cambridge, MA: Harvard University Press, 2001), 60. A later smallpox epidemic was deadly in southern New England, with some Native communities entirely wiped out; see Kathleen J. Bragdon, *Native People of Southern New England, 1500–1650* (Norman: University of Oklahoma Press, 1996), 28. She says that by 1650, it is estimated that the Native population in the area was "reduced to one-tenth its former strength" (28). Much was due to the susceptibility of indigenous people to European diseases.

14. Mary Chapman, introduction to *Ormond; or, The Secret Witness*, ed. Mary Chapman (Peterbourgh, ON: Broadview Press, 1999), 17.

15. Fiedler, *Love and Death*, 134.

16. Chapman, introduction, 17–22.

17. Alan Lloyd-Smith, *American Gothic Fiction: An Introduction* (London: Continuum, 2004), 3. Godwin married Mary Wollstonecraft; their daughter was Mary Shelley.

18. *Ormond* was the first American novel translated into German and was credited with being from the English of Godwin. Philip Barnard and Stephen Shapiro, "A Note to the Text," in *Ormond; or, The Secret Witness*, ed. Philip Barnard and Stephen Shapiro (Indianapolis, IN: Hackett, 2009), liii.

19. See Edgar Allan Poe, *Essays and Reviews* (New York: Library of America, 1984), 480 and 1342.

20. Donald A. Ringe, *Charles Brockden Brown*, rev. ed. (Boston: Twayne, 1991), 2.

21. H. P. Lovecraft, *The Annotated Supernatural Horror in Literature*, rev. ed., ed. S. T. Joshi (New York: Hippocampus Press, 2012), 37–38.

22. Peter Kafer, *Charles Brockden Brown's Revolution and the Birth of American Gothic* (Philadelphia: University of Philadelphia Press, 2004), xi.

23. Kafer, *Charles Brockden Brown's Revolution*, xviii.

24. Alan Axelrod, *Charles Brockden Brown: An American Tale* (Austin: University of Texas Press, 1983), xiii.

25. Kafer, *Charles Brockden Brown's Revolution*, xxi.

26. Axelrod, *Charles Brockden Brown*, 53–54.

27. Brown, "Advertisement," in *Wieland, or The Transformation*, ed. Philip Barnard and Stephen Shapiro (Indianapolis, IN: Hackett Publishing, 2009), 3. Hereafter cited in the text. Another case is the Beadle murders. In 1782 William Beadle, in Wethersfield, Connecticut, killed his wife and four children and then committed suicide. See *Wieland*, 284–91.

28. Clive Bloom, *Gothic Histories* (London: Continuum, 2010), 78.

29. The novel includes a possible explanation for its dark events through the actions of Carwin, the ventriloquist. He steals voices and incites some of the awful events. This is a naturalistic explanation that Brown at times seems to be suggesting. But perhaps Brown is really uncovering a problem with our perceptions of our world. Brown's novels demonstrate "the unreliability of the senses in providing knowledge," according to Beverly Lyon Clark, "Charles Brockden Brown's Contagious Unreliability," *International Fiction Review* 8, no. 2

(1981): 91. In a sense, the novel is investigating an epistemological problem. For example, Clara distrusts what she hears and also her ability to reason in the midst of the chaos taking over Mettingen.

30. Nicolas Abraham, "Notes on the Phantom: A Complement to Freud's Metapsychology," trans. Nicholas Rand, *Critical Inquiry* 13, no. 2 (1987): 289–90.

31. Abraham, "Notes on the Phantom," 287.

32. Weinstock, *Charles Brockden Brown*, 54.

33. Brown, *Ormond; or, The Secret Witness*, ed. Mary Chapman (Peterborough, ON: Broadview Press, 1999), 79–80. Hereafter cited in the text.

34. *28 Days Later*, DVD, directed by Danny Boyle (2003; Century City, CA: 20th Century Fox Home Entertainment, 2004). See also Jovnaka Vuckovic, *Zombies: An Illustrated History of the Undead* (New York: St. Martin's Griffin, 2011), 116.

35. Weinstock, *Charles Brockden Brown*, 29.

36. Brown, *Edgar Huntly, or Memoirs of a Sleepwalker*, ed. Philip Barnard and Stephen Shapiro (Indianapolis, IN: Hackett, 2006), 4. Hereafter cited in the text.

37. Joshua David Bellin, *The Demon of the Continent* (Philadelphia: University of Pennsylvania Press, 2001).

38. Francis Murphy, introduction to *Of Plymouth Plantation 1620–1647*, by William Bradford (New York: Modern Library, 1981), xv.

39. Bradford, *Of Plymouth Plantation*, 26.

40. Mary Rowlandson, "A Narrative of the Captivity and Restauration of Mrs. Mary Rowlandson," in *Early American Writing*, ed. Giles Gunn (New York: Penguin, 1994), 219.

41. Cotton Mather, "A Notable Exploit: wherein, Dux Faemina Facti: from *Magnalia Christi Americana*," in *Women's Indian Captivity Narratives*, ed. Kathryn Zabelle Derounian-Srodola (New York: Penguin, 1998), 58.

42. Mather, "A Notable Exploit," 60.

43. William S. Simmons, "Cultural Bias in the New England Puritans' Perceptions of Indians," *William and Mary Quarterly*, 3rd series, 38, no. 1 (1981): 67. Simmons described the Mystic River massacre of May 26, 1637, when Puritan soldiers, under Captain John Mason, slaughtered at least 400 inhabitants, mostly women and children, in a Pequot stockade.

44. Perhaps a source for Poe's "The Pit and the Pendulum," as suggested by Axelrod, *Charles Brockden Brown*, 9.

45. J. Hector St. John de Crèvecoeur, *Letters from an American Farmer* (New York: Penguin Classics, 1986), 77.

46. Roderick Frazier Nash, *Wilderness and the American Mind*, 4th ed. (New Haven, CT: Yale University Press, 2001).

47. Roger B. Salomon, *The Mazes of the Serpent: An Anatomy of Horror Narrative* (Ithaca, NY: Cornell University Press, 2002), 11.

48. Salomon, *Mazes of the Serpent*, 13.

49. *The Village*, DVD, directed by M. Night Shyamalan (2004; Burbank, CA: Buena Vista, 2005).

50. Teresa Goddu, *Gothic America: Narrative, History, and Nation* (New York: Columbia University Press, 1997), 11.

51. Charles L. Crow, *American Gothic* (Cardiff: University of Wales Press, 2009), 2.

52. Lovecraft, *Annotated Supernatural Horror*, 37.

53. Nash argues the wilderness became "a dark and sinister symbol" to settlers. *Wilderness and the American Mind*, 24.

54. Lovecraft, *Annotated Supernatural Horror*, 38.

55. Goddu, *Gothic America*, 34.

56. Crow, *American Gothic*, 25.

57. Donald A. Ringe, *American Gothic: Imagination and Reason in Nineteenth-Century Fiction* (Lexington: University Press of Kentucky, 1982), 49.

58. Clark, "Charles Brockden Brown's Contagious Unreliability," 97.

59. Crow, *American Gothic*, 1.

60. Toni Morrison, *Playing in the Dark: Whiteness and the Literary Imagination* (Cambridge, MA: Harvard University Press), 33.

61. Crèvecoeur, *Letters from an American Farmer*, 178.
62. Albert E. Stones, introduction to *Letters from an American Farmer*, 7.

Chapter Two

Poe's "The Fall of the House of Usher"

A Predecessor to Lovecraft's "The Outsider"?

"The Outsider" (written 1921; published 1926) is a keystone story in H. P. Lovecraft's body of horror fiction. It has been widely reprinted, it was one of his early professional stories, and it headlined the Arkham House first collection. The story has also been extensively and variously interpreted: Carl Buchanan, Donald R. Burleson, S. T. Joshi, Dirk W. Mosig, Robert H. Waugh, and others have all studied and commented on the story. All spy the hand of Poe in the tale.[1] Several of Poe's stories are identified as precursors, for example, "William Wilson," "The Masque of the Red Death," "The Facts in the Case of M. Valdemar," and "Berenice." This chapter suggests that it may be a sequel to "The Fall of the House of Usher" (1839). Peter Cannon implied this when he wrote that Lovecraft's underground castle "rivals Poe's *House of Usher* as a symbolically potent image."[2] Robert H. Waugh proposes "an antecedent to the *Outsider* in the figure of Madeline Usher"[3] and identifies parallels between the stories. However, Perry and Sederholm do not mention "The Outsider" in their wide-ranging review of the influence of Poe's tale on many of Lovecraft's stories. Overall, they argue that Lovecraft's work in horror fiction was, in part, to "explore new dimensions from 'Usher's' hints about cosmic horror."[4]

In a fashion, "The Outsider" imagines the aftermath of Poe's story, or at least one possible afterworld. Although sometimes distorted, similar images and themes haunt the stories. Some of the key common images are the House of Usher and the underground castle in "The Outsider"; the library of Roderick Usher and the "rows of antique books"[5] in the underground castle; the reflecting tarn in Poe's tale and the mirror in "The Outsider"; the wasteland surrounding the House of Usher and the wasteland the outsider travels; an escape from a tomb; and a climactic scene of coming face to face with one's terrifying destiny. The thrall of time and space over humans are thematic links. There is a life-to-death sequence in Poe's tale, while there is a sort of death-to-life ascent in Lovecraft's. In a way, there is a resurrection in both. A key question may be: "Is the outsider the imaginary spawn of Roderick and Madeline—the last of the Ushers—and an abomination at that?" Leslie Fiedler saw incest as a major theme in "The Fall of the House of Usher," along with the theme of a death wish.[6] Barton Levi St. Armand argues that the end of Poe's tale was not destruction "but a new genesis."[7] More importantly, is "The Outsider" a signpost toward a new Gothic horror?

Lovecraft was not an imitator: "The Outsider" is an early story and it bears the signs of homage,[8] but there is a shift in the locus of horror in the story. Richard Wilbur argues that Poe broke wholly new ground[9] in a sequence of stories published between 1835 and 1839, including "The Fall of the House of Usher."[10] Lovecraft also opened new ground in the Gothic. Perry and Sederholm suggest that Lovecraft went beyond Poe, and by melding "the mundane to cosmic realism as an additional source for the weird and uncanny, Lovecraft helps plot the course of twentieth-century Gothic horror fiction."[11]

Poe's influence is of a piece with the omnipresence of the past. The story itself seems from the past—a dusty set of pages found in an old tomb. But is it a jumble? S. T. Joshi notes several inconsistencies in the story.[12] William Fulwiler claims that the story is virtually a transcript of a dream and is best understood as a dream.[13] This echoes Richard Wilbur's surmise that "we must understand 'The Fall of the House of Usher' as a dream of the narrator's."[14] Louise Norlie suggests that a dreamer experiences a cascade of images and morphing events that, while dreaming, make sense; but awake, everything seems irrational and absurd.[15] It is a trance state, and this trance is also evident in "The Fall of the House of Usher." Wilbur contends, among other things, that Poe's tale be viewed as illustrating the experience as one slips from the wakeful world to that of dreams, when consciousness reels before plunging into dreams—a phantasmagoria state.[16] In "Between Wakefulness and Sleep," Poe wrote about this unique transition when the "confines of the waking world blend with those of the world of dreams" that is at "the very brink of sleep." It is thronged with "shadows of shadows."[17] "The Fall of the House of Usher" is, then, a passage from the living world of light to a world of night where the past and death reign. "The Outsider" also is a tale of the interstices between being awake and being asleep, between light and dark. "Light" is used eight times, and "dark" or "darkness" is used six times. They are point and counterpoint words in the text of the story. "The Outsider" is a tale of the nightmarish passage from sleep to being awake, or from death to life, where neither dream nor reality offers solace. In a manner,

Roderick is going to sleep (the sleep of death, admittedly) while the outsider is just awakening.

Both "The Outsider" and "The Fall of the House of Usher" drown in the tides of past time, as manifested, in part, by their primary abodes. In Poe's tale, the Ushers had lived in the hoary house through the "long lapse of centuries."[18] The architectural twin in "The Outsider" is the underground castle resting upon the "piled up corpses of dead generations" (46–47). Time itself is embodied in the decomposing castle "infinitely old and infinitely horrible" (46). The unnamed narrator "cannot measure the time" (47) he has lived in the castle of darkness where the only light comes from candles. The Usher House is "of excessive antiquity" where the "discoloration of the ages had been great" (400) and it suffers a fracture scoring from its roof to "the sullen waters of the tarn" (400).

The Ushers are shuttered within the confined space of their house. Darkness and an "irredeemable gloom hung over and pervaded all" (401) in the House of Usher. Upon arriving, the unnamed (as in "The Outsider") narrator, who is a boyhood friend of Roderick Usher, proceeds through "many dark and intricate passages" (400) to Roderick's study, which is hung with "dark draperies" and the "eye . . . struggled in vain to reach . . . the remoter angles of the vaulted and fretted ceiling" (401). The outsider lives in a shadowy castle and is restricted to roaming "dark passages" and "dismal chambers with brown hangings" (46). In the underground castle (not known to be buried by the outsider early in the story), there are "high ceilings where the eye could find only cobwebs and shadows" (46). Yet even with these heights, both the house and castle are confined spaces, constricted spaces, limiting the movement of the main characters. Even the forest seems to prevent escape from the castle, as the outsider learns when "farther from the castle the shade grew denser and the air more filled with brooding fear" in the forest so that he dreaded losing his way "in a labyrinth of nighted silence" (47).[19] Both the house and castle are enclosed spaces, haunted with a sense of capture, of a prison. In "House of Usher," both Ushers are sick and dying, seemingly drugged by the age of the house into a somnambulistic trance of pre-death. Roderick "for many years . . . had never ventured forth" (403). He is chained to the house, as is his sister, Madeline, who is a shadowy figure in the story. D. H. Lawrence calls them "inmates"[20] of the Usher House. The outsider has been enclosed, but he is different; he longs for light and freedom from the infernal gloom of the underground castle and from isolation and loneliness.

Both the house and the castle seem to be alive—especially the stones. Roderick tells his friend the house is sentient—evident in the "gray stones of the home of his forefathers" (408), which had a particular order and were overspread with fungi and a "certain condensation of an atmosphere of their own about the waters and the walls" (408). Seemingly, the house breathed. The castle is more of a dead place, but its "worn and aged stone"[21] (47) seems like flesh. When the outsider ruminates, "I think that whoever nursed me must have been shockingly aged, since my first conception of a living person was that of somebody mockingly like myself, yet distorted, shriv-elled, and decaying like the castle" (47), he is really personifying the castle as alive, almost like a parent.

The books of Usher are named: Christopher Rollason points out that they range from classical times up to Poe's time in European literature and en-compass a diversity of genres, come from seven different countries, and are in four different European languages.[22] Moreover, Thomas Ollive Mabbott confirms that the volumes in the library of Roderick Usher were not imagi-nary but for the most part real. Mabbott also convincingly shows that the particular books were seemingly chosen by Poe to give "greater insight into . . . [Roderick's] character."[23] The books are the reification of his intel-lect and are unusual and of a dark cast, as Mabbott explained. For example, *Belphegor* is a novella about a fallen archangel and demoniac possession. Swedenborg's work is of visions and mystical experiences. The *Subterra-nean Voyage* tells of a land inside the earth where the people are trees who walk and talk. The works on chiromancy are about predicting the future. The novella by Tieck tells of Gloriana, the Faerie Queene, who reigns in a para-dise inside a mountain, where the souls of great poets live. Campanella's work recounts a visit to the inhabitants of a Utopia in the Sun. The *Director-ium Inquisitorium* contains instructions to priests examining heretics and includes a list of forbidden books. And a tome on the vigils for the dead according to the church at Mainz is also part of the odd collection of read-ing.[24]

In "The Outsider" the books are not named. The outsider has read at least some of "the mouldy books" (47) but generally muses on the pictures. In the underground castle, the books of Usher decompose on rotting shelves, per-haps becoming unreadable, now moldering, mirroring the corruption of Ush-er's intellect. Perhaps these odd books have affected the mind of the outsid-er—he is confused about what is reality. The books are unnamed, replicating the inchoate nature of the outsider's intellect.

The outsider escapes from his tomb. He undertakes a perilous journey, scaling up the tower of the castle to touch the sky, as if on a vision quest. He dares go beyond his enclosed space. His struggle is a devilish version of birth, as he claws up the tower. This is an escape from the womb in contrast to Poe's tale, which presents a return to the womb, illustrated by Madeline's premature burial. And, in both tales, there is a live burial, with the outsider alive in the castle as a tomb and Madeline entombed by her brother. But she also breaks out of her tomb. She is resurrected, and her struggles in escaping from the tomb parallel the terrifying ascent of the outsider. His climb ends as he heads a trap-door open and falls unto a level space shrouded in darkness. In dread, he feels his way to a "portal of stone" (49) and forces it open. A flood of silver moonlight showers him. He is elated but also confounded. He has attained level ground, not a lofty height. Venturing out, he finds "marble slabs and columns . . . overshadowed by an ancient stone church, whose ruined spire gleamed spectrally in the moonlight" (49). This is the beginning of the wasteland[25] he crosses. Driven by a deep memory, he sorties across a land of "ruins" (50).

This is prefigured by the wasteland surrounding the House of Usher, the badlands that infect the mood of the unnamed narrator as he rides toward the dire and fissured house and looks upon "a few rank sedges—and upon a few white trunks of decayed trees" (397). At the house he seems to sink into "its image in the pool" (399) and is overcome with "a fancy . . . that about the whole mansion and domain there hung an atmosphere . . . which had reeked up from the decayed trees, and the gray wall, and the silent tarn" (399–400). The desolation of the land and the house is paralleled by the "acute bodily illness" (398) of Roderick and by the "long-continued illness" (403) of his sister. The narrator was summoned by Roderick to bring "some alleviation of his malady" (398). Perhaps he is a knight to rescue Roderick and the land— as if the narrator, who is an outsider to the Ushers, is the mythic hero of Grail Quest tales as told by Jessie L. Weston.[26] His deed is to restore Roderick as the Fisher King or Maimed King, and healing him will return the land to fecundity. Instead, perhaps the narrator becomes enmeshed in the delirium world of Roderick; he gives in "by slow degrees [to] the wild influences of [Roderick's] own fantastic yet impressive superstitions" (411). He becomes a bit player in Roderick's hallucinogenic world of his sister's death and resurrection, according to Rollason.[27] St. Armand identifies Roderick's role as the Fisher King and the house as the Hidden Castle.[28] Forrest C. Helvie argues that Roderick Usher embodies many aspects of the Maimed King.[29] The landscapes in both thematically present the Gothic wastelands and ruins. But there are differences in the stories; the land and house are emphasized in Poe's tale, but in Lovecraft's it is the relics of previous structures, a wasteland of human ruins.

After his journey, the outsider arrives at a "venerable ivied castle" (50), another distorted mirror image of the House of Usher in this tale. Lovecraft deploys this ivied castle, alive and full of merriment, in contrast to the House of Usher, which is a "mansion of gloom" with "bleak walls" and "vacant eye-like windows" (397). The ivied castle has "open windows—gorgeously ablaze with light" (50), and the interior resounds with revelry. The outsider recalls vanished towers and wonders at the added wings, again calling on deep memory, as if, like Lovecraft wrote, "The past is *real*. It is *all there is*."[30] The past is buried in our memories and structures our world, the shape of our architecture and our landscapes, and it spawns the ideas that form our perceptions. The past is the ground of our living but also our death. However, perhaps the outsider is disoriented—he has escaped in a landscape he dreamed of and is now realizing in a dizzying fashion. In a sense, the outsider emerges from the unconsciousness realm into consciousness, but the disturbing element is the absence of solid epistemological ground to understand himself and the strange, but familiar, world he now inhabits.

Peering through the ivied castle's windows, the outsider observes a crowd of people in high spirits and joy. He yearns to join their company. His hope of escape from loneliness and the dark is at hand. Entering through a window, he witnesses a colossal commotion among the revelers. They scream and hide their faces and stumble over one another in a mad rush to flee the castle. At first he thinks some danger is lurking in the room. Cautiously he surveys his environs. Alarmed, he senses some movement and cries out as he sees an "inconceivable, indescribable, and unmentionable monstrosity" (51). In the presence of the monster one cannot reason, portray, or speak. In confusion and terror, the outsider reels forward and seemingly touches the "paw of the monster" (51). But the paw is his;[31] it is himself in the mirror.[32] He is "unclean, uncanny, unwelcome, abnormal and detestable" (51); he is abject. At the climactic moment, he discovers he is the monster. He is an outcast. Julia Kristeva posits that "abjection" is the way we react to the loss of any distinction between self and other. This arises from an encounter with an abject object, something disgustingly other. It is as if the world loses sense or meaning for us—it becomes unspeakable. The collision with the abject in the story is the outsider touching the looking glass. According to Kristeva, when we confront the abject we both fear and identify with it; we are attracted to and repelled by the abject; nausea is a biological recognition of it. Its looming presence provokes fear. For the outsider it is himself. Moreover, in Kristeva's psychological terms, abjection is something we must experience in forming a sense of self. This notion is illustrated by the outsider's trials toward self-discovery through self-revulsion.[33]

This reflection, or rather the revelation, of a hidden self that has been darkly repressed is crushingly unsettling to the identity of the outsider. In a sense, the outsider's time in the underground castle was a time of stifled identity or buried self-awareness. It is similar to Roderick's attempt to repress his shadow-self—Madeline—a burial that does not last. The confrontation of the outsider with himself, leading to self-revulsion through self-revelation, is paralleled by the final embrace of Madeline with Roderick, who had knowingly entombed her alive in the catacombs of their ancient abode, after her seeming demise to the narrator. In the climactic scene, Roderick is in the narrator's chamber within the house, which is assaulted by an external tempest. The narrator feels the creeping near of an internal doom accompanied by a sequence of increasingly disturbing sounds. These sounds appear to echo the events in the "Mad Trist" by Sir Launcelot Canning (the one imaginary book in the tale), the adventures of the knight Ethelred, which the narrator is reading to Roderick. The sounds start with "cracking and ripping," followed by "low and apparently distant, but harsh, protracted, and most unusual screaming or grating sound" (414), and then "a distinct, hollow, metallic and clangorous, yet apparently muffled reverberation" (415).[34] Then the aged antique panels of the chamber door open languorously, revealing Madeline "lofty and enshrouded" (416), resurrected, as the outsider was from the underground castle. She trembles and reels to and fro in her "final death-agonies" (416). Her white robes are soaked in blood and she bears the marks of the grave. She is abject; like the outsider, she is a figure of horror and pathos. Then she lurches forward and with a "moaning cry, fell heavily inward upon the person of her brother" (415–16), with whom she shares "sympathies of a scarcely intelligible nature"[35] (410), and "bore him to the floor a corpse" (416). She falls upon her brother as if she is being absorbed into his person in their embrace of death, as if the shadow has returned home. As the narrator flees, the house collapses into the tarn, engulfed by its mirror image.

Similar to the concept of the "abject" is Kelly Hurley's notion of the "abhuman," which she borrows from William Hope Hodgson. The abhuman is typified by a "morphic variability" and is "in danger of becoming not-itself, becoming other."[36] The abhuman is a being that retains part of its human identity but is or is becoming an unspeakable other thing. Such a thing is loathsome as it threatens or indeed overcomes human identity. The abhuman is on the threshold between human and beast. Hurley contends that the modern Gothic shows and ignites cultural anxieties and conflicts through the figure of the abhuman. When the outsider sees his reflection, at first he identifies it, as Waugh noted, "as someone else or, more subtly as a travesty, a creature dressed as a human but not one."[37] Lovecraft's story vividly illustrates the process of becoming not-itself, becoming other, becoming alien. In Poe's tale Madeline also becomes not-herself, arising from the grave in a monstrous form, no longer truly human.

Leslie Fiedler argues that American literature is a "chamber of horrors," where readers face "inter-reflecting mirrors, which present us with a thousand versions of our own face."[38] The chambers include "The Fall of the House of Usher" and "The Outsider." Before entering the House of Usher at the beginning of the story, the narrator stares into the stagnant tarn and sees the reflected image of the house; it is a mirror.[39] In "The Outsider," the unnamed protagonist looks into a mirror and becomes a stranger to himself, or finally knows himself. Or has he stepped through the mirror into a wonderland of terror? Or is he taken over by the thing in the mirror? In "The Fall of the House of Usher," the mirror reveals the crack in the castle, foretelling its demise. In "The Outsider," the mirror reveals the monster, arisen from death, and the loss of hope. The mirror parallels the tarn and, of course, the mirror image of the monster is like seeing one's rotting self in all its desolation. But it is the mirror of the old Gothic that Lovecraft's story breaks.

Chris Baldick argues that "The Fall of the House of Usher" is an exemplar Gothic short story. Poe shifted the Gothic from cruelty to decadence, according to Baldick, who further maintains that for the Gothic effect a story needs to express a "fearful sense of inheritance in time with a claustrophobic sense of enclosure in space."[40] Both of these are central to Poe's story, with its plot of a sickening descent into intellectual and emotional disintegration predestined by the ancestral Ushers as atavistic denizens of the house. The traditional Gothic uses the chains of time and the constriction of space as both alluring and repulsive. These themes are explored explicitly in Lovecraft's "The Tomb" (1917), in which Jervas Dudley yearns for the dead, for confinement, and for a return to the past. And he ends up being committed in an asylum, realizing his dream with a Lovecraftian twist. "The Tomb" is another story of the dead hand of the past—the Gothic strangulation of the present. In this story Dudley is confined (in either imagination or reality—the story leaves some ambiguity) by his volition in a crypt for a time and then involuntarily confined by his parents. Dudley seems to "know the way" into the depths of the "vault."[41] The vault is a counterpart to the underground castle. Later, he seems aware of a sub-cellar of a burned mansion (a parallel of the above-ground castle) that "had been unseen and forgotten for many generations,"[42] as if guided by past memories or as if possessed. Tombs, of course, abound in "The Outsider"—indeed, at the end of the story the Great Pyramid is the final tomb.

"The Fall of the House of Usher" is one of the landmark tales in the American Gothic. Lovecraft praised Poe's story in *Supernatural Horror in Literature* and conjectured that the house and two Ushers, brother and sister, "an abnormally linked trinity of entities,"[43] shared one soul—one source of being—and perished at the same moment, really a story of a sickness of the soul. The house in Lovecraft's view seems alive. "The Fall of the House of Usher" riffs on the themes of the decline and extinction of a family line, of the dissolution of identity, and of obsessive mental states. The house is the family—is the personality of Roderick Usher—is the world of the living dying. At the end of the story, the Ushers all die, the house cracks apart and falls into its mirror image in the tarn—it is the end of life—the house is like a human body in its decay. But the house is also a killer: it seems as if it has pervaded the mind of Roderick, who walls up his sister in a tomb, and she resurrects in vengeance. In "The Outsider," the castle gives a sort of life-in-death to its offspring.

Poe's tale is an archetypal story, with its elegance of language, its striking characterizations, its symmetry of images, its slow yet building pace to the climax, and its clarity in plot. Lovecraft's "The Outsider" is rough-hewn; yet there is a staying power in the story with its disturbingly familiar strangeness as Lovecraft unchains a spirit into a world of loneliness and dread. Lovecraft denigrated the story later in his life, but Burleson says it is "central to an understanding of Lovecraft's thematic continuity," focused on the "soul shattering consequences of self-knowledge."[44] For Waugh the moment when the outsider touches the polished glass "presents a paradigm of Lovecraft's most authentic fiction"[45] and the words that stream forth represent Lovecraft's lexicon of horror.

Although the story is stylistically reminiscent of Poe and, as argued here, it reflects "The Fall of the House of Usher," it is not merely an imitation; it is a keystone at the start of Lovecraft's reshaping of the Gothic away from the confines of old houses, away from decadence out into cosmic dread. The story is distorted and there are inconsistencies, as if Lovecraft were experimenting during the writing of the tale—illustrating indeterminacy.

Both stories have been interpreted in manifold ways. As Perry and Sederholm catalogue, "The Fall of the House of Usher" is the subject of hundreds of critical articles and chapters exploring the story's endless ambiguities.[46] "The Outsider" also yields to alternate readings. That is part of its allure, its ambiguity imaging the indeterminacy of our experience of the world. Readers can see what they want in the story. It may be a weird coming-of-age story—a deformed perspective on an introverted, lonely teenager's agony and failure in shaping an identity in an unfriendly world, as the outsider's personality goes from one obsessive state to another. Or is it a tale of alternate times or of doubles, as Waugh suggests,[47] among other interpretations, with the outsider playing multiple parts? Perhaps "The Outsider" is a tale of the "uncanny" as described by Freud, "that class of the terrifying which leads back to something long known and to us, once familiar."[48] The uncanny is in the interstices between the living and the dead and the figure of the double. And the double eventually becomes a "vision of terror,"[49] as the outsider experiences. Or is it a story of self-discovery leading to self-revulsion—a moral drama of fear and trembling in the face of death? In this story it is the monster we feel sympathy toward, not the fleeing revelers. But that is because readers participate in the outsider's agonizing struggle for self-discovery. And perhaps the story appeals because readers experience a distressing epiphany as the outsider journeys away from home, fearfully venturing out and finding only rejection, disgust, sadness, and despair.

"The Outsider" reveals the disturbing nature of Gothic fiction. The inconsistencies and contradictions in the tale reflect the unreliability of storytelling and story-reading, which in turn reflect the contradictions and the underside of society and the chaos and horror of the cosmos within which we live. The story is akin to a disquieting initiation rite into the new Lovecraftian horror Gothic, which is pronounced by its epistemological instability, its raw images and power of disgust, its cosmic dread, its pervasive despair, its solitary fear, and its existential loneliness.

In summary, "The Outsider" reflects images and actions from "The Fall of the House of Usher" and works with similar themes of the impact of the tentacles of the past and the cells of space on personality. "The Outsider" takes place after the collapse of the Usher House. The house is re-imagined in the form of the underground castle and later as the castle of light and joy and then despair. The books of Roderick mold and rot in "The Outsider." In both stories, there is a wasteland. Mirrors appear in each. Madeline and the outsider are both resurrected. Both have a climactic confrontation scene of revelation and dread. And both predict, in a fashion, current literary theories on the Gothic.

The underground castle is the fallen House of Usher. But more so, it is the Gothic castle appearing in many traditional Gothic fictions that is scuppered. Lovecraft seems to be using up or mocking the old Gothic castles of dungeons and clanking chains and decadent protagonists to illustrate that what emerges is dead literature for his time. In "Cool Air" (1926) Lovecraft's narrator considers it "is a mistake to fancy that horror is associated inextricably with darkness, silence, and solitude. I found it in the glare of mid-afternoon, in the clangour of a metropolis, and in the teeming midst of a shabby and commonplace rooming-house with a prosaic landlady and two stalwart men by my side."[50] "The Outsider" bears the burden of the past in explicit form in the beginning paragraphs as it takes place in a closed foreboding space; but it emerges into the moonlight, and Lovecraft takes the Gothic off into limitless space—the indifferent void—more terrifying than any bounded space. The decadence of Poe is revealed to conceal the unknowable, the unspeakable true horror experienced in vast open space adrift in endless, meaningless time, that is just around an ordinary corner.

The monster of "The Outsider" ends up riding the night wind with ghouls; he leads a company of monsters as they extend the frontiers of horror literature. Freedom is illusory, and any continuing life is a sort of death-trance in a zombie world.[51] The marks left by the dead rune the end of all. At the culmination the hero embraces his alien nature, his otherness, even though all is hopeless—an existential freedom in nightmare.[52] He welcomes "the bitterness of alienage" (52) as foreshadowed in the first paragraph when his thoughts try to "reach beyond to *the other*" (46). Lovecraft's story illustrates "the mystery of the recognition of otherness."[53]

Lovecraft admired Poe and acknowledged the importance and influence of his work in horrific supernatural literature. In part, Poe saw art as a way to break free from ordinary consciousness into a domain of beauty and wonder; for Lovecraft, in his fiction, breaking free only means more fear and dread. There is no sublime in Lovecraft. "The Outsider" is an embryonic state of Lovecraft's later great stories, as it creates unease in its indeterminacy, which reveals an emerging artistic response to a world of chaos and dread. It bears lineage to "The Fall of the House of Usher," but it births a new line of horror fiction.

NOTES

1. There are other influences, for example: S. T. Joshi in *H. P. Lovecraft: A Life* (West Warwick, RI: Necronomicon Press, 1996), 253, notes Mary Shelley's *Frankenstein*. In the novel, the monster is unnamed. It is rejected and causes panic by its appearance, which Dr. Frankenstein describes, "Oh, no mortal could support the horror of that countenance. A Mummy again endued with animation could not be so hideous as that wretch," Mary Shelley, *Frankenstein*, ed. Joanna M. Smith (London: Palgrave Macmillan, 2000), 61.

2. Peter Cannon, *H. P. Lovecraft* (Boston: Twayne, 1989), 47.

3. Robert H. Waugh, *The Monster in the Mirror: Looking for H. P. Lovecraft* (New York: Hippocampus Press, 2006), 145.

4. Dennis R. Perry and Carl H. Sederholm, *Poe, "The House of Usher," and the American Gothic* (New York: Palgrave Macmillan, 2009), 69–70.

5. H. P. Lovecraft, "The Outsider," in *The Dunwich Horror and Others*, ed. S. T. Joshi (Sauk City, WI: Arkham House, 1984), 46. Hereafter cited in the text.

6. Leslie Fiedler, *Love and Death in the American Novel* (New York: Criterion, 1960), 398–99.

7. Barton Levi St. Armand, "The 'Mysteries' of Edgar Poe: The Quest for a Monomyth in Gothic Literature," in *The Tales of Poe*, ed. Harold Bloom (New York: Chelsea House, 1987), 50.

8. Bradford Morrow and Patrick McGrath continue the homage to Poe as the fountainhead of the new Gothic: introduction to *The New Gothic*, ed. Bradford Morrow and Patrick McGrath (New York: Random House, 1991), xi–xiv.

9. Richard Wilbur, "The House of Poe," in *The Recognition of Edgar Allan Poe: Selected Criticism since 1829*, ed. Eric W. Carlson (Ann Arbor: University of Michigan Press, 1966), 277. This is similar to Ezra Pound's praise of Walt Whitman in "A Pact" that he "broke the new wood" of open verse. Ezra Pound, "A Pact," in *New Selected Poems and Translations*, ed. Richard Sieburth (New York: New Directions, 2010), 39.

10. The other stories were "Berenice," "Morella," "Ligeia," and "William Wilson."

11. Perry and Sederholm, *Poe*, 81.

12. Joshi, *Lovecraft: A Life*, 252.

13. William Fulwiler, "Reflections on 'The Outsider,'" *Lovecraft Studies* no. 2 (Spring 1980): 1–4.

14. Wilbur, "The House of Poe," 265.

15. Louise Norlie, "Existential Sadness in H. P. Lovecraft's 'The Outsider,'" *Bewildering Stories* no. 208 (August 2006). http://www.bewilderingstories.com/issue208/outsider_article.html (accessed November 2011).

16. Richard Wilbur, introduction to *Poe: The Complete Poems*, ed. Richard Wilbur (New York: Dell, 1959), 26.

17. Edgar Allan Poe, "Between Wakefulness and Sleep," in *The Unknown Poe*, ed. Raymond Foye (San Francisco: City Light Publishing, 1980), 42.

18. Edgar Allan Poe, "The Fall of the House of Usher," in *Tales and Sketches*, vol. 1, ed. Thomas Ollive Mabbott (Urbana: University of Illinois Press, 2000), 399. Hereafter cited in the text.

19. This is a striking phrase, shifting mazes from space to sound, painted black. It rings of Jean-Jacques Rousseau's "Absolute silence leads to sadness. It is the image of death." Rousseau, *The Reveries of the Solitary Walker*, trans. Charles E. Butterworth (Indianapolis, IN: Hackett, 1992), 70.

20. D. H. Lawrence, *Studies in Classic American Literature* (London: Martin Secker, 1933), 79.

21. "Stone(s)" is the most frequently used non-common word in the story, appearing twelve times, followed by "castle."

22. Christopher Rollason, "The Character of Phantasm: Edgar Allan Poe's 'The Fall of the House of Usher' and Jorge Luis Borges' 'Tlön, Uqbar, Orbis Tertius,'" *Atlantis: Journal of the Spanish Association of Anglo-American Studies* 31, no. 1 (June 2009): 14–15.

23. Thomas Ollive Mabbott, "The Books in the House of Usher," *Books at Iowa* 19 (November 1973): 1.

24. Mabbott, "The Books in the House of Usher," 1–5.

25. Lovecraft developed the theme of the wasteland more elaborately in "The Colour Out of Space," in *The Dunwich Horror and Others*, 56. The "blasted heath" is a zone of death where the thriving Gardner farm once stood.

26. See Jessie L. Weston, *From Ritual to Romance* (Mineola, NY: Dover, 1997).

27. Rollason, "The Character of Phantasm," 13.

28. Barton Levi St. Armand, "The 'Mysteries' of Edgar Poe," 25–54.

29. Forrest C. Helvie, "'The Fall of the House of Usher': Poe's Perverted Perspective on the Maimed King," *452 M F.: Electronic Journal of Theory of Literature and Comparative Literature* 1 (2009). http://www.452f.com/pdf/numero01/01_452f-mon-helvie.pdf (accessed November 2011), 42–51.

30. H. P. Lovecraft, *Selected Letters*, vol. 3, ed. August Derleth and Donald Wandrei (Sauk City, WI: Arkham House, 1971), 31.

31. Even though the underground castle had no mirrors and was seeped in darkness, the outsider lit candles and looked at books, yet did not notice his own hand? Perhaps this and other incongruences reflect the clash of the ideal and materiality.

32. Jorge Luis Borges in "The Other" has a more sanguine confrontation with himself on a bench on the banks of the River Charles in Cambridge. St. Armand enumerates the synchronicities of Borges and Lovecraft: "Synchronistic Worlds: Lovecraft and Borges," in *An Epicure in the Terrible: A Centennial Anthology of Essays in Honor of H. P. Lovecraft*, ed. David E. Schultz and S. T. Joshi (Rutherford, NJ: Fairleigh Dickinson University Press, 1991), 298–323.

33. Julia Kristeva, *Powers of Horror: An Essay on Abjection* (New York: Columbia University Press, 1982), 2.

34. Roderick sums it up: "To-night—Ethelred—ha! ha!—the breaking of the hermit's door, and the death-cry of the dragon, and the clangor of the shield!—say, rather, the rending of her coffin, and the grating of the iron hinges of her prison, and her struggles within the coppered archway of the vault!" (416). Roderick recounts how he has been aware of Madeline's struggles yet was paralyzed with agony, as if he knew she would come to him to join her in the grave, or as if he knew the penalty for his crime.

35. A hint of incest.

36. Kelly Hurley, *The Gothic Body: Sexuality, Materialism, and Degeneration at the Fin de Siècle* (Cambridge: Cambridge University Press, 2004), 3–4.

37. Waugh, *The Monster in the Mirror*, 50.

38. Fiedler, *Love and Death*, xxi.

39. In "Tlön, Uqbar, Orbis Tertius," in *Collected Fictions*, trans. Andrew Hurley (New York: Viking, 1998), Borges writes about mirrors as abominations: "There is something monstrous about mirrors" (68). Early in the tale a mirror "troubled the far end of a hallway" and "hovered, shadowing" (68) the fictive Borges and Bioy Casares. Later he writes of the Uqbar "stone mirrors" and then of an engineer who still lingers in the "illusory depths of the mirrors" (70) of a hotel. These are images of the cruelty of mirrors, their true and false reflections of reality, their distorted revelations, and their haunting duplications.

40. Chris Baldick, introduction to *The Oxford Book of Gothic Stories*, ed. Chris Baldick (Oxford: Oxford University Press, 1992), xix.

41. H. P. Lovecraft, "The Tomb," in *Dagon and Other Macabre Tales*, ed. S. T. Joshi (Sauk City, WI: Arkham House, 1986), 8. As in "The Outsider," "stone" is a very frequent word, used ten times in "The Tomb," but more frequent are "tomb," "vault," "door," and "time."

42. Lovecraft, "The Tomb," 10.

43. Lovecraft, *The Annotated Supernatural Horror in Literature*, rev. ed., ed. S. T. Joshi (New York: Hippocampus Press, 2012), 59.

44. Donald R. Burleson, "On Lovecraft's Themes: Touching the Glass," in Schultz and Joshi, *An Epicure in the Terrible*, 135.

45. Waugh, *The Monster in the Mirror*, 17.

46. Perry and Sederholm, *Poe*, 1.

47. Waugh, "Landscapes, Selves and Others in Lovecraft," in Schultz and Joshi, *An Epicure in the Terrible*, 233.

48. Sigmund Freud, "The 'Uncanny,'" in *Collected Papers*, vol. 4, ed. Ernest Jones, trans. Alix Strachey (London: Hogarth Press, 1950), 370–71.

49. Freud, "The 'Uncanny,'" 389.

50. Lovecraft, "Cool Air," in *The Dunwich Horror and Others*, 199.

51. Jovanka Vuckovic, *Zombies: An Illustrated History of the Undead* (New York: St. Martin's Griffin, 2011), 8, suggests that the zombie has emerged as the modern monster in popular culture from "films, to video games to musicals, comic books and even global 'zombie walks.'"

52. In one of his faces of the outsider, Yōzan Dirk W. Mosig, *Mosig at Last: A Psychologist Looks at H. P. Lovecraft* (West Warwick, RI: Necronomicon Press, 1997), 16, sees him as going insane and that accounts for the chaotic nature of the ending. Carl Buchanan, "'The Outsider' as Homage to Poe," *Lovecraft Studies* no. 31 (Fall 1991): 12–14, sees it as the outsider accepting his existential lot.

53. Lawrence, *Studies in Classic American Literature*, 78.

Chapter Three

The Realm of Suffering

*Ambrose Bierce and the Phantoms of the
American Civil War*

Ambrose Bierce (1842–1914?) is a keystone author within the Gothic tradition and a master of the short story form. Lawrence I. Berkove says Bierce's "oeuvre includes some of the best short stories ever written."[1] He is the most important author actually to fight in the American Civil War and he was in it from beginning to nearly the end.[2]

Bierce was a Union soldier, miner, journalist, short story writer, and general cynic, but also a humanist. He survived a number of major battles in the Civil War, achieving an officer's rank during his service. He disappeared into Mexico in 1913, leaving behind a fog of mystery. His stories are haunted by that war, as if his wound never healed, as if Blue and Gray battalions of unburied soldiers still wander lost in his head. And it is not just in his "Tales of Soldiers," but a realm of suffering and death also pervades his "Tales of Civilians" and the stories of *Can Such Things Be?* Indeed, these stories etch most achingly the consequences of war and peace: despair, suffering, slaughter, and devastation, all under the dominion of an unknowable, dark fate. It is an uncompromising literature that paints a dark dread in people, society, and the world. His work also seems to keep something away, a little concealed, as if he were hiding part of himself or part of his experience—perhaps too horrible to say directly. Bierce is a writer concerned with human emotions and knowledge within the maze of the military, social, and political duplicity of his time. His stories are tinged with a deep sorrow and a deep sadness, and are nearly elegiac in their mourning for all the dead. Bierce journeys far into the realm of the suffering.

BIERCE'S GOTHIC BATTLEFIELDS

American Civil War battlefields were killing grounds and burial grounds, or sometimes just littered with the dead. Death was everywhere; it was the purpose of the Civil War. All the dead haunted Bierce. In a letter of June 8, 1864, he writes of them to Clara Wright: "so many good men who could ill be spared from the army and from the world. And yet *I* am left."[3] As David W. Blight notes, Bierce's stories and nonfiction accounts of the war "are riddled with the randomness of soldiers' deaths."[4]

Bierce always remembered the war. Perhaps he still lived his Civil War experiences, for he fought in some of the fiercest battles of the Civil War, including "Chickamauga, Chattanooga, Murfreesboro, Franklin, Nashville, Shiloh, and so forth,"[5] as he listed in a letter of September 21, 1913, to Amy Wells. He wrote about these battles years after, but his words ring true. These are collected in *A Sole Survivor: Bits of Autobiography*, where S. T. Joshi and David E. Schultz confirm that Bierce composed "some of the most memorable accounts . . . of the conflicts . . . and they harmonize in every significant particular with the known facts."[6] Some of these accounts were written forty years later, attesting to their impact on Bierce. It is as if the battles were seared permanently in his memory. His daughter, Helen Bierce, writes that when "soldiering in the army, he had seen many shattered bodies, and could never rid himself of the horror of them."[7] In 1894 he was wounded in the head at the battle of Kennesaw Mountain. He suffered headaches ever after,[8] as if the bullet was the keeper of his time in the war.

So many died in the American Civil War: 620,000 according to Drew Gilpin Faust.[9] However, J. David Hacker's very recent re-estimation of Civil War deaths suggests 750,000 as the best estimate, with a range of 650,000 to 850,000.[10] Bierce survived; he fought in bloody battles and traversed the fields of wounded, dying, and dead men. Faust writes of the reign of death during the war, and she often goes to Bierce to help understand the catastrophe and its effects on participants. Three times she uses the same quotation from Bierce: that he was haunted always, by "visions of the dead and dying."[11]

The Civil War battlefields were rife with bodies and screaming men. Shiloh had close to 24,000 casualties, with about 1,700 dead on each side.[12] These were killing battlefields. The touch of death was everywhere—before, during, and after the bullets and the artillery shells. First there was the killing, then the burying, often in mass graves. Frequently, the fallen were left in the open as the troops withdrew.

The Civil War took an awful toll in human life. John A. Wyeth, a Confederate cavalryman, describes the feeling of men in battle as they watched an attacking Union charge: "there was no defiance from us, only the courage born of despair, for we knew we were doomed."[13] Bierce felt the same way about the battle of Pickett's Mill, where General Hazen, Bierce's commander, was ordered to attack. The Confederate forces were prepared and Hazen's forces were slaughtered. Bierce writes that Hazen nodded grimly when given the order and "he uttered never a word, rode to the head of his feeble brigade and patiently awaited the command to go. Only by a look which I knew how to read did he betray his sense of the criminal blunder."[14] Across a narrow open space the North and South forces raged in battle, and now and then a group of the Federal troops would push forward, "moved by a common despair."[15] The scything rain of bullets would cut them all down. Hazen's action is mirrored in such stories as "The Affair at Coulter's Notch" (1889).

Bierce escaped the doom of war but not the doom of living. In a 1912 letter to George Sterling, he wrote about his visit to Richmond: "a city whose tragic and pathetic history . . . is some fifty years old . . . it is always with me . . . making solemn eyes at me."[16] He was haunted by the war. He felt "sentenced to life"[17] after the Civil War. Perhaps he went to Mexico to face death on his own terms and not have it visit him in the quiet of the night, but on a battlefield where he felt at ease or elated.

Bierce's stories of war are not battlefield reports. They are fictional accounts of the human condition in dangerous circumstances where individuals face a crisis of the soul through a confrontation with the unknown in war.

GOTHIC WAR STORIES

Bierce's stories echo the violence of the American Civil War. They are fierce, relentless tales; there is no relief from the overwhelming feeling of dread and impending ruin. Bierce's stories recount despair, suffering, and death. The battlefields are both real and symbolic in his short stories. He was not bitter, I think, but disillusioned, brave in war and brave, after that trauma, in peace. Bierce's stories are raw, but sometimes are laced with humor to relieve the horror. It is a military humor, a humor of biting satire, and ironic distance within disaster. It is a dark humor, born in the chaos of grim battles and the long waits for death. It is sardonic and physical. There is a cynicism often directed toward the leadership and war strategy. The war stories are about loyalty, and brothers-in-arms, and despair, and death. They speak to the randomness of killing, the folly of battle tactics, and the effects of fear and courage.

In his nonfictional "What I Saw of Shiloh" (1874), Bierce describes the scene before battle. At first there were the "great guns" firing with "a dull distant sound like the heavy breathing of some great animal. . . . The long deep sighing of iron lungs."[18] This sparked the army's attention and anxiety, as the guns throbbed with "the strong, full pulse of the fever of battle" (11). Then came the bugle call for assembly, and the men ran to their guns. He describes the feeling as exhilarating. The bugle notes bring a "wild intoxica-tion" that stirs the "heart as wine and the blood like the kisses of a beautiful woman" (12). The actual battle is in deep contrast. The battles of the American Civil War were often fought in dense forests. At Shiloh, Bierce tells of going into a "valley of death," where he "sank into ashes to the ankle" (21). The forest had a thick blanket of leaves, and it had come aflame. The valley was full of dead men. Some had died from bullets; others were in "postures of agony," having died in the "tormenting flame" (22). The scene was ghastly. On a battlefield, he writes of "all the wretched debris of the battle" (19): dead horses, disabled caissons, knapsacks, rifles, and dead men. One sergeant is suffering and dying gruesomely. He breathed in "convulsive rattling snorts . . . blowing it out in sputters of froth," and his "brain pro-truded in bosses, dropping off in flakes and strings" (19). A sympathetic soldier recommends bayoneting the sergeant, but Bierce demurs: "it was unusual, and too many were watching" (19). Bierce transforms this wartime experience in "The Coup de Grâce" (1889), where Captain Madwell, in agony, decides to kill a friend in death-throes to save him more pain, only to see stretcher-bearers emerge from the forest, like ghosts, just as he bayonets his friend in the heart. Good intentions turn out dreadfully.

"What I Saw of Shiloh" is a magnificent piece, so evocative of the frenzy, despair, and horror of combat. It seems Bierce is writing from a recording in his head. He captures the fear and anticipation of an army advancing at night and the sense of unreality, wondering where the enemy may be. It seems they are ghosts already, as the troops move through the "black-dark" (16), rainy night. He describes the advance of his regiment over the bodies of soldiers, some dead and others dying. As morning begins to glimmer, he wonders: "Where was the enemy?" and "What protected our right? Who lay upon our left? Was there really anything in our front?" (17). The soldiers are weary and tired and afraid of the unknown. Then there harks "the long weird note of a bugle . . . that seemed to float in the gray sky like the note of a lark." It electrifies the troops.

Bierce's Civil War stories are not records of the Civil War akin to "What I Saw of Shiloh." They are authentic Gothic texts about war re-imagined through the sensibility and creativity of Bierce. He keeps trying to under-stand the shadow of fate in war, the darkness over the soldiers. He is reflect-ing on what happens to people in moments of crisis, how reason fails at critical times, and he is expressing compassion toward those who were caught in the snares of fate. Through all the stories there is a lament for those long-lost days and for all the men who died. Reading several of Bierce's short stories in a sitting is brutal. You feel it is too much: the suffering, the irony, the gallows military humor, and the doom pounding in your ears like cannon.

In his stories, it seems war is where the military code of honor means a Union son kills his Confederate father, as in "A Horseman in the Sky" (1889). A sentry shoots a shadowy figure who is his beloved twin brother in "The Mocking-Bird" (1891). War is pitiless. For Lieutenant Brayle, in "Killed at Resaca" (1887), it means to prove your courage to your lover you must die. There is no relief from the suffering. In "One of the Missing" (1888), Jerome Searing is virtually buried alive with his own Springfield rifle aimed directly between his eyes. Following orders seems to mean slaughtering your fellow soldiers in "One Kind of Officer" (1893). War is the setting for General Masterson to utter bombastically: "It was the beautifulest fight ever made"; however, "the beauty and greatness were attested by a row of dead,"[19] as in "An Affair of Outposts" (1897). In "A Tough Tussle" (1899), a soldier is commanded by illusion and fear to kill himself, while in "One Officer, One Man" (1889), an officer is self-slain by disgrace. Captain Coulter cannonades his home, wherein his wife and child die, in "The Affair at Coulter's Notch." Some of these and others are explored in more depth in the following.

"The Story of a Conscience" (1890) demonstrates the brutal logic of war. In the story, Dramer Brune is a Confederate spy uncovered by Captain Hartroy. However, Brune had once saved Hartroy's life. The captain orders the execution of Brune. Then he commits suicide to balance the grotesque commands of war in a supernatural space.

Private Carter Druse is asleep at his post of duty at the beginning of "A Horseman in the Sky." He is a soldier alone. There are several perspectives in the story. At first we are given a picture of Druse positioned on a spur of a cliff with a view, "had he been awake" (660) (as the scolding narrative voice says), of a road and a rock jutting over the cliff. Below the sleeping man, there are five regiments of Federal troops planning to take the road. Druse is the sentinel to secure the road to allow an attack on a Confederate camp. The next perspective is of Druse. He is a Southerner by birth, raised in luxury and love, but he elected to fight for the North. It is never clear why. Druse is awakened by "some invisible messenger of fate" (661), to see a Confederate on horseback on the cliff. He thinks it is a beautiful sight, silhouetted against the blue sky, in perfect proportions. The rider peers into the valley below where the Federal troops are. Druse aims at the horseman. The Confederate soldier turns and seems to "look into his brave, compassionate heart" (662). At that point Druse knows it is his father, but the reader does not. Druse then debates with himself. Whatever he chooses, he is lost. If he does not shoot, his father will inform the Confederate forces, and the Federal troops will likely be annihilated. But shoot your father? What can one do in that circumstance? With the voice of his father in his ear: "Whatever may occur, do what you conceive to be your duty" (663), Druse aims at the horse and fires.

The following scene is from the view of a Federal officer in the valley. Astounded, he watches a man on horseback plunge down 1,000 feet. The suffering of Private Druse's father, as he falls, is not told in the story. The officer stumbles at the sight and hears the horse and man crash into the pines. It seems unreal. He searches but is unable to find them. In the final scene a sergeant crawls up to Private Druse and asks him if it was his shot they had heard. Druse says yes, he shot a horse, on which sat his father. The sergeant is aghast. So Druse pays for his neglect of duty by having to kill his father. Berkove says that Private Druse has destroyed his own mind along with the body of his father,[20] as duty won out over family. Duty has killed both father and son. There is a deep silence after the last sentence of the story. Nothing more can be said.

Private William Grayrock is an isolated sentry at night where "in the gloom of the wood the darkness was deep" (790). The darkness of "The Mocking-Bird" will overtake Grayrock. The narrator has an aside on the need for pickets, after what happened at Shiloh, but then he is not to portray the "fate of an army" (791), but Private Grayrock. In his fiction, Bierce is concerned with the individual, not the grand, perhaps overblown, drama of the tactics of generals and the conflict of divisions. This story focuses on what happens to one soldier, as he comes up against the supernatural. As the night wears on Grayrock becomes increasingly disoriented. His environment becomes "unfamiliar" (791). He has crossed a frontier and slipped into the unknown. He has "lost his bearings" (791). Spying a shadowy form, he challenges it. He fires, and this is echoed by shots along the picket line. The men are nervous. Then the pickets retreat, fearing the "evolving enemies from . . . [their] imagination" (791). Not Grayrock; he does not know which way to go. He is commended for not running away. Grayrock returns to the wood to hunt for the body, but finds nothing at first. Then he rests and dreams of a happy time with his twin brother. It was broken by the death of their mother. They are separated, one raised in the North, the other in the South, by kinsmen who were enemies. Grayrock re-experiences the joy and sorrow of childhood, but now he is a soldier. Awakening, he finds the body of the intruder. It is akin to looking into a mirror; it is his face. He has killed John Grayrock, his brother, dead now on the ground in his uniform. William Grayrock will reunite with his brother in death. Their fates are twined. The American Civil War split the country, split states, split families, and sundered brothers. In this story, the killed brother is a "masterwork of civil war" (794). This is an unsettling story of brothers linked by love, but separated by the death of their mother and driven by military duty and fear toward a shared doom as if by supernatural fate.

"A Son of the Gods" (1888) starts with the Federal army in doubt and confusion about the exact position of the enemy. An open field halts its advance. A half-mile in front rises a crest of a hill, behind is a hedge, and behind the hedge, tops of trees. It has a "sinister look" (599). Is the enemy up there? Eric Solomon says this story depicts the soldiers "in awe of the incomprehensible."[21] As the troops wait for orders, a "young officer on a snow-white horse" (600), and in full uniform, rides along the edge of the open ground, as if challenging the enemy. He argues with the commanding officer, then wheels and dashes toward the crest. It is a glorious sight as he rides so grandly and gallantly. The Federal troops themselves seem to be in wonder, as if the rider is miraculous. Solomon argues that the story is replete with religious symbolism.[22] Indeed, the young officer is called a "military Christ" (602). The soldiers seem to experience a religious ecstasy watching the horseman race toward the crest of the far hill. The young officer changes course to ride parallel to the crest, calling for the fire of the enemy. He gallops directly toward the crest again, but wheels and races back "toward his friends, toward his death!" (602). The wall comes alive with fire and smoke. Lead shoots across the field. The young man escapes a few volleys, but eventually his horse falls under the heavy fire of the guns. He stands briefly and salutes his fellow troops. The troops explode into the open space, as if commanded by the fallen hero. Or is it mob behavior? The enemy mows them down, leaving a field of dead. The enchantment of the spectacle is broken by the realities of war. The sacrifice of the young man to identify the enemy's position and save lives instead has led to death. It is doom again. With elegiac alliteration and irony, Bierce laments the force of "the pitiless perfection of the divine, eternal plan" (603).

War is heartless, as Lieutenant Brayle in "Killed at Resaca" finds out. This story is similar in part to "A Son of the Gods." But here Brayle must die to prove his courage to his lover. Brayle is "vain of his courage" (507) and, in contrast to most soldiers, he does not take cover when "hissing lead and screaming iron" (508) assaulted the troops. He seems indifferent toward death. A topographical engineer, as Bierce was during part of the American Civil War, narrates the story. The Federal troops are in a wooded area just behind an open field. Across the field the enemy lurk in another wood. Brayle is commanded to take an order to Colonel Ward and "leave your horse" (509). Instead, Brayle rides out into the open on his horse, where "it meant absolutely certain failure to deliver the message" (509). He rides into a "storm of bullets and grape" (508). Troops rush into the open to fire back at the enemy, and many fall and die. The artillery joins in the battle. The narrator sees Brayle standing on the "shot-swept space"; he is "awaiting death" (510). Then he is down. The firing stops, and both sides rush out to secure the fallen hero to take up the "sacred burden" (510), as if he were another sacrifice. From the enemy side a dirge sounds to honor the fallen brave man. The narrator takes Brayle's pocketbook. He finds a letter to Brayle from his lover. It implies that he may be a coward, and she says she could bear his death more than his cowardice. After the war the narrator travels to see Marina Mendehall, to confront her with what she caused. She recoils at the blood on her letter. She is a "detestable creature" (511) to the topographical engineer. With bitterness he tells her Brayle was "bitten by a snake" (511). This story has many interpretations. Was she the snake that caused Brayle's death? Or was Brayle caught in his own trap of valor? Or could it be that in the end the narrator recognizes the vainglorious actions of Brayle, who did not deliver his message, as a good soldier would do, but is "the cause of the carnage" (510)?

"The Affair at Coulter's Notch" is a story, on the surface, of the power of army rank to cause suffering and tragedy. The colonel is baffled by Captain Coulter's hesitation and by the general's orders to have Coulter's artillery engage the Confederates' dozen cannon. Coulter is described in great detail early in the story, as gray-eyed, thin, with a blond mustache and hair, and casualness in his uniform. The artillery duel is also told in great detail. When it ends, Coulter and his men "looked like demons of the pit . . . their reeking skins black with blotches of powder and spattered with gouts of blood" (688). The duel had turned them into beasts. The gun was alive, "bleeding at the mouth" (688). It is savage. Coulter becomes "a fiend seven times damned" (688). With "teeth flashing between his black lips, his eyes . . . burning like coal" (689), he is not recognized by the colonel. Coulter is also not recognized later in the cellar of the house where he is clasping his wife and child. The colonel and others think the man is dead. When he lifts his head and gazes "tranquilly into their faces . . . his complexion was coal black; the cheeks were apparently tattooed in irregular sinuous lines from the eyes downward. The lips, too, were white, like those of a stage negro. There was blood upon his forehead" (690).

Captain Coulter is broken by the war, and the malice of army rank, and perhaps by his own pride and honor as a soldier. He follows the order to engage the Confederate force, which is near his house. Coulter is a Southerner. The general had some trouble with the lady of the house and he had been transferred; his order is revenge on the whole family. Coulter's rewards for following military discipline are the dead bodies of his wife and child. He is now in hell. Bierce captures the horror and derangement of the captain in his description of Coulter's face. It seems a mask: a horrid mask with the characteristics of sorrow and loss, of a slave, and a mad killer. Coulter's eyes reveal a vacancy, as he has died in mind and spirit there in the cellar. He is transformed into a Gothic monster.

Daniel Aaron points out that Bierce's clear sense of topography helps the reader see "every copse or ravine or stream"[23] in his stories. This is his realism. Aaron also alludes to Bierce's keen ability to shift from reality to surrealism.[24] In "Chickamauga" (1889), Bierce contrasts the reality of war with the idealism of war, in a very surreal story. Able neither to talk nor hear, a child wanders from his home and encounters an army of retreating, wounded solders. "They crept upon their hands and knees. They used their hands only, dragging their legs. They used their knees only, their arms hanging idle at their sides" (650). The child knows not what he sees. He sees them as playthings, as he sees his father's slaves. He rides them, as he had ridden the slaves, both odious. The boy imagines himself a great and fearless general leading his troops into victorious battle. This is set in sharp contrast to the reality of war, as attested by the dreadful state of the wounded. The men are "like a swarm of great black beetles" (650). They have lost their humanity in the war. They crawl continuously through their "haunted landscape," casting "monstrous shadows" (650). It is a Gothic scape. Then the boy is attracted by a "guiding light" and heads toward it, "confident of the fidelity of his forces" (652). The light is his plantation, which is now a blazing ruin. His mother is a burnt and disfigured corpse. It is an awful revelation. He utters "a startling, soulless, unholy sound, the language of a devil" (652); the howl of suffering. It is also an inarticulate howl in the face of inexpressible horror. War has claimed yet another victim. In this story, Bierce contrasts the distorted perspective of the child to the reality of the wounded soldiers. The perspectives are merged into the grotesque image of the child's dead mother, as war kills not only soldiers but also civilians.

Death is omnipresent in war, but it is the response of the individual to it that interests Bierce. In the beginning of "Parker Adderson, Philosopher" (1891), Adderson, the Union spy, seems nonchalant and flippant about death. The Confederate General Clavering, with whom he is philosophizing, on the other hand respects death, knows its horrors. After the general orders Captain Hasterlick to have Adderson shot immediately, the philosophy changes hands. Reality is a killer. Perhaps all philosophies are flawed in the face of death. Adderson panics and a fight ensues. Hasterlick dies and the general is mortally wounded, while Adderson suffers only a broken arm. General Clavering repeats his order and Adderson, while "begging incoherently for life, was shot to death by twenty men" (722). The general seems to welcome the silence and passes away with a smile, as if at the cruel jest of life.

In "One of the Missing," fate rules, as it "was decreed from the beginning of time that Private Searing was not to murder anybody" (527) on that day. He is a Union "scout" (525) with orders to approach enemy lines and gather what intelligence he can. He finds a good observation point on a tottering, small building and spots the withdrawing Confederate army. It is his duty to return and report, but he dallies and takes up his Springfield rifle, refitted as a sniper's weapon. He aims at the retreating enemy with the hope of making "someone a widow, or an orphan, or a childless mother" (527). This seems an ignoble reason to kill, and, moreover, Searing is neglecting his duty.[25] But at that moment of firing, a Confederate captain of artillery, having "nothing better to do . . . amused himself" by firing toward "what he mistook for some Federal officers." The missile is off its mark and shatters the building where

Searing stands. He finds himself covered with timbers, "caught in a trap like a rat" (528). Even in his trap, Searing tries to extract himself, not giving up right away. But in the end he is in the bull's-eye of fate. He dies there staring into his Springfield rifle, while waiting for the rats to "attack his face, gnaw away his nose, cut his throat" (531). Bierce is exploring the Gothic archetype of the double in this story, along with the fragility of identity in the American Civil War, where many died anonymously. Herman Melville eulogizes: "In glades they meet skull to skull / Where pine-cones lay—the rusted gun, / Green shoes full of bones, the mouldering coat / And cuddled-up skeleton; And scores of such."[26] All these dead are still unburied in Bierce's head; they kept arising and returning again and again.

The first set of doubles is Searing, a private and a sniper, off on his own, and his unknown assailant, the Confederate captain of artillery, with his troops, preparing to retreat. They both seem to want to fire off their weapons needlessly for the pursuit of the war. The captain takes out Searing. The one does not know of the other, as is the case most often in war, illustrating the anonymity of war and the randomness of death. The second set of doubles is Private Searing and his brother, Lieutenant Adrian Searing. The lieutenant, leading a picket guard, comes upon the bombed building and sees a body. It is covered in dust and seems to be in a gray coat; he notes the anguished face and does not recognize his brother. In death Searing becomes the enemy and one of the anonymous dead. Soldiers even in death suffer. Often in Bierce, identities seem to shift, as the war changes people forever.

Captain Graffenreid, the protagonist of "One Officer, One Man," considers himself brave, as does Harker Brayton in "The Man and the Snake" (1890). Here, Bierce explores the frailty of perceptions both of oneself and of one's surroundings. Graffenreid misreads himself and misreads the battle circumstances. He is in the front ranks of his company, looking out over an open field to the wood beyond. He does not see the enemy; indeed, he never has seen an "armed enemy" (655). His views are contrasted with those of the soldiers, where "every man in those miles of men knew that he and death were face to face" (655). The captain can imagine "nothing more peaceful than the appearance of that pleasant landscape with its long stretches of brown fields" (654–55). The first shot of the skirmish blows apart his peace. He hears the gun's roar, the whine of the missile, and an explosion. Thinking it is near, he "dodged and threw up his hands" (656), but then realizes it exploded far to his left. Graffenreid is mortified. The narrator says he "heard, or fancied he heard" (656), his men laugh at him. The captain is shaken. He is isolated, alone in an army. Graffenreid tries to understand his feelings. He finds it difficult to be still and "fancied that his men observed it. Was it fear? He feared it was" (656). He thinks he is disgraced. He does not understand what is happening to him. Then he hears the crackle of rifles, and the hissing of lead through the air. At his side, a soldier is hit and falls. As do all the soldiers, the captain hits the deck. But he is beside the dead man and is appalled by his hideousness. Graffenreid looks across at the wood and once again fails to see. He imagines soldiers lining up to attack, pushing heavy guns forward. He "fancied he could see their black muzzles" (657). All around him there is the sound and fury of an army rising to attention, of men readying for combat. The captain stands at the head of his troops, noting "the sinister silence of the forest in front" (657). His body seems to fail him, as he is hot, then cold; he pants and forgets to breathe. Looking down, he spies his sword, thinks of Rome, and with one last "fancy" (658) falls on the sword. Only two soldiers die in the skirmish. Bierce may be using an old Roman code of honor to suggest that the captain is not a coward but honorable, because he felt disgraced. He is an individual who did not know what war was. He did not really know himself and was unforgiving about his own fear. Yet he embraces death in the end as his only escape from his fear of fear. It is a story about distress, and how individuals respond to fearful situations.

Roy Morris, Jr., thinks fear is one of Bierce's major themes.[27] Bierce fought in many battles, received numerous commendations,[28] and always stood up to death. In "A Little of Chickamauga" (1898), Bierce writes about soldiers moving "toward the sound" of guns, toward the center of a battle, as he "did so himself."[29] Michael W. Schaefer sees this as a distinguishing characteristic of Bierce. He was brave and is forthright in his war stories. Schaefer concludes that Bierce created a "body of work that for the first time in American literary history does not . . . gloss over the physical and psychological terrors of battle."[30]

Bierce is trying to understand the unforgiving universe, which is replete with suffering and death. He treats war as a personal event and not a grand tapestry of anonymous soldiers under the thoughtful and grand command of an abstract general. He is about the individual experience, as if he is trying to understand his own life. He emphasizes the solitary soldier—his stories are about individuals in extraordinary circumstances. As Cathy N. Davidson shows, Bierce, in most of his stories, presents a character "who must respond to reality but who often does not know what is real, what imagined, and what an inextricable intermingling of both."[31] Schaefer concurs, saying that Bierce's stories are about the "stresses an isolated protagonist feels before or after battle."[32] These traumas often impel a character to desperate actions leading to tragic ends.

Bierce also explores the problem of perception and the problem of reason under duress. Reason may not always be the best guide, as the condition may be irrational. However, reason is a way to make some sense of the world, at some times, under some circumstances. It is also a tool used by the powerful to cover their emotional drives. Bierce was conflicted. He saw logic as a way of overcoming ignorance. He was also aware of its limitations, or perhaps more correctly put, the limitations of humans as rational beings, as shown by modern behavioral economists. Trying to rationalize away fear may only lead to more suffering and death, as in "A Tough Tussle" (1899).

The main character, Lieutenant Brainerd Brying, is horrified by dead bodies, but considers himself a superior war strategist, perhaps better than Napoleon. However, he finds himself trapped in a "monstrous . . . alliance . . . of night and solitude and silence and the dead" (620). He is alone with a corpse, although he thinks it may be alive. He smokes and the sight vanishes, as if light scares away the dead. But it returns, and he cries, "Damn the thing" (621), as if cursing the night. The corpse persists, visibly and horribly. It is as if he is visited by something alive yet dead. He senses "the supernatural" (621) nearing. Brying tries to reason his way out of his dread of "a dead body, a malign thing" (621). The fear is irrational but real, yet Brying ignores the reality of his fear and ends up believing in the reality of the corpse. He thinks how brave he is to face his fear, so he stares at the body. This is a poor strategy for this lieutenant, for his final action is to panic. He goes through a series of physical changes akin to Captain Graffenreid in "One Officer, One Man." The dead man seems to move, as Brying hallucinates. He is becoming something else. He attacks the corpse, stabbing it repeatedly in a frenzy, and then kills himself.

We live in a disordered world, and our reason is often a slave to our passion and works against out best interests. In this, Bierce is nearly a modern in his short stories. Davidson says he anticipates modernism through his fragmentary and non-chronological style of writing, such as "The Suitable Surroundings" (1889) and "A Watcher by the Dead" (1889). Bierce seems to be as disillusioned with narrative form as he was with the grandeur and heroism of war and the fairness of life. In his writing, Bierce expresses his sense of the randomness of life.

"An Occurrence at Owl Creek Bridge" (1890) is perhaps Bierce's most renowned story. It is narrated in three stages. It starts with Peyton Farquhar standing on a bridge about to be hanged. There are Union soldiers at attention. A sergeant is standing on an end of a plank; Farquhar at the other, between two ties with a rope around his neck. The sergeant steps off the plank. The following scene tells of Farquhar. He is a wealthy Southern plantation owner with slaves. His family is highly respected in Alabama, but he is not a soldier. Others fight for his right to own slaves. One evening a gray-clad soldier stops at his plantation and asks for water. He tells Farquhar that Union soldiers are repairing Owl Creek Bridge and recruits him as a saboteur. The gray-clad man is a Federal spy. In the third scene, we return to the bridge, or rather the stream. Farquhar plunges down into the water, miraculously surviving the rope. In the stream, he eludes rifle shots, cannonballs, and grapeshot. Leaving the river, he travels through a dense forest back to his wife and family. But it is all a fantasy. There are two worlds depicted in the story, the bridge of reality and the stream of fantasy. The most frequent non-common words in the story are "bridge" and "water." Both are used nineteen times. The bridge is the fate of Farquhar; it is the site of his attempted sabotage, and the site of his death. The water is a dream escape, the rippling stream (which is used eleven times) a contrast to the solid bridge. Time is distorted for Farquhar. In reality, as he swings below the timbers of the bridge, high above Owl Creek, Farquhar finds only "darkness and silence" (732).

Bierce turns on its head George Eliot's insight, expressed in *Middlemarch* (1871–72), that "we should die of that roar which lies on the other side of silence."[33] This is the dread and the tragedy in everyday life, which is often ignored. Here Bierce evokes the silence on the other side of the roar of the guns of war. In his stories of soldiers, civilians, or the supernatural, he conveys that tragedy of everyday life, that great silence.

That silence is in "A Resumed Identity" (1908). The story starts with a description of a solitary man on a low hill in the pre-dawn hour. It is a lonely scene, and the man is not sure where he is. Then he sees a long column of cavalry, artillery, and infantry marching along a road. But there is silence. He thinks himself "deaf" (1036). But he speaks; he hears, but it seems not his voice. He believes the army is a Confederate force and hides, but looking back, the army has "passed out of sight" (1037). He cannot "comprehend it," perhaps because he seems to have "lost his sense of time" (1037). Looking again at his surroundings, the man is bewildered to see that "on every side lay cultivated fields showing no sign of war and war's ravages" (1037).

Then the narrative structure shifts to Dr. Malson returning to his home. An elderly man in civvies accosts him. The man claims he is a lieutenant assigned to General Hazen. The man asks the doctor where the armies have gone. He says he is twenty-three and had only a "brief unconsciousness" (1039) from a glancing blow by a bullet. He must return to his unit. The man and his seemingly inane questions and answers perplex the doctor. Struggling with what he thinks is lunacy, Dr. Malson departs across a field, leaving the man alone on the moonlit road. The story plays with varying perspectives.

This is what war can do: even if you live, it will eventually take your mind and your life. War always takes something from the soldiers who survive, as Morris reads the story.[34] In the final paragraphs, the man sees his aged face in a pool of rainwater, a mirror. Seeing it, he dies from heart failure, decades of his life seemingly lost.

Mary E. Grenander places this story in her mimetic tales of passion category, and for this story it is one of pathos. A mimetic tale portrays human experience in such a fashion that it will elicit in the reader a feeling similar to that of the protagonist in the story.[35] She says the story is based on two incidents in Bierce's life: the actual battle, at Stone River, and his return years later to the same battlefield.[36] The Stone River battle site is one space and two times for the man in the story, as it was for Bierce. Grenander reads the story as depicting the way the protagonist's life has been split; neither is complete and both are shattered by the war. In a way, the man is a double in one. He has had two lives, neither of which knows the other. He is incomplete, broken by the war. It could be read as a commentary on the difficulty faced by soldiers in returning to civilian life. They are burdened with terrible images, which they try to keep buried. But their young selves may arise again and their civilian lives vanish, and they are back on the battlefield.

STORIES OF A DARK PEACE

As Berkove argues, Bierce's work goes beyond the horror of the Civil War; his stories have the "theme of man in a hostile universe."[37] The stories of soldiers "make common cause with his tales of 'civilians.'"[38] Bierce's war stories harmonize with his supernatural stories. Roger B. Salomon argues that Bierce's war stories and his horror stories have a "seamless relationship."[39] Davidson says: "one cannot conclusively divide the ghost from the war story."[40] She goes on to say that, in Bierce, "the only reality is the reality of the 'haunted mind.'"[41] One of the haunted minds is Bierce's. Davidson thinks Bierce examines "the human mind in crisis."[42] Perception often fails and language cannot articulate fully or truthfully some dreadful experiences. She sees Bierce as a very modern writer experimenting with form, style, and content to express the individual's hopelessness in the face of the ineffable. She argues that Bierce's fictions are purposely disruptive of normal plotting and style to reflect the ultimate indeterminacy of our language. The disruptive techniques are akin to the chaos of battle.

Bierce's supernatural tales are grim and hallucinatory. In "The Death of Halpin Frayser" (1891), it seems your dream in a "haunted wood" (806) may be a killer. What is more, a stuffed snake with glowing eyes can kill you, as in "The Man and the Snake" (1890). These eyes appear again in "The Eyes of a Panther" (1897) and in "The Boarded Window" (1891). Houses are not safe, as Bierce's "The Spook House" (1889) features a sort of reverse panic room, wherein people are trapped in a killing darkness. Reading a ghastly manuscript is murderous in a haunted house next to a dead man, as in "The Suitable Surroundings" (1889). A similar tale is "A Watcher by the Dead" (1889), where Jarette succumbs to "the superstitious awe with which the living regard the dead" (699). When Bierce's ghosts speak, as in "An Inhabitant of Carcosa" (1886) or "The Moonlit Road" (1907), they are still suffering; they are lonely and live in desolation. A few of Bierce's supernatural stories will be explored in more detail to understand how these have common cause with his war stories.

"The Man and the Snake" features Hacker Brayton, who is proud of his bravery. In this story, Bierce illustrates how irrational fear in a home environment can lead to death, just as it does in war. Brayton is a bachelor of thirty-five and is visiting his friend Dr. Druring, a biologist and collector of toads and snakes. Brayton seems a bit of a dilettante, "a scholar, idler . . . rich, popular and of sound health" (721).

Lounging on a sofa in his room in the house, he is reading *Marvells of Science*. Brayton scoffs at the notion that a snake's eyes have hypnotic power. Putting the book aside, he catches "two small points of light" (719) in the darkness under his bed. He fancies they gleam brighter and have a greenish hue. Perhaps the eyes moved. Starting to rise, he is startled when he sees "the coils of a large serpent" (720) under his bed. The eyes look into his with "a malign significance" (720). He thinks at first it is an absurd circumstance. Standing, he feels the eyes burn with "more pitiless malevolence than before" (721). Hesitant at creating any impression that he is fearful, he does not ring a servant. Previously, snakes had escaped from their menagerie and roamed the house. Brayton's suffering and agony are told in excruciating detail. He is captured by the eyes, or perhaps by his own fear. He takes baby steps, holding on to a chair as if it were a lifeline, but then it falls, abandoning him. He is alone with a snake. Brayton groans in fear. But the snake still has not moved; just its eyes gleam. He is overcome by his fear and his misperception in the room. He thinks he hears a "great drum throbbing" (722)—it is his heart. He imagines himself in some jungle where there is a gigantic serpent. Brayton falls, striking his head. All through this he dares not break eye contact with his chimerical snake. There is blood everywhere. Now he is close to his enemy. He begins to convulse with a "serpentile undulation" (723), as if he is becoming what he fears. The final scene has Dr. Druring and his wife in the library. After hearing Brayton's wild scream, they find him on the floor, dead. But it was only a stuffed snake; irrational fear can drive one to death in peace as well as war.

"The Damned Thing" (1893) is more than a story of an invisible thing. The setting is a corner's inquest into a death. The witness for the jury is William Harker, a reporter, who "sometimes write[s] stories" (859), blurring nonfiction with fiction. For him the breakdown of the orderly world "is incredible" (858). But only he and Hugh Morgan, the dead man, had experienced the invisible thing. It had attacked Morgan. The jury returns a verdict of death by mountain lion for the dead man. The witness's story is overthrown to preserve the orderly world. The witness is not raving, but reports the facts as he saw them. However, the facts disrupt the ordinary world as viewed by the jury. Here perception is not disoriented, but those perceptions are not congruent with a rational world. Harker thinks: "We so rely upon the orderly operation of familiar natural laws that any seeming suspension of them is noted as a menace to our safety, as warning of unthinkable calamity"

(860). This is similar to H. P. Lovecraft's view of the cosmos. The thing is an anomaly in the wilderness, which tears to shreds one hunter. But staid members of an inquest, who want only their reasonable world, will not accept it. Harker is discounted, as if he had witnessed only an illusion. Reason here overrides facts. This story is in four sections, each with a macabre heading. The first section, for example, is titled: "One Does Not Always Eat What Is on the Table." Hugh Morgan's body is on the table. Bierce continues his grim military humor in stories of the dark peace.

In "An Inhabitant of Carcosa" (1886), a ghost speaks through the medium Bayrolles. A man is wandering, alone, through an unfamiliar wilderness. It is a bleak, dark, and desolate place. But the landscape is alive: "the wind sighed . . . and the gray grass bent to whisper its dread secret to the earth" (457–58). Stones "exchange looks" (457). The wanderer does not know where he is at first. He remembers having a fever and worries that he has roamed away from his house. He is from Carcosa, but now he is in a place of "mystery and dread" (458). He wonders if he has lost his mind. His shouts at a lynx go unheeded, as it trots casually by. Next he spies a man in animal skins and tries to stop him, but the man passes by as well. The wanderer can "hear the silence" (459). This is that silence that is behind the roar of life. It is also in "The Death of Halpin Frayser." After Holker and Jaralson discover Frayser's body, they are overcome with a "dread unspeakable" when they hear a "soulless laugh" that rose from and "sank to silence" (815). In "An Inhabitant of Carcosa," the wanderer discovers his own tomb and the ruins of his once grand city. It seems that here, as in "The Stranger" (1909), there is only desolation, and what we encounter is a "darkness that seemed to enclose . . . like a black wall" (1047).

Bierce seems wounded by human suffering, but there is toughness to his writing. There is no hand-wringing, just saddle up and charge no matter what. We are under the sway of a fate, but there is still a responsibility for honor, duty, and action. It is the individual's response in crisis that Bierce writes about, and that individual bears some responsibility—not just to oneself but as homage to those who went down even if they were braver and stronger. It was just dumb luck. The grotesque or supernatural provides a lever upon which Bierce turns these tales from solitary events into universal tales. It makes them un-orderly, in chaos as war is. The divide is there between the civilian and soldier, but there are ghosts, so to speak, everywhere, and there are wars away from a battlefield.

In "Beyond the Wall" (1907), reason works to kill happiness. The narrator listens to the sad tale of Mohun Dampier. They are talking in Dampier's ugly dwelling. Gloomy grounds, "destitute of either flowers or grass" (1029–30), surround it. It is a "dismal environment" (1030) somewhat similar to that around the House of Usher. Dampier's "prescience of death" (1030) is also similar to Usher's sickness. From a wall the narrator hears a gentle tapping, and Dampier stares fixedly at the sound. He seems in mourning. Dampier laments his past life. He refrained from acting outwardly on his love for a beautiful and caring young lady because she "was not of . . . [his] class" (1032). He blames it on his ancestors, those long-dead ones whom he will soon join. But he was a cad back then; he conspired to obtain a room adjacent to the young woman's. He starts a conversation of taps on the wall. She responds, and he is in joy. But she falls silent, and he blames her. Then one night there is a faint tapping, but he is brutal and does not respond. It turns out that the young woman had been sick for weeks, and with her last hope she had tried to call for him with taps through the wall. He did not respond to her plea, and he bears the scar forever. Now he is waiting for her to come and claim him. Her taps announce her return from the tomb, similar to Lady Madeline Usher.

As Berkove argues, many of Bierce's characters are rationalists.[43] They use reason to make a choice that is not always in their best interests, and sometimes reason only supports an emotional reaction. Bierce has anticipated the work of behavioral economists such as Daniel Kahneman,[44] who studies the biases to which people are prone in judgments. His studies have found that people have several behavioral prejudices, such as bounded willpower, which is the failure of people to do something even when they know it is in their best interests—think of Captain Coulter. He also has identified a number of common deviations from rational behavior, such as overconfidence, where people rate themselves better than they really are—think of Captain Graffenreid. People also exhibit a framing bias, which is a tendency to draw conclusions according to the way something appears—think of Hacker Brayton. Kahneman also finds that people often use reason to support pre-held beliefs and not as some impartial arbiter, also like Bierce.

In Bierce's fictional world the familiar laws are overthrown; characters enter a nightmare world, a world that seems "inimical to life, hope and happiness,"[45] according to Salomon. This is the world of war but also the world of the civilian. In the end, their familiar places turn out to be in the realm of suffering. It is where they all are "prey to apprehension and despair" (1020), as the ghost exclaims in "The Moonlit Road."

HONORING THE DEAD

Ambrose Bierce's Civil War stories are not mere transcripts from the killing fields, but rather merge fact and fiction with a supernatural touch that elevates the stories into a great literature of the human situation in times of crisis and chaos. Schaefer rightly asserts that Bierce "aspired to produce serious, artful literature."[46] These stories are unredemptive, grim, take-no-prisoners writing. They chronicle the realm of suffering in life. Grenander suggests that

Bierce felt we are all "poised precariously on the abyss of anguish, despair and death."[47] This is when we are alone in a crisis, and many of Bierce's stories are just that: how an individual behaves at such a time. He writes of that existential anxiety in the face of "forces that are . . . dark and mysterious,"[48] as Grenander says. At that instant a person is tried by how he or she will react. Will there be self-revelation, or self-loathing, or self-denial, or just fear and trembling? It is confrontation with self or with the indifferent universe. We are alone in a great void within which we must make our being.

Bierce honors the phantoms of the Civil War. Blight argues that Bierce's work was "antiheroic . . . at odds with modern nostalgia for Blue-Gray Valor."[49] Rather, it is anti-heroic and heroic at the same time. Yes, in war bravery does not always determine if you live or die. For Bierce, it is luck, but bravery still counts among the soldiers. Blight says that Bierce understood "the nature of Soldiers' sacrifices."[50] That is why he shows the dead in both his nonfiction and his fiction. It is not just the war they are confronting but also themselves and the great unknown. This is also true for civilians.

Bierce was a craftsman of short fiction. He is very good at descriptions of unusual landscapes and with a brevity of genius sketches the settings into life. Donald A. Ringe notes Bierce's "clear, precise and simple style even when depicting his most gruesome horrors."[51] He goes on to say that Bierce "creates a real sense of horror or terror."[52] Bierce's stories exhibit a "literary craftsmanship of a high order," and the "intensity and pain in his stories rang true,"[53] according to the editors of *The Short Fiction of Ambrose Bierce*. His stories are realistic in settings, although the reality is malleable and has various levels of experience, including the realm of the unknown that intrudes unpredictably.

Bierce affected the work of writers in both mainstream and genre literature. Daniel Aaron identifies Bierce's fundamental role in portraying the differences between soldier and civilian taken up by Stephen Crane, Ernest Hemingway, and Norman Mailer. Aaron sees Bierce lifting the idealistic and patriotic fog that obscured the cruel realities of war and combat.[54] John Berryman notes in his biography that Stephen Crane expressed admiration for the short stories of Bierce, especially "An Occurrence at Owl Creek Bridge," saying: "Nothing better exists."[55] Faust says that Bierce is often cited as a major influence of Crane and Hemingway.[56] Davidson suggests that Hemingway's "The Snows of Kilimanjaro" has Bierce as one of its models.[57] She also argues for Bierce's influence on such moderns as Jorge Luis Borges. In particular, she sees Borges's "The Secret Miracle" owing a debt to "An Occurrence at Owl Creek Bridge." In Borges's story, Jaromir Hladik is standing before a firing squad, but time stops to allow him to complete his play in his head, as Farquhar enjoyed a fantasy of freedom before being hanged.[58] Roy Morris, Jr., argues that Bierce was the first to treat war as an absurd and hallucinatory experience. It was "revolutionary"[59] and influenced all modern writing about war. Bierce also influenced H. P. Lovecraft, who calls Bierce's stories "grim and savage," which "admit the malignly supernatural and form a leading element in America's fund of weird literature."[60] Solomon says, "Bierce might be called the first truly modern war writer working in the English language."[61] He goes on to identify five ways in which Bierce affected future writers: "the treatment of time, the process of animism, the approach to nature, the use of religious symbolism and . . . the development from innocence, through war, to experience."[62]

Bierce writes in the Gothic tradition. There is a haunting quality to his fierce realism. In his nonfictional "Four Days in Dixie" (1888), he tells of coming upon a small group of Confederate soldiers: "The men were asleep; the sentinel was asleep."[63] He has a sense of the supernatural; it seems they were already dead or soon to be, so he slips "silently back into the shadow"[64] of the forest. There is perhaps only a small difference between realism and fiction. In Bierce's fictions there are no Gothic castles, no family curses, no clanking chains: his tales happen out in the open air or in old shacks. Bierce does deploy several of the Gothic archetypes, but adds his sense of loss, suffering, and inevitable doom. He reinvents the haunted house with "The Spook House" into a meat locker of silence and death for the unfortunate who enter it. "A Vine on a House" (1905) centers on an old house with an "evil reputation" (984), which protects and shelters the roots of a vine to help reveal the brutal murder of Mrs. Harding, a former inhabitant. But most fundamentally these haunted spaces are part of a haunted world, a place where the dead lie unburied. Bierce makes everything a haunted space, including his characters' minds.

Bierce tries to understand his war experience through his fiction and nonfiction. Neither really seemed to get at what he was searching for, or exorcise it from his head, as he went back to those old battlegrounds at the end of his life. The war was violent, bloody, and horrifying. He creates a great fiction out of his years in that war. That is part of his legacy. He honors all his former comrades in arms, on both sides, by telling stories of individuals caught up in an incomprehensible world. They try to overcome their fears, often failing due to fate, or the actions of others, or even themselves. Many soldiers were mustered out of the army at the end, and they went on to other lives. These lives may have been just as incomprehensible as those during the war, so Bierce tried to tell their stories as well.

Bierce was scarred by the Civil War, as is America to this day. In his writing, you sense that a part of him is still out there on the bloody fields strewn with dead soldiers, the air reeking of corruption and death, and gunpowder smoke rolling over the bodies. Or maybe he is in a wood as the artillery roared, spitting grape and canisters down from the fortifications. Or perhaps he is crawling across an open field to measure the topography, assess the battle lines, while a sniper draws a bead on his head. Or he is moving toward the sound of guns, over dying and dead soldiers in the dark. All those dead are in his head. Bierce kept "in memory the dear dead comrades"[65] left on the battlefields. He honored their sacrifice; many were ill prepared for the bewilderment, suffering, and horror of the Civil War. Today, "among the heroes in blue and the heroes in gray," Bierce takes his place in the formation, now joined with them in "sleeping their last sleep."[66]

NOTES

1. Lawrence I. Berkove, *A Prescription for Adversity: The Moral Art of Ambrose Bierce* (Columbus: Ohio State University Press, 2002), x.

2. Bierce enlisted on April 19, 1861, shortly after President Lincoln's call to arms, "the second man in Elkhart County, Illinois," according to Roy Morris, Jr., *Ambrose Bierce: Alone in Bad Company* (New York: Crown, 1995), 19.

3. Ambrose Bierce, *A Much Misunderstood Man: Selected Letters of Ambrose Bierce*, ed. S. T. Joshi and David E. Schultz (Columbus: Ohio State University Press, 2003), 1.

4. David W. Blight, *Race and Reunion: The Civil War in American Memory* (Cambridge, MA: Harvard University Press, 2001), 244.

5. Bierce, *A Much Misunderstood Man*, 242.

6. Ambrose Bierce, *A Sole Survivor: Bits of Autobiography*, ed. S. T. Joshi and David E. Schultz (Knoxville: University of Tennessee Press, 1998), x.

7. Helen Bierce, "Ambrose Bierce at Home," *American Mercury* 30, no. 4 (December 1933): 458.

8. Morris, *Ambrose Bierce*, 88–89.

9. Drew Gilpin Faust, *This Republic of Suffering: Death and the American Civil War* (New York: Vintage, 2008), xi.

10. J. David Hacker, "A Census-Based Count of the Civil War Dead," *Civil War History* 57, no. 4 (2001): 307–48.

11. Faust, *This Republic*, 196, 209, and 266.

12. Faust, *This Republic*, 55–56.

13. John A. Wyeth, quoted in Ronald S. Coddington, "A Gallant Officer," *New York Times* (June 29, 2013), http://opinionator.blogs.nytimes.com/2013/06/29/a-gallant-officer/?_r=0 (accessed June 2013).

14. Bierce, *A Sole Survivor*, 39.

15. Bierce, *A Sole Survivor*, 42.

16. Bierce, *A Much Misunderstood Man*, 221.

17. Quoted in Berkove, *A Prescription for Adversity*, 38.

18. Bierce, "What I Saw of Shiloh," in *A Sole Survivor*, 11. Hereafter cited in the text.

19. Bierce, "An Affair of Outposts," *The Short Fiction of Ambrose Bierce*, ed. S. T. Joshi, Lawrence I. Berkove, and David E. Schultz (Knoxville: University of Tennessee Press, 2006), 919. All citations from Bierce's fiction are taken from this edition and will occur in the text.

20. Berkove, *A Prescription for Adversity*, 111.

21. Eric Solomon, "The Bitterness of Battle: Ambrose Bierce's War Fiction," in *Critical Essays on Ambrose Bierce*, ed. Cathy N. Davidson (Boston: G. K. Hall, 1982), 191.

22. Solomon, "The Bitterness of Battle," 191–92.

23. Daniel Aaron, *The Unwritten War: American Writers and the Civil War* (New York: Knopf, 1973), 183.

24. Aaron, *The Unwritten War*, 184.

25. Donald T. Blume views the tale as depicting Searing as detestable, as a shirker of duty, and one who kills for the fun of it, not out of necessity. *Ambrose Bierce's Soldiers and Civilians in Context: A Critical Study* (Kent, OH: Kent State University Press, 2004), 85.

26. Herman Melville, "The Armies of the Wilderness," in *The Battle-Pieces of Herman Melville*, ed. Hennig Cohen (New York: Thomas Yoseloff, 1963), 100.

27. Morris, *Ambrose Bierce*, 204.

28. See Russell Duncan and David J. Klooster, introduction to *Phantoms of a Blood-Stained Period: The Complete Civil War Writings of Ambrose Bierce* (Amherst: University of Massachusetts Press, 2002), 8–9.

29. Bierce, "A Little of Chickamauga," in *A Sole Survivor*, 31.

30. Michael W. Schaefer, *Just What War Is: The Civil War Writings of De Forest and Bierce* (Knoxville: University of Tennessee Press, 1997), 130.

31. Cathy N. Davidson, introduction to *Critical Essays on Ambrose Bierce*, 8.

32. Schaefer, *Just What War Is*, 103.

33. George Eliot, *Middlemarch* (London: Folio Society, 1999), 173.

34. Morris, *Ambrose Bierce*, 51.

35. Mary E. Grenander, *Ambrose Bierce* (New York: Twayne, 1971), 93.

36. Grenander, *Ambrose Bierce*, 99.

37. Berkove, *A Prescription for Adversity*, 38.

38. Berkove, *A Prescription for Adversity*, 38.

39. Roger B. Salomon, *Mazes of the Serpent* (Ithaca, NY: Cornell University Press, 2002), 13.

40. Davidson, introduction to *Critical Essays*, 8.

41. Davidson, introduction to *Critical Essays*, 9.

42. Cathy N. Davidson, *The Experimental Fictions of Ambrose Bierce* (Lincoln: University of Nebraska Press, 1984), 5.

43. Berkove, *A Prescription for Adversity*, 85.

44. Daniel Kahneman, *Thinking Fast, Thinking Slow* (New York: Farrar, Straus & Giroux, 2011).

45. Salomon, *Mazes of the Serpent*, 46.

46. Schaefer, *Just What War Is*, 18.

47. Grenander, *Ambrose Bierce*, 77.

48. Grenander, *Ambrose Bierce*, 77.

49. Blight, *Race and Reunion*, 246.

50. Blight, *Race and Reunion*, 248.

51. Donald A. Ringe, *American Gothic: Imagination and Reason in Nineteenth-Century Fiction* (University Press of Kentucky, 1982), 183.

52. Ringe, *American Gothic*, 185.

53. S. T. Joshi, Lawrence I. Berkove, and David E. Schultz, general introduction to *The Short Fiction of Ambrose Bierce*, vol. 1, xvii.

54. Aaron, *The Unwritten War*, xvi.

55. Stephen Crane, quoted in John Berryman, *Stephen Crane: A Critical Biography*, rev. ed. (New York: Cooper Square Press, 2001), 170. See also Berryman, *Stephen Crane*, 248, and Roy Morris, Jr., *Ambrose Bierce*, 215.

56. Faust, *This Republic of Suffering*, 196.

57. Davidson, *The Experimental Fictions*, 133.

58. Davidson, *The Experimental Fictions*, 125. Jorge Luis Borges, "The Secret Miracle," in *Collected Fictions*, trans. Andrew Hurley (New York: Viking, 1998), 157–62.

59. Morris, *Ambrose Bierce*, 180.

60. H. P. Lovecraft, *The Annotated Supernatural Horror in Literature*, rev. ed., ed. S. T. Joshi (New York: Hippocampus Press, 2012), 65–66.

61. Solomon, "The Bitterness of Battle," 183.

62. Solomon, "The Bitterness of Battle," 183.

63. Bierce, *A Sole Survivor*, 51.

64. Bierce, *A Sole Survivor*, 51.

65. Bierce, *A Sole Survivor*, 32.

66. Bierce, *A Sole Survivor*, 33.

Chapter Four

Suffering and Evil in the Short Fiction of Arthur Machen

"There are sacraments of evil as well as of good about us,"[1] writes Arthur Machen (1863–1947) in "The Red Hand." A "sacrament," according to Iris Murdoch, "provides an external visible place for an internal invisible act of the spirit."[2] Murdoch was writing about the nature of the good, but for Machen a sacrament is a visible ritual that reifies the supernatural—good or evil.

This chapter will explore the rituals of suffering and evil in Machen's short weird fiction as exemplified in four stories: "The Great God Pan" (written 1890; published 1890–94); "The Inmost Light" (written 1892; published 1894); "The Shining Pyramid" (written and published 1895); and "The White People" (written 1899; published 1904).[3] The rituals center on the sacrifice of women. The sacrifices are founded within a web of mystery, where the sacrifice, in most cases, is intended to rip away the veil of reality or open the wonders of the universe. The sacrificial act is engineered by men, men with power, and in part within a nexus of scientific exploration.

These are stories of the mystery of being in a universe of horror. One of the protagonists, Vaughan, in "The Shining Pyramid," says mystery is a "veil of horror."[4] The events of "The Inmost Light" take place in London, which often "veiled in faint blue mist" its "deformities."[5] As central to the Gothic tradition, the stories are nested within Victorian societal, scientific, and sexual nightmares, with violence at their heart. The stories' lead female characters all die violently, and they are the sacrificial beings to rend the veil of the world, to reveal the mysteries.

PERSPECTIVES ON ARTHUR MACHEN

Machen was a prolific writer with many publications, but he is best noted for his work in the Gothic or horror genre. H. P. Lovecraft appraises Arthur Machen as one of the great writers of weird fiction.[6] Although differing substantially in their overall assessment of Machen's body of work, S. T. Joshi, Wesley D. Sweetser, and Mark Valentine agree that his short horror fiction is noteworthy and influential, especially the short fiction written in the 1890s. Sweetser contends that Machen opposes modernity in many of its forms, such as big business, industrialization, communism, atheism, democracy, materialism, and science. Machen's work is a constant interrogation of the modern and an exploration of the moral effects of the collision between the modern and the past, according to Sweetser.[7] Joshi argues that the whole of Machen's work is based on only one notion, "the awesome and utterly unfathomable mystery of the universe."[8] This sense of wonder and awe at the world is central to Machen's short fiction, and as Joshi shows, that wonder is an awful wonder at times. Joshi also argues that Machen's work is best exemplified in the decade when the stories studied in this chapter were written. Valentine also sees Machen as a visionary who pens a sense of wonder tinged by strangeness.[9]

Vincent Starrett was an early advocate, virtually a publicist for Machen, and he viewed Machen as a writer of the frontier between reality and mystery. Starrett writes, "Machen is a novelist of the soul. He writes of a strange borderland, lying somewhere between Dreams and Death."[10] Starrett saw Machen as striving to unveil and provide a view of the mysteries, which are not marvelous but awful. Dorothy Scarborough seemed to be scandalized, as she says that Machen wrote the "most revolting instances of suggestive diabolism"[11] and "[one] feels one should rinse his mind out after reading . . . [Machen's] stories."[12]

MYSTERY

In "A Fragment of Life" Machen writes: "Man is made a mystery for mysteries and vision."[13] As a first approximation, Machen explores three levels of mysteries. The first is akin to solving a puzzle or unraveling a riddle—very much like a detective story. Another level harkens back to the Mysteries— the ancient mystery religions with their hidden initiations and secrets forbidden to tell. These religious cults were entered through special initiations— mysteries. Walter Burkert notes that "to initiate" is *myein*, in Greek, "the initiate" is called *mystes*, and the whole process is the *mysteria*.[14] Part of the mystery celebrations was a jolt from normal customs, often as a descent into the primitive. The Mysteries always involved some initiation into an arcane and precious knowledge or experience. There was a ritual or rite of passage—a journey beyond the everyday, beyond the veil of normal sense. In some initiations there were tests or trials. Marvin W. Meyer notes that the Mysteries were sacred and much is still not known about their ceremonies, as classical writers themselves were silent on some matters. Mystery, Meyer says, is *mysterion* in Greek and comes from the Greek verb *myein*, whose root meaning is "to close."[15] The Mysteries were a secret set of ceremonies not to be disclosed. Such a visionary experience must have had a profound effect on adherents. This is the force of belief.

Burkert defines the Mysteries as "initiation rituals of a voluntary, personal and secret character that are aimed at a change of mind through experience of the sacred."[16] The initiations were often trying and perhaps painful and meant to disrupt the beliefs and personalities of initiates, to cause a change in consciousness. As Meyer points out, in the Eleusinian Mysteries the initiates went through rituals of life and death, and they emerged into a new light, as if reborn. The initiation rituals were to upset initiates' knowledge and give them a new set of beliefs. From a religious perspective, the Mysteries led to an encounter with the divine. In the stories studied in this chapter, Machen links the awe from the ancient mystery religions to Celtic worldviews. He treats the ancient Greek and Roman times, not as idealized images of reason and realism, but as locales for an underworld of magic and witchcraft, alive with the unquiet dead who bring fear and dread.

The third level of "mystery" is the hidden essence of creation that it is not possible to comprehend through reason or science or perhaps any means. In a way, the Mysteries are the process of achieving insight into the hidden essence. It is the revealing of the *arcana mundi*, the secrets of the universe. Machen is adept at evoking a sense of awe at the world, sometimes wondrous, but more often, in the stories, dreadful. There is something beyond our perceived world, but it is not a spiritual realm of goodness and beauty. Our world of sense is profane, and it seems from the stories that the world beyond is not sacred but evil. In the stories there are rituals for attaining esoteric knowledge. Marco Pasi calls it being able "to have access to aspects of reality that normally cannot be the object of perception or experience. These aspects belong to other levels of reality, and esotericism claims to provide access to these levels."[17] Alfred North Whitehead wrote of two kinds of experience. One is our sensory world, which is precise and open for all and is primarily the arena for the work of science. But the other, more fundamental, primitive level of experience is "vague, haunting, unmanageable . . . heavy with the contact of things gone by."[18] Machen evokes this primitive level of experience.

Mysteries, as phenomena, are outside of rational explanation and are dangerous. Machen's landscapes, either in the dark wood or in the dark streets of London, arouse a sense of dread. He explores the porcelain nature of our commonplace worldview and also the fragility of all epistemological or narrative meaning. The jumble of narrators and narrative techniques in his stories reflects the confusion that abounds in the world. Our perception is like glass and easily shattered by the intrusion of the malevolence released by scientific curiosity or indolence, or ancient beliefs, smoldering just below the surface of the everyday. Machen deploys the pagan god Pan and the Little People as reifications of cosmic panic, as Lovecraft uses the phrase. Pan is the totem, so to speak, of an aspect of the esoteric, or of the world normally hidden from us, but not a bucolic world. Machen demythologizes Pan's image as a pleasant and playful being and renders him back as the power of the dark wood. As Sweetser suggests, the Little People are symbolic of timeless evil,[19] but they also arise from the Victorian fear of the lower classes, say miners or laborers or servants, who were asserting more societal power and threatening the ancient order of classes in Britain.

Horror narrative at its core leads to the loss of hope—leads to the denial of the stability that the forces of society and culture strive relentlessly to build, maintain, and reinforce. The mysteries, the past, the evil sacraments snuff out the soul, as happens in "The Inmost Light" under Dyson's boot heel. In these stories of darkness there is no ultimate salvation. The core of the ultimate mystery is malignant; there is suffering and evil everywhere. Machen is exploring the tragedy of being. There is torment in the stories, as the world is for Mephistopheles, who, responding to a question from Faustus on why he was not in hell, shudders: "Why this is hel, nor am I out of it: Thinkst thou that I who saw the face of God, and tasted the eternal ioyes of heauen, am not tormented with ten thousand hels, in being depriv'd of ever-lasting blisse?"[20]

Machen's fictional world is a sort of hell, a world where innocents suffer not because of the indifferent hostility of the universe but because of the deliberate acts of men. The sacrifices of women are the sacraments of evil carried out by men, often men of science in the stories.

SACRIFICE

Henri Hubert and Marcel Mauss define a type of sacrifice as "communication between sacred and profane worlds, through the mediation of a victim, that is, of a thing that in the course of the ceremony is destroyed."[21] The profane is our world and the other beyond is generally thought of as the good. The question is: What is the other world really? Is it good or evil or beyond good and evil? Machen explores these questions. And sacrifice is intended to link us in our everyday world with the world of the supernatural. The offering—the sacrifice—brings a return to those who sacrifice, say a view of the sublime, or grace from a god, or societal control. But what it gives to the victim is only violent death. Communication with the supernatural in this context is the aim of sacrifice. In the stories the sacrifice is at the borders of experience,[22] and the rite is the suffering and death of women. The Gothic exemplified in these stories is what Clive Bloom calls the expression of a passion of fear and torment into a distorted eroticism transformed into a sadistic ritual.[23]

The sacrifice of women is the "dark, primordial manifestation of evil still lurking in men."[24] These acts spawn such abominations as "flaming eyes in a formless thing staring from a window,"[25] as Sweetser describes Dr. Black's wife in "The Inmost Light" after a successful experiment to capture her soul. Another abomination is the "child that embodies all the unspeakable evil in the world,"[26] as Scarborough describes the ultimate effect of Dr. Raymond's experiment on Mary's brain in "The Great God Pan." The sacrifice turns out to be dreadful, terrible, seemingly a homage to an elemental power, to evil itself. Mephistopheles answers Faustus's question about whether the demons of hell have many ways to torture: "As great as haue the humane soules of men."[27] In this set of stories Machen creates "embodied deviance,"[28] as Judith Halberstam calls the work of the Gothic. Machen explored taboo areas of Victorian culture, although it seems that he yearned to be a protector of that culture and his stories were cautionary tales. There are excesses in his work, but this is a hallmark of the Gothic—not a failure but rather necessary for his expressions of what was the underside of life.

The core of this chapter is on the ritual of sacrifice to reveal the mysteries. In some of the stories Machen injects elements of a detective narrative to set a tableau against which the real mysteries will stand out. He also uses textual devices of a return or reversion to the past, or perhaps an interaction of the past with the present, to illustrate the connection to the ancient mysteries. This is likely also a warning about the loss of true religion and a warning against the danger of devolution, of a slipping back to primitive pagan time, because "an awful lore is not yet dead."[29] A warning that the old mysteries had real meaning and real danger.

THE FOUR STORIES OF SACRIFICE

In "The Great God Pan," the sacrificed one is a young woman, Mary, the ward of Dr. Raymond. It is perpetrated in order to see "the real world" that is "beyond a veil," and the sacrifice is to allow Dr. Raymond "to see it lifted" (170). Vivisection is the method. Dr. Raymond performs a lobotomy of sorts: he penetrates her brain with a "glittering instrument" (178); afterwards, he "kissed her mouth" and then she "crossed her arms upon her breast as a little child about to say her prayers" (177–78). The young woman is defenseless and treated as an object by Raymond. Indeed, the scientist says: "I rescued

Mary from the gutter, and from almost certain starvation, when she was a child; I think her life is mine, to use as I see fit" (173). There is a witness, Clarke,[30] to the experiment, as Dr. Raymond calls the sacrifice.

The experiment is founded on the notion that what we see every day with our senses is only the shadow of a deeper reality. But Dr. Raymond believes that a simple surgical procedure on the brain will unlock the mysteries of the esoteric. After the surgical knife cuts into her brain, Mary dozes for a few minutes and then starts awake:

> Her eyes shone with an awful light, looking far away, and a great wonder fell upon her face, and her hands stretched out as if to touch what was invisible; but in an instant the wonder faded, and gave place to the most awful terror. The muscles of her face were hideously convulsed, she shook from head to foot; the soul seemed struggling and shuddering within the house of flesh. (178–79)

She falls with a shriek and becomes vegetative. Dr. Raymond observes that it was to be expected, as she had seen the Great God Pan, although earlier he had said there was no danger in the incision. On the surface this is the failure of parental, or moral, or societal responsibility to provide proper care and protection to the innocent. Moreover, it portrays a scientist as able to do anything with human subjects with no concern for their care. There is also an undercurrent of a more sinister kind in the relation between Mary and Dr. Raymond.

Mary is deformed by the brain surgery, but there is more to come. She dies nine months later after spawning a child,[31] who goes under various names, but mostly Helen Vaughan. The remainder of the story is, in a sense, a Victorian shocker about the sexual exploits of Helen Vaughan, the she-devil, the embodied deviance. Helen is a sort of antichrist, born from Mary and Pan, who is akin to Lucifer. The experiment unleashes vengeance and terror in the green hills of England and the shining streets of London; it calls up an ontology of evil in the mating of Pan and Mary. The textual element of the scientific experiment is central to the story's trajectory.[32] The only supernatural effects produced by science are horror. Machen calls this "transcendental medicine" in "The Great God Pan" and "occult science" in "The Inmost Light." Here the Gothic is used to reveal what some thought might be the underside of science, which was becoming the arbiter of truth in place of religion, perhaps exemplified in Victorian times by Darwin and evolution.

Pan in this story is the fetish for evil and suffering and the danger and dread of the wilderness of the ancient woods, a primal fear landscape. Machen links his Pan with the ancient Celtic forms in the great forests of Wales, still dark and haunted. His is the Pan of dread. There are at least two images of Pan, one the bucolic satyr or goat-god, who is playful and amorous but not threatening. W. R. Irwin itemizes the differences between the two images.[33]

There is also a dead Pan, as an ancient rumor had it, although Irwin shows this was a mistranslation and writes that, in fact, Pan was the only ancient god to survive classical times. However, Elizabeth Barrett Browning expressed a view of the vanished god in "The Dead Pan." She imagines an ancient lament:

> And that dismal cry rose slowly
> And sank slowly through the air,
> Full of spirit's melancholy
> And eternity's despair;
> And they heard the words it said,—
> "Pan is dead! Great Pan is dead!
> Pan, Pan is dead!"[34]

John Boardman suggests that the poem is an expression of the death of the pagan world, with Pan as the image for the end of the old gods and Pan as the passing of the wild darkness, now overcome by light.[35] Perhaps this is symbolized by a city standing brightly where the woods were. Machen transforms the city of comfort into a nest of evil, a den of iniquity, filling it with the bodies of men who have committed suicide. London is a "city of nightmares" (222) and is as threatening "as the darkest recesses of Africa."[36]

Pan is a witch god: Robert Graves in *The Greek Myths* identifies Pan as the devil of the Arcadian witch cult and links him with the witch cults of northwestern Europe.[37] In *The White Goddess*,[38] Graves also identifies Pan with the goat-Dionysus, who on the Day of Atonement had a scapegoat, under the name of Azazel, sacrificed to him. E. R. Dodds notes that the god Pan causes panic and evokes a variety of religious experiences or mental disturbances from possession and personality change.[39] Burkert in *Greek Religions* has only brief comments on Pan but suggests that Pan symbolized uncivilized procreation. Georg Luck writes that the Celts worshipped a horned god that the Romans associated with Pan. These two horned gods combined and formed a powerful deity for the pagans. Out of necessity they tried to keep their worship secret and hidden, as the early Christians were barbaric in the war to wipe out the old pagan gods, Greco-Roman or Celtic. Luck argues that Pan was transformed into the devil and that female pagans were characterized as witches, as they often used herbs and natural remedies for sickness.[40] Machen returned Pan to his ancient image of terror and frenzy[41] and overturned the cosmeticized image of Pan as a playful satyr[42] and harmless woodland goat-god—he is not Peter Pan.

The sacrifice of a woman is an attempt by men to open the doors of perception; but it is also the killing off of the old ways, especially the traditions and practices of strong women. "The White People" contains several tales, one of which is about Lady Avelin or Cassap. She was one of the white people, perhaps the league of witches so feared by the church in the Middle

Ages as theological and social protesters and a threat to its powers and authority. Hence, in the story the white people are, in a sense, underground and hidden. Lady Avelin ends up burnt at the stake, illustrating the force of the church and state against women and the old folk beliefs.

The progeny of Pan and Mary, Helen Vaughan, is painted as an independent woman, a sybarite, personifying the fear of Victorian men. She has multiple aliases, travels the world, disappears for a time, and has wealth and independence. In Victorian times, the "New Woman," as Kelly Hurley suggests, must be in league with the devil or with Pan.[43] In the story Helen precipitates the suicide of several men, as if her sexual power were draining away their will to live. This is a twisting of passion into demonic pagan death rites. Joshi says the story "degenerates into a frenzied expression of horror over illicit sex."[44] She is the image of the all-powerful, threatening woman. The image of a woman as succubus is clearly expressed in the "Novel of the Iron Maid." Machen describes a large green bronze statue of a naked woman, with a smile on her lips and "about the thing an evil and a deadly look."[45] The "Iron Maid" was a mechanical torture device with the arms tightening around the neck of a victim. In the story, the statue starts up and reaches out for Mathias, who had acquired the piece, and the bronze head bends toward him and "the green lips"[46] bite onto the man's lips, as if to suck out his soul.

Helen Vaughan has numerous crimes on her hands, stretching back to when she was a young girl. These crimes are mostly treated obliquely in the story, as they are unspeakable and hence unwriteable. And perhaps they should not be read, just as Austin discards, without reading, the manuscript detailing the "entertainments" of Mrs. Beaumont (that is, Helen Vaughan). A husband, Mr. Herbert, is said to have died of fright. Another of her victims, Crashaw, hangs himself. Earlier, Villiers passed Crashaw and saw "a devil's face." It was as if Villiers had looked into "the eyes of a lost soul." In Crashaw's eyes was "furious lust and hate that was like fire" (225). This is similar to Mrs. Black in "The Inmost Light"—the bargain with the devil means giving up your soul, but men make the bargain for the women.

At the end, Helen Vaughan's "suicide" with a "hempen cord" (234) when threatened seems improbable, although this is hard to say in a story with so many improbabilities. As the rumor of the death of the Great God Pan was merely a mis-hearing, here Helen's suicide is perhaps disinformation. It is yet another sacrifice of a woman, a strong woman. Here the killing is portrayed as a self-sacrifice, but it seems really to be a mock suicide with Helen, like Thetis or Pan,[47] changing forms and shapes as she escapes or dies or perhaps returns to her primordial[48] or aboriginal embodiment, from which she will be called forth yet again. Helen Vaughan is a shape-shifter, her body wavers "from sex to sex, dividing itself from itself, and then reunited." It "descends to the beasts whence it ascended" and dissolves into "a substance like jelly" before becoming "a horrible and unspeakable shape, neither man nor beast" (237). In the "Novel of the White Powder,"[49] Francis Leicester goes through a similar metamorphosis when he is found as "a dark and putrid mass, seething with corruption and hideous rottenness, neither liquid nor solid, but melting and changing before our eyes, and bubbling with unctuous oily bubbles like boiling pitch. And out of the midst of it shone two burning points like eyes, and . . . a writhing and stirring as of limbs."[50] This last image is echoed in "The Shining Pyramid" at the bowl in the deep of night as Vaughan observes the Little People. He "peered into the quaking mass and saw faintly that there were things like faces and human limbs, [in] that tossing and hissing host." And "in the uncertain light [he saw] the abomina-ble limbs, vague and yet too plainly seen, writhe and intertwine" (37–38), yet another warped erotic image.

These descriptions also represent a regression to chaotic disorder and social decay. Or perhaps this is an expression of the awfulness or fear of the human body, perhaps especially the female body. The New Woman of the late Victorian time was a threat to the male-dominated culture. The common image was of mother, wife, and sister, as Kelly Hurley notes, characterized or idealized by childlike innocence.[51] The *fin de siècle* was a time of the morphing of gender roles, and perhaps many men rebelled against such a shift. At that time, Bram Stoker portrayed the vampire women in *Dracula* as sexual aggressors, perhaps she-devils or monster women. This is Helen Vau-ghan.

Machen deploys science as the tool that sacrifices and results in the intru-sion of extra-normal events. It is the experimental work of a scientist that leads to the intrusion, as if he is a modern counterpart to ancient pagan priests. Knowledge is now lodged in the sciences. It brings the imperative to believe, an autonomous authority, the power to compel. But science with all its enlightenment drags in more horror. The more we know the more we have to fear, as H. P. Lovecraft argued.

"The Great God Pan" is "an old story, an old mystery" (232) told in episodic fragments from different perspectives, as if the truth is too horrible to see directly. And it is told with different narrators, as if to give credibility through collaboration to an incredible tale. There are supporting documents referenced, like the note by Dr. Matheson. The diffusion in the telling is reflective of the imperative of the Gothic to be disruptive and subversive, especially disruptive of the "dominant rational, empirical and progressive ethos of modern Western culture."[52]

"The Inmost Light" is a story of roaming the mysterious environs of London and the sacrifice of a woman. The experimenter here is named Dr. Black.[53] In "The White People" a stand-in for the devil is called the black man. At first Dr. Black and his bride live bucolic lives in a suburban abode. But Dr. Black tires of the routine of medical practice and duties as a husband and returns to his occult science studies and experiments. The experimenter wants to confirm his power over the forces of the universe. He coerces his wife into becoming an experimental subject to confirm his theories. He takes away her soul, capturing it in a jewel. But his wife is transformed into evil, or she becomes the embodiment of the ancient pagan world, starkly staring from a window in that obscure suburb of London. He eventually kills her, but is not prosecuted, as two doctors at the autopsy could find no evidence of foul play. Her death had been caused by an obscure disease that had malformed her brain. Dyson hunts down one of the doctors, who confesses that he believes that Dr. Black killed his wife. And he thinks it was justified because Mrs. Black's brain was, in fact, "the brain of a devil" (269).

The story starts with Dyson telling Salisbury of his encounter with the monster created by Dr. Black. Dyson had traveled to the quiet suburb and happened by chance to rest in a meadow near a row of houses including the Blacks.' Dyson relates:

> As I glanced up I had looked straight towards the last house in the row before me, and in an upper window of that house I had seen for some short fraction of a second a face. It was the face of a woman, and yet it was not human . . . as I saw that face at the window, with the blue sky above me and the warm air playing in gusts about me, I knew I had looked into another world . . . and seen hell open before me. (254)

Dyson relates his physical shock at the sighting of Mrs. Black: around her face there "was a mist of flowing yellow hair, as if it were an aureole of glory round the visage of a satyr" (255), very much like a fire and linking this story to Pan.

Thus begins the journey into a "world of mystery" (255) across London, resulting in marvelous coincidences or improbable revelations or more obscurities. This story is replete with improbable and deliberately overdone coincidences, not least of which is the purloining of the jewel from Dr. Black and the scrap of paper that Salisbury has thrown at his feet while he takes shelter from the rain in an archway, hidden from view. There is duplicity everywhere and unlikely discoveries always, culminating in Dr. Black's all-telling notebook discovered after his death. After the visit with one of the autopsy physicians, Dyson actually chances upon Dr. Black, who appears drained of life, on one of his London walks and befriends him for a spell, visiting his hovel, where there is "an odour of corruption" (272). Dyson leaves London for a time and on returning finds that Dr. Black is dead.

Machen is mocking mystery stories. Upon arriving at home, Salisbury spreads that thrown scrap of paper out on his table "as if it had been some rare jewel" (263), in a howling portent. Or perhaps Machen is arguing that all things are connected and that coincidences or improbabilities are merely the manifestations of the vast mystery we live in but do not really know.[54]

The story continues with Salisbury telling Dyson about the scrap of paper and its strange phrases. On yet another one of his haunts through London, Dyson finds the shop hinted at on the paper and uses a phrase to extract a case, which contains the jewel and the pocketbook of Dr. Black. In the story, the most treasured object is the "opal with its flaming inmost light" (286): the work of the husband [55] in his lab while the human subject of his study is made mad and then killed. The wondrous colors of the jewel do not enchant Dyson, and at the close of the story he crushes it underfoot, yet another sacrifice of the wife. And at the end a small fire blazes forth briefly—a faint reflection of the burning pyramid of fire in "The Shining Pyramid."

"The Shining Pyramid" is perhaps the thinnest of the four stories. It seems to be a sketch of the contrast between the ease of a British gentleman and the terror of the sacrifice of a young woman to pagan, sybaritic forces. Vaughan and Dyson, especially Dyson, savor the intellectual challenge of the mystery of the ancient flints. Perhaps Machen is mocking common mystery tales again, with their focus on clues, facts, [56] and figuring out a solution through reason. In this story, the protagonists do not use sacrifice to attain arcane knowledge, but they use suffering and evil to display their puzzle-solving abilities.

The story is set in the Welsh countryside. Vaughan has invited Dyson to his home to help solve the matter of some flints being left in varying patterns near an ancient pathway beside his garden wall. The flints are very ancient and rare. After the flints, oblong eyes begin to appear on the pathway garden wall. Vaughan is mildly concerned it might be messages of potential thieves after his old sliver plate. The disappearance of a young woman, Annie Trevor, is a background element, which foreshadows the horror to come. The heroes ignore or discount the event, focusing their efforts on the hidden meanings of the flints and oblong eyes.

On the surface, the sacrifice and the horrid violation are of a young woman, Annie Trevor, by the Little People. Her sacrifice begins with her disappearance, or rather kidnapping by the Little People, continues through an ugly orgy of horror, and ends in flame, leaving only her brooch, as her body and soul are consumed. However, the real sacrifice is the young woman by English gentlemen to the forces of darkness and "embodied deviance" (the Little People) for their viewing pleasure. The perpetrators of the sacrifice seem to be the Little People, but at that natural bowl at night Dyson and Vaughan are observers, like objective scientists gathering data on their field study, detached from their subject.

After Dyson figures out the clues, like an amateur sleuth getting the what, when, and where, they enjoy "six days of absolute inaction" (34), forgetting about Annie Trevor. At the end of this sojourn in comfort, they finally go out at night to the site of a "circular depression, which might well have been a Roman amphitheater, [with] ugly crags of limestone . . . [like] a broken wall"

(33). They hide on the rim among the limestone rocks "grim and hideous . . . [like] an idol of the South Seas" (33). They sprawl on the ground and wait in the dark. At last they hear a low sound and then see a moving to and fro in the bowl. A mass of restless forms begins to appear, and these forms seem to speak to one another with a "hissing like snakes" (36). The two men watch as the hideous forms swell around a central object. They hear "more venomous" hissing and see "abominable limbs" (38) grope and grind—another twisted erotic image. Then they hear a faint moan but do not move. Suddenly, the things draw back and they glimpse "human arms," and then a large flame (the shining pyramid) erupts, and they hear screams in utter anguish and horror. Not once during this scene is Annie's name used; she has become a non-being, objectified, a sacrificial object. One of the real horrors in this story is the spinelessness of the heroes—they are voyeurs. Dyson is satisfied at the end of his unraveling of the mystery and reasons away his failure to intercede in the sacrifice of Annie.

The Little People are the imaginative re-creation of fairies in a form of terror. This is similar to Machen's work with Pan; he goes back to the original panic, the original forms. These are not the fairies of children's stories; here as elsewhere Machen uses atavisms to reverse time and invert morality. Graves in *The White Goddess* suggests that fairies can be thought of as displaced early tribes forced into the wilds and woods, where they continue to haunt the imagination.[57] Leslie Fiedler suggests that gnomes or kobolds are "the surviving image in the mind of homo sapiens of the stunted proto-men that they destroyed, the first dispossessed people, whose memory survives to haunt our fairy tales and nightmares."[58] In the story itself, the Little People are identified with "prehistoric Turanian inhabitants" (45). The stories imagine the return of these beings, bearing savagery upon the innocent. They are part of the awful aliveness of the landscape for Machen.

In the story, two Englishmen ruminate on an archaeological mystery in the wilds but do nothing to help a young woman in danger. What is of value to those two men? It is old silver plate, especially a silver bowl. But mostly the solving of a puzzle, like doing a crossword puzzle while smoking a pipe. To Dyson and Salisbury the small flints left in varying patterns are of value and worth pondering, as are the increasing number of oblong eyes on a wall, but not the disappearance of a young woman of a lower class. In a sense, Machen is mocking the search for false knowledge or a false search for knowledge, the unraveling of a superficial mystery. It is as if the protagonists focus on the lowest level of mystery, as in a detective story, and are unaware of or ignore the deeper mystery. They are voyeurs at the end, watching Annie Trevor's awful death from a hiding place. They are witnesses or perhaps accomplices to a sacrifice and seem to be so self-focused as to be blinded to the world.

The most carefully sketched character is the lurking wilderness, with its feral nature and deep dread. Vaughan's house is "in the west with the ancient woods hanging all about it, and the wild, domed hills and the ragged land" (13). The landscape seems more alive than the male leads, especially "the ancient woods, and the stream drawn in and out between them; all grey and dim with morning mist beneath a grey sky in a hushed and haunted air" (23–24). There is a "desolate loneliness and strangeness of the land" (33) similar to the landscape in "The White People." Underneath everything, the story hints there are currents of great forces at work, which Machen personifies as a grand conspiracy against humans.

In "The White People" the elaboration of this theme of sacrifice is completed. Here we hear the voice of the sacrificed one herself, through her journal or diary. Here we get to see an imaginary manuscript, which in the other of these stories is only hinted at or mentioned and not elaborated. She appears to be an only child, living in the countryside and ignored by her father. A nurse initiates her into the mysteries embedded in the wild landscapes surrounding her home and into ancient rituals that appear magical and terrifying. It seems to be nearly an alternative religion, and the "nurse must have been a prophet."[59] The diary recounts the child's experiences with the nurse and on her own after the nurse has been let go. These latter adventures become increasingly strange and wonderful, all within a deepening feeling of existential loss and elegiac despair. The child finds a most secret place within the "secret wood which must not be described" (161) and performs a series of rituals, and something is revealed to her. The diary ends with her writing of the nymphs both dark and bright and how she called them and a dark nymph appeared and "turned the pool of water into a pool of fire" (163). The "diary" is framed with a prologue and epilogue where Cotgrave listens to Ambrose ruminate on good and evil.

This is a tale from innocence and of innocence violated, as there is a hint of sexual abuse. In the frame tale, when Ambrose is about to lend his green book to Cotgrave, "He fondled the fading binding" (123), as if he were fondling the young girl, whom he knew. The girl's father is detached and in a sense not there at all, while a nurse plays the role of parent for a time for the young girl. We read of her experiences in fragments, and much is hidden of the wonders and strangeness that she experiences. She uses wonderful words, such as the Chian language, Aklo letters, the Mao games, or the Dols, Jeelo, and voolas, along with the Xu language and voorish things and shib-show. These all dance in the voice of the child narrator,[60] giving a sense of the surreal to her experiences. But the central mystery is with the white people.

Keepers of the old pagan faith appear in the story. There is Lady Avelin, who may be a leader of an underground secret society of witches. She is being forced into marriage but rebels and uses occult means to kill her suitors one by one, nearly a retelling of the suicides caused by Helen Vaughan. And in this story she is also found out and is sacrificed by fire. Each of the four stories has a scene or two with fire as an emblem of death. Perhaps Machen intended this to be a cleansing of evil through fire or a specter of hell. Machen injects distorted erotic images of women into the telling. Lady Avelin cavorts with great serpents in the woods; they "twisted round her, round her body, and her arms and her neck, till she was covered with writhing serpents" (150). The serpents always blessed her with a glame stone (a magical totem) for her pleasures. But Lady Avelin is also emblematic of women who rebel against the rules ordering women into certain roles. Hence she is sacrificed for social control, although perhaps Machen had her sacrificed for being in league with the devil. That lesson for the young girl may result in what is apparently her "self-sacrifice" in a sacred grove near a Roman statue, where "she poisoned herself[61]—in time." But "in time" against what? Or was it a suicide? Is Ambrose to be trusted, or did he drive her to death through abuse that was not caught by her non-observant father, who is distant, aloof, away from the events, and ignorant of what is happening to his own daughter? Mark Valentine suggests it was the fear of becoming like Helen Vaughan or Helen's mother, Mary—that is, becoming the she-devil or spawning one.[62]

The girl's travels through the wild landscapes are like dreamscapes. Jack Sullivan characterized the story as having a "trance-like lyricism and spontaneity" where "beauty and horror ring out at precisely the same moment."[63] H. P. Lovecraft extolled the merits of the story, calling the narrative "a triumph of skilful selectiveness and restraint [that] accumulates enormous power as it flows on in a stream of innocent childish prattle."[64] Lovecraft admired the craft and praised the overall sense of a horrid sentience behind the words of the young girl.

The landscape she travels is foreboding and alive with danger. As she clambers among the megaliths, she describes them:

> . . . dreadful rocks. There were hundreds and hundreds of them. Some were like horrid-grinning men; I could see their faces as if they would jump at me out of the stone, and catch hold of me, and drag me with them back into the rock, so that I should always be there. And there were other rocks that were like animals, creeping, horrible animals, putting out their tongues, and others were like words that I could not say, and others like dead people lying on the grass. (128–29)

This is all under a sky, "heavy and grey and sad, like a wicked voorish dome in Deep Dendo" (128). Ordinary things come alive. Matter seems to be malleable.

The girl's language is akin to stream-of-consciousness writing, as pointed out by Joshi.[65] It is a wondrous stream, but also there is something beyond or below the surface. There is an overall sadness and feeling of loss and vulnerability in the story. It tells of abandonment and the torture of separation and loss; and there seems to be something non-childhood about her experiences, as if she has been robbed of her innocence. There is a deep despair and a feeling of absence in the marvelous flow of words.

After the nurse is let go, the girl roams the wild countryside on her own with no friends or companions or chaperons. She is alone in a landscape of bewitchment. And the landscape is not in one form but in many forms, a shape-shifting world, a world with a broken epistemology. The little girl thinks of it this way: "all alone on the hill I wondered what was true" (156).

The frame tales of this artifact may be characterized as a "Luciferian philosophy,"[66] to use Murdoch's turn of phrase. It articulates a voyeuristic sordidness, expressed through the fingering of the green book, as if it were flesh. The book is one of Ambrose's "choicer items" and is treated as a specimen, or rather a trophy. He lingers over the book and parts "with diffi-culty, it seemed, from his treasure" (124), as he hands it to Cotgrave. This story is a treasure from the horror zone. The frame tale speaks of mysterious-ness including both good and evil. In a sense they are both indefinable and can only be hinted at or spoken of in allusions, like the ancient mysteries.

Murdoch jokes that only angels could define the good,[67] so perhaps only devils define evil, and this seems to be the point of the frame tale.[68] It is as if there is a deep, old urge to worship, to strive toward the sacred, as Murdoch argues; but in Machen's tales this urge does not reach the good or the sacred but delivers suffering and evil.

LANDSCAPES OF WONDER AND TERROR

As Machen writes, "if there is a landscape of sadness, there is certainly also a landscape of a horror of darkness and evil."[69] Barton Levi St. Armand argues that this is the natural corollary to a theory assuming that nature possesses a spirit as well as a self, that it is, in some measure, conscious and alive.[70] Valentine sees Machen's landscapes as replete with "active, brooding evil" yet also a "sacred splendor."[71] There are atavistic haunts in these four stories. Over the wonder or terror of existence there is a mask or cloak or veil. The great weeping beauty of nature hides a terror, as in "The Damned" of Alger-non Blackwood, where the hero flees in panic from the woods as he hears the despairing clamor at the gates of hell. There is a deep fear of the forest as it takes us back to the primitive, to the campfires and howling of the wild. But Machen also transforms the streets of London into a forest of dark night.

In each story's landscapes, there are objects, relics, or statues from the past which personify evil or are fetishes reifying a fear. Megaliths appear in these stories like sentinels from the pagan world, along with relics from

Rome. The use of ancient images, ruins, or statues is common in Machen and signals the return of the past, the revolt of the dead, an awful history.

In "The Shining Pyramid" there are contrasting objects. First there are the flints left by the Little People, but there is also the silver, symbolic of old England and the stability of the world. There are the limestone megaliths in the hills and a limestone pillar by Vaughan's garden wall that was "a place of meeting before the Celts set foot in Britain" (46).

The landscape in "The White People" is overwhelming, "a strange, deso-late land" (165). The green book itself—a journal of the evil years, so to speak—is the prime relic. There are megaliths in abundance. And there is the stone image, "of Roman workmanship . . . white and luminous" (166), where Ambrose found the young girl's body. He demolishes it to kill the pagan world or hide his own sin.

In "The Inmost Light" the landscape is the foreboding, dank atmosphere of London and its maze of streets. The dying Dr. Black resides in an area where the houses seem to have been "sordid and hideous enough when new" but aged in "foulness with every year and seemed to lean and totter to their fall" (271). In this urban landscape of darkness, the key object is the jewel, the host of Mrs. Black's soul. Its crushing snuffs out any hope for transcen-dence.

There is "the stone head of grotesque appearance" that was "of the Ro-man period" (186) in "The Great God Pan." The view of this head causes such a shock to the boy Trevor, in whom Helen had precipitated a vision of "the strange naked man," that it leads to a "weakness of intellect" (184), as if Helen had stolen away his knowledge. In the closing pages of "The Great God Pan," Clarke writes to Dr. Raymond about the life of Helen Vaughan and recounts his recent stay at Caermaen with its "mouldering Roman walls" (239). Near the grounds of an old temple to the god of the deeps was the house where Helen had lived when younger. Off the old Roman road Helen had seduced her first victim, Rachel, who was introduced to the powers of night in the "maze of the forest" (239).

A SCIENCE OF EVIL

The sequence of stories is close to a critique of Victorian scientific research with human subjects. There are observers and non-interventionists of natural events in "The Shining Pyramid." Observational reason here views the suf-fering of the innocent but does nothing. Is it simply fear or the failure of morality, or the mocking of scientific objectivity? There is experimentation on human subjects, without consent,[72] in "The Great God Pan" and "The Inmost Light." Finally we witness complete detachment and theorizing in "The White People," akin to a single-subject case study design. A child is heard, but her voice is framed by the voyeuristic, perhaps abusive, voice of a man. In the end it is all about the sacrifice of women to appease the desires of men for knowledge and control. And the sacrifice calls up cosmic terror. In a way the stories, solidly in the Gothic tradition, give voice to an underclass against a distorted and immoral ruling order, which uses whatever means it can to maintain its control. In the stories, men engineer the intrusion of horror by sacrificing women. It is as if women are scapegoats to appease the great unknown and allow the gathering of data and knowledge by men. The troubling center of these stories is precisely the act of violent sacrifice of women.

These stories may be seen as critiques of the cult of science as the highest form of human activity. Christine Ferguson writes of decadence as the logical conclusion of one of the most fundamental of all Victorian values, scientific positivism.[73] Roger B. Salomon argues that Machen, along with Lovecraft and Bierce, attacked the accepted worldview of nineteenth- and twentieth-century scientific positivism and empiricism, which rejected any horror or disorder or atavistic haunts from the past as having any place in a narrative structure. Salomon sees Machen as disrupting the accepted sense of truth as given to us by empiricism; he also hints that this disruption applies to conventional morality and ethics.[74] The dominance of positivistic science and logical positivism was distasteful for Machen. Ferguson argues that if science is too worshipped for its mathematical logic and the fruits of its experimental methodology, then the moral practice of its experiments is secondary and ethical considerations are unnecessary.[75] Machen exposes this. The *reductio ad absurdum* is that in science all is allowed and that the resulting knowledge sanctifies all means for its achievement.

The Victorian anti-vivisectionist and feminist Frances Power Cobbe warned of the consequences of science penetrating into "regions where it has no proper place,"[76] such as emotions and ethics. Cobbe argues that the over-veneration of science could lead to a disruption of common human morality. Cobbe's *Wife Torture in England* unveils the Victorian-age beatings of women. Susan Hamilton writes how Cobbe let light into the horrid details of the violent acts against Victorian women's bodies. For her the Victorian age was a culture of violence against women.[77] The central core of Machen's four stories is violence against women; it is as if the search for knowledge and the power structure sanctify suffering and evil.

A NEGATIVE VISION

Machen's quartet of stories deconstructs established Victorian notions such as empiricism, rationality, social control, and sexuality. Although part of this is like a Romantic reaction to reasoning and the praise of vision to experience being, Machen's sundering of the veil reveals horror. The invisible world is not like the Romantic ideal, as Emerson wrote of:

> If the Reason be stimulated to more earnest vision, outlines and surfaces become transparent, and are no longer seen; causes and spirits are seen through them. The best moments of life are these delicious awakenings of the higher powers and the reverential withdrawing of nature before its God. [78]

In these stories the god, so to speak, brings panic, not wonder; it is a revealing of a negative vision. The dropping of a veil is revolting and hideous, the mysteries infected with blasphemy and despair. There are only fear and trembling, and the face of god revealed is of a corpse or worse. The sight does not elicit feelings of the sublime but rather of dread and panic. Of course, this is the Gothic. There is no sublime, only an unnameable dread.

The sacrifices are the terror. In each of the four stories there is a sacrifice of a woman at the hands of men. Although the sacrifices take on different forms and the actions of the men, as agents or abettors of the sacrifices, are somewhat different, the essential theme is the killing of women. These sacrifices are set in a pornography of suffering and evil. The rituals are performed in alien landscapes misted in misery, haunted by atavistic relics, and distorted with repellent erotic images.

In "The White People," Ambrose says that real evil is akin to trying to take heaven by storm. Perhaps that is what the men in these stories are doing by sacrificing women—women who end up like Mrs. Black, "a cinder, black and crumbling to the touch" (286); or Annie Trevor, "a heap of grey ashes" (40); or the young woman's beloved statue in "The White People," "dust and fragments" (166); or Helen Vaughan, "a horrible and unspeakable form" before her "death" (237).

NOTES

1. Arthur Machen, "The Red Hand," in *The White People and Other Stories*, ed. S. T. Joshi (Oakland, CA: Chaosium, 2003), 11.

2. Iris Murdoch, *The Sovereignty of Good* (London: Routledge Classics, 2001), 67.

3. See S. T. Joshi, *The Weird Tale* (Austin: University of Texas Press, 1990), 39–41, for a comprehensive list of dates for the works of Machen.

4. Machen, "The Shining Pyramid," in *The Shining Pyramid* (New York: Knopf, 1925), 17. Hereafter cited in the text.

5. Machen, "The Inmost Light," in *The House of Souls* (New York: Knopf, 1922), 247. Hereafter cited in the text.

6. H. P. Lovecraft, *The Annotated Supernatural Horror in Literature*, rev. ed., ed. S. T. Joshi (New York: Hippocampus Press, 2012), 81.

7. Wesley D. Sweetser, *Arthur Machen* (New York: Twayne, 1964), 116–28.

8. Joshi, *The Weird Tale*, 13.

9. Mark Valentine, *Arthur Machen* (Bridgen, Wales: Seren, 1995), 23–24.

10. Vincent Starrett, *Arthur Machen: A Novelist of Ecstasy and Sin* (Chicago: Walter M. Hill, 1918), 11.

11. Dorothy Scarborough, *The Supernatural in Modern English Fiction* (New York: G. P. Putnam's Sons, 1917), 139.

12. Scarborough, *The Supernatural*, 237.

13. Machen, "A Fragment of Life," in *The House of Souls*, 86.

14. Walter Burkert, *Greek Religion*, trans. John Raffan (Cambridge, MA: Harvard University Press, 1985), 276.

15. Marvin W. Meyer, introduction to *The Ancient Mysteries: A Sourcebook of Sacred Texts*, ed. Marvin W. Meyer (Philadelphia: University of Pennsylvania Press, 1999), 4.

16. Walter Burkert, *Ancient Mystery Cults* (Cambridge, MA: Harvard University Press, 1987), 11.

17. Marco Pasi, "Arthur Machen's Panic Fears: Western Esotericism and the Irruption of Negative Epistemology," *Aries* 7 (2007): 64.

18. Alfred North Whitehead, quoted in William Beer, *Women and Sacrifice: Male Narcissism and the Psychology of Religion* (Detroit, MI: Wayne State University Press, 1992), 9.

19. Sweetser, *Arthur Machen*, 18.

20. Christopher Marlowe, *The Tragicall Historie of Doctor Faustus*, in *The Works of Christopher Marlowe*, ed. C. F. Tucker Brooke (London: Oxford University Press, 1910), 155.

21. Henri Hubert and Marcel Mauss, *Sacrifice: Its Nature and Function* (Chicago: University of Chicago Press, 1964), 97–98.

22. The sacrifice is to bridge the "unthinkable gulf that yawns between two worlds; the world of matter and the world of spirit" (Machen, "The Great God Pan," in *The House of Souls* [New York: Knopf, 1922], 172; hereafter cited in the text); and "the fathomless abyss that separates the world of consciousness from the sphere of matter" (Machen, "The Inmost Light," 268).

23. Clive Bloom, *Gothic Histories: The Taste for Terror, 1764 to the Present* (London: Continuum, 2010), 78. For Machen it may be that these stories lament the dying of Christian religious ritual and a reversion to pagan rites.

24. Sweetser, *Arthur Machen*, 81.

25. Sweetser, *Arthur Machen*, 82.

26. Scarborough, *The Supernatural*, 139.

27. Marlowe, *The Tragicall Historie of Doctor Faustus*, 160.

28. Judith Halberstam, *Skin Shows: Gothic Horror and the Technology of Monsters* (Durham, NC: Duke University Press, 2000), 5.

29. Machen, "The Red Hand," 11.

30. Clarke is one of several witnesses to the events of the whole story.

31. One wonders if Dr. Raymond is the father.

32. In a letter to John Lane in 1894, Machen rejects a suggestion to cut out the first chapter of "The Great God Pan" because it contains "the motive." Machen, *Selected Letters*, eds. Roger Dobson, Godfrey Brangham, and R. A. Gilbert (Wellingbourough, UK: Aquarian Press, 1988), 218. He argues that the credibility of the story rests on a scientific basis, as the supernatural itself is not credible.

33. W. R. Irwin, "The Survival of Pan," *PMLA* 76 (June 1961): 159–67.

34. Elizabeth Barrett Browning, *The Complete Poetical Works of Mrs. Browning* (Boston: Houghton Mifflin, 1900), 190.

35. John Boardman, *The Great God Pan* (New York: Thames & Hudson, 1998), 7.

36. Machen, "Novel of the Iron Maid," in *The Three Imposters and Other Stories*, ed. S. T. Joshi (Oakland, CA: Chaosium, 2001), 188.

37. Robert Graves, *The Greek Myths: I* (Baltimore, MD: Penguin, 1968), 102–3.

38. Robert Graves, *The White Goddess* (London: Faber & Faber, 1961), 218.

39. E. R. Dodds, *The Greeks and the Irrational* (Berkeley: University of California Press, 1951).

40. Georg Luck, *Arcana Mundi* (Baltimore, MD: John Hopkins University Press, 1985), 7.

41. Machen's portrayal of the awful power of Pan influenced subsequent writers such as Edgar Jepson in *The Garden at 19*. Valerius Flaccus caught this aspect of Pan in *Argonautica*. "Pan had driven the doubting city distraught, Pan fulfilling the cruel commands of the Mygdonian Mother, Pan lord of the woodlands and of war, whom from the daylight hours caverns

shelter; about midnight in lonely places are seen that hairy flank and the soughing leafage on his fierce brow. Louder than all trumpets sounds his voice alone, and at that sound fall helm and sword, the charioteer from his rocking car and bolts from gates of walls by night; nor might the helmet of Mars and the tresses of the Furies, nor the dismal Gorgon from on high spread such terror, nor with phantoms so dire sweep an army in headlong rout." Valerius Flaccus, *Argonautia*, trans. J. H. Mozley (Cambridge, MA: Loeb Classical Library, 1934), 131.

42. This image of Pan is detailed by John Boardman, *The Great God Pan*. It is still a potent salutary symbol as evidenced by the April 12, 2010, cover of the *New Yorker* of "Spring Is Sprung" by Edward Sorel. The cover depicts Central Park overrun by satyrs and lascivious naked women, who seem to be the sexual aggressors. Most interesting is the pictorial of a balding, bearded satyr with eyeglasses pushing a baby carriage: the Great God Pan fully domesticated.

43. Kelly Hurley, "British Gothic Fiction: 1885–1930," in *The Cambridge Companion to Gothic Fiction*, ed. Jerrold E. Hogle (Cambridge: Cambridge University Press, 2002), 199–201.

44. S. T. Joshi, introduction to *The Three Impostors and Other Stories*, 21.

45. Machen, "The Novel of the Iron Maid," 190.

46. Machen, "The Novel of the Iron Maid," 191.

47. Pan changed shape when the gods battled the Titans, as did most of the gods out of terror. C. Julius Hyginus (c. 64 BCE–17 CE) writes that Pan took on the shape of fish for his lower half and a goat for his upper half. Hyginus, *Astronomica*, part 2, trans. Mary Grant, http://www.theoi.com/Text/HyginusAstronomica2.html (accessed May 2012).

48. Sweetser, *Arthur Machen*, 111–12, suggests that Machen has her become a "hideous protoplasm," because it represents the "primordial slime" back to which we could all slide. It is symbolic perhaps of original sin for Machen and an expression of the fear of the return to the primitive.

49. In both this story and "The Great God Pan," an attending physician provides the descriptions of the transformation as an analytic and objective viewer.

50. Arthur Machen, "Novel of the White Powder," in *The Three Impostors and Other Stories*, 207.

51. Kelly Hurley, *The Gothic Body: Sexuality, Materialism, and Degeneration at the Fin de Siècle* (Cambridge: Cambridge University Press, 1996), 121–122.

52. Roger B. Salomon, *Mazes of the Serpent* (Ithaca, NY: Cornell University Press, 2002), 117.

53. This is an old textual ploy to make it appear as if one is hiding the real name and have readers suspend disbelief. The devil was historically portrayed as black. Cotton Mather, *On Witchcraft* (Mineola, NY: Dover, 2005), 102, wrote that witches call the devil the "Black Man."

54. It is expressed this way in "The Children of the Pool": "Any man who cares to glance over his experience of the world and of things in general is aware that the most wildly improbable events are constantly happening." Machen, "The Children of the Pool," *Tales of Horror and the Supernatural* (New York: Pinnacle, 1983), 315.

55. Tellingly, over the course of the tale, Dr. Black shrivels, as if the jewel that he hoards in his hovel drains his life force.

56. In "The Red Hand," Phillips, searching for a commonplace solution to a murder with a primitive flint knife, says to Dyson, "I warn you I have done with mystery. We are to deal with facts now." Machen, "The Red Hand," 5. But this is not how it all works out.

57. Graves, *The White Goddess*, 171.

58. Leslie Fiedler, *Love and Death in the American Novel* (New York: Criterion, 1960), 369.

59. Arthur Machen, "The White People," in *The House of Souls* (New York: Knopf, 1922), 161. Hereafter cited in the text.

60. The book is "full of secrets" and she has written "a great many other books of secrets . . . hidden in a safe place" (Machen, "The White People," 125); but not everything is written down, as if she is aware that someone may take her books, as in fact happens.

61. Shortly before the journal breaks off abruptly, the young girl, after her moment of rapture, writes: "I wished that the years were gone by, and that I had not so long a time to wait before I was happy for ever and ever." Machen, "The White People," 161.

62. Valentine, *Arthur Machen*, 62.

63. Jack Sullivan, *Elegant Nightmares* (Athens: Ohio University Press, 1978), 114.

64. Lovecraft, *The Annotated Supernatural Horror*, 84.

65. S. T. Joshi, *The Weird Tale* (Austin: University of Texas Press, 1990), 22.

66. Murdoch, *The Sovereignty of Good*, 47.

67. Murdoch, *The Sovereignty of Good*, 96.

68. Ambrose says that sin "is an effort to gain the ecstasy and the knowledge that pertain alone to angels. And in making this effort man becomes a demon." Machen, "The White People," 117. This is traced through the stories.

69. Machen, "The Children of the Pool," 320.

70. Barton Levi St. Armand, "The 'Mysteries' of Edgar Poe: The Quest for a Monomyth in Gothic Literature," in *The Tales of Poe*, ed. Harold Bloom (New York: Chelsea House, 1987), 25–54.

71. Valentine, *Arthur Machen*, 24.

72. In a sense, these are cautionary tales about the lack of ethics in the conduct of research on human subjects; this attitude reached its epitome in Nazi Germany. After the war, the Nuremburg Code finally elaborated a set of principles to guide such research, one of which was that researchers should be willing to subject themselves to any research. The principles, standards, and controls over research with human participants have evolved since then.

73. Christine Ferguson, "Decadence as Scientific Fulfillment," *PMLA* 117 (May 2002): 465.

74. Salomon, *Mazes of the Serpent*, 115.

75. Ferguson, "Decadence as Scientific Fulfillment," 468.

76. Frances Power Cobbe, quoted in Ferguson, "Decadence as Scientific Fulfillment," 486.

77. Susan Hamilton, "'A Whole Series of Frightful Cases': Domestic Violence, the Periodical Press and Victorian Feminist Writing," *TOPIA* 13 (2005): 89–101.

78. Ralph Waldo Emerson, *Works* (London: George Routledge & Sons, 1883), 558.

Chapter Five

The Haunted Wood

Algernon Blackwood's Canadian Stories

In "The Wendigo" (1910),[1] Algernon Blackwood (1869–1951) portrays the character Simpson alone in the great northern Ontario forest. Simpson hears footsteps and whispering voices in the woods. He sees figures "crouching behind trees and boulders."[2] The murmur of the wind surrounds him, and "the shadows of the woods" (188) threaten. Within this haunted wood, "nameless doom lurked" (188). It is a "world of wizardry and horror" (189). Yet in the forest, "untrodden by foot of man," Simpson is "enchanted by its austere beauty" (165). And "his heart drank in the sense of freedom and great spaces" (165). The wilderness is a grand otherness of hope and awe in Blackwood's stories, along with the counterpoint: the woods are a Gothic space.

The Canadian wilderness was a powerful force in the life of Algernon Blackwood.[3] John Robert Colombo writes, "the forests and mountains have a Canadian cast"[4] in Blackwood's fiction. Colombo also contends, "Imaginatively Canada would come to him [Blackwood] repeatedly during . . . his active, writing life."[5] David Punter observes that Blackwood set "some of his best-known stories"[6] in Canada. Greg Gatenby asserts, "Canadian imagery haunted Blackwood's writing,"[7] and Jeff Gardiner sees Blackwood's travels in Canada as "a great influence on him."[8]

As a young man, Blackwood toured across Canada in 1887 with his father, Sir Arthur Blackwood. From 1890 to 1892, prior to moving to New York City, Algernon Blackwood lived in Canada, primarily in Toronto and then on an island in the Muskoka Lakes area of Ontario.[9] From April to October in 1894, Blackwood returned to Canada to pursue a mining venture and spent six weeks in the Rainy River district in Ontario. His journeys there and back seemed more fruitful for him than the venture, which came to naught. On the journey, Blackwood rhapsodized, "Out of New York City into this primaeval wilderness produced intoxication. No more cities of dreadful night for me!"[10] Mike Ashley suggests Blackwood was in the Muskoka Lakes area in the summer of 1896. He was back in Canada moose hunting in 1898.[11]

Blackwood's experiences in Canada helped cast his sense of wonder with nature. His travels across Canada and his time in the forests aroused a feeling for the vastness of the country and the unbearable stretch of the wilderness. In *Episodes before Thirty* (1923), Blackwood exalted the island in the Muskoka area and his joy in the natural setting. His rhapsody in Nature is at the core of his life and his works. S. T. Joshi points out the deep significance of Nature for Blackwood.[12] At times Nature is a Garden of Eden full of awe and wonder. In *Episodes before Thirty*, Blackwood stated that Nature "offered an actual sense of companionship no human intercourse could possibly provide."[13] He experienced "a strange sense of oneness with nature."[14] In his fiction, sometimes Nature is an escape, as in "The Camp of the Dog" (1908). The narrator rejoices as the campers head into the wilderness: "the horror of trains and houses was far behind us, the fever of men and cities, the weariness of streets and confined spaces."[15] At times Blackwood writes of reconciliation within Nature, as William Blake depicted in "Night" when the lion says, "And now besides thee, bleating lamb, / I can lie down and sleep."[16] In Blackwood's *The Centaur* (1911), Terence O'Malley speaks of "the call to childhood, the true, pure, vital childhood of the Earth—the Golden Age—before men tasted of the Tree and knew themselves separate; when the lion and the lamb lay down together and a little child could lead them."[17] However, this idyllic vision of Nature is not always shown in Blackwood's short stories. In some, the natural world is at best indifferent and in others menacing. Gatenby believes "it was in Canada that he [Blackwood] best became aware of the often hostile power of Nature."[18]

There is a mix of awe, loneliness, wonder, and fear in the wild. In "The Wendigo," Simpson feels "the forest pressed round him with its encircling wall: the nearer tree-stems like bronze in the firelight: beyond that—blackness, and, so far as he could tell, a silence of death" (171). On the other hand, "the vigorous air of the wilderness brought its own powers of healing" (173). Is a forest sinister in itself or is it our estrangement from Nature? Is it our alien presence that provokes the terror? Or is it that the wilderness in the Canadian stories is Nature infested by men who cannot understand it, who are cut off from the grand "stream of a Consciousness far bigger"[19] than they? Peter Penzoldt suggests that "Blackwood's idea is that nature is good, beautiful, right and healing."[20] Indeed, a substantial body of research supports Blackwood's notion of the healing power of Nature.[21] David Punter sees "a kind of euphoria, a kind of rapture, in the visions which conclude many of Blackwood's stories."[22]

Blackwood's Canadian stories conjure both visions. And this perspective of the wood pervades Blackwood's work. There is an ambiguity about the wilderness: it is foreign yet familiar; it is dangerous but beautiful; it is uncanny. This chapter explores Blackwood's Canadian stories to help understand the tension between these two views of Nature and perhaps to contribute to an understanding of how Blackwood's Canadian experience shaped his literary perspective on the wilderness and our place in that dark but glorious space.

Blackwood seemed to have had an idiosyncratic mythology of Nature. The Canadian wilderness may have been a key element in the elaboration of that myth. Karen Armstrong states that myth "looks into the heart of a great silence."[23] That great silence is the unknown, or what at first we have no words to express. She contends that mythology is not opting out of the world; rather, it enables us to live more intensely within it. Blackwood seemed to believe that our perception limits our experience of the world. There is more to the world than we normally experience. But to achieve transcendence, which is a key to the myth, there is a harrowing journey. It is as if one must find a way to leap over the ontological ravine between humans and the rest of Nature. As Armstrong argues, myth is about going beyond our ordinary experience. For Blackwood, "an expansion of normal consciousness"[24] will bring the numinous vision of nature.

Joshi argues that this is what Blackwood sought.[25] Perhaps it arises from those moments of epiphany when we intuit something greater than what is shown in the world. In Blackwood this happens in Nature, in a place outside of the constructed world of cities and towns. Out there in the wilderness all things seem more bound up together, not always in peace, often in conflict, but composed of the same substance, of the same spirit.

THE CANADIAN CONTEXT

Several of Blackwood's stories are set in Canada.[26] Mike Ashley has identified the following: "A Haunted Island" (1899), "Skeleton Lake: An Episode in Camp" (1906), "The Wendigo" (1910), "Running Wolf" (1920), "First Hate" (1920), and "The Valley of the Beasts" (1921).[27] John Robert Colombo in his collection *Algernon Blackwood's Canadian Tales of Terror* includes "The Camp of the Dog" (1908) and "Confession" (1921), which are not set in Canada but have Canadian characters. "Confession" is a traditional ghost story of a Canadian soldier suffering post-traumatic shock syndrome in London.[28] "The Camp of the Dog" is set on an isolated island in Sweden and features the character Peter Sangree, who is called "the Canadian" and is of aboriginal heritage.

The Canadian landscape has influenced many writers who traveled through or lived in Canada. Gatenby has compiled an anthology of pieces by non-Canadians about Canada. He discovered 1,200 writers who have written about Canada. Gatenby observes that non-Canadians have focused on the vastness of the nation, including "a looming wilderness of savage purity and Promethean scale."[29] Algernon Blackwood is in the anthology with a selection from *Episodes before Thirty*.

The Canadian wilds are not idyllic; Northrop Frye notes a "deep terror in regard to nature," which is "a terror of the soul"[30] in Canadian poetry. Frye identifies a "garrison mentality"[31] in Canadian literature about the wilderness. Susanna Moodie in *Roughing It in the Bush* (1852) wrote that Canada was a "strange, stern landscape" where "lofty groves of pines frowned down in hearse-like gloom."[32] She felt "a stranger in a strange land."[33] It was a country "only fit for wild beasts,"[34] a "landscape, savage and grand in its primeval beauty."[35]

Margaret Atwood, Justin D. Edwards, and Margot Northey have explored the continuing influence of the Canadian wilderness, in mythic and real form, on Canadian Gothic literature. Atwood classifies four key obsessions in Canadian literature, centering on the wilderness. These include the "North" as mythic and real landscape, the appropriation of indigenous identity by whites, the Wendigo as forest monster and call of the wild, and women writers using the wilderness as locale.[36] Northey argues there is an "unresolved duality of awe and fear"[37] in the Canadian experience of Nature. There is a haunted wilderness in Canada. She sees a strong and enduring Gothic tradition in Canadian literature, starting with John Richardson's *Wacousta* (1832). In a wide-ranging exploration of the meaning of the Gothic in Canada and beyond, Edwards argues that "the wilderness is a haunting presence for the newcomer, [and] it is also haunted for those who call it home."[38]

For American Gothic writers like Charles Brockden Brown and Nathaniel Hawthorne, the woods in America are the abode of the devil and witches. There is no grandeur, just terror. Steve Duffy writes about "the smell of fear engendered by an incautious foray into the woods."[39] The wilderness scares people. Does the wilderness take a part of your soul, or does it enlarge your soul? Or is it really the person who makes the difference? Think of a time in a real woodland, away from civilization, not a grand park or reforested area, but a dark expanse of woods far from the concrete of cities, away from the noise of machines and people. Blackwood describes this wilderness in "The Wendigo," as "leagues of endless, crowding Bush, desolate in its lonely sweep and grandeur" (165). It is a "tangled backwood . . . merciless and terrible" (166). But it is also beautiful. You step into the forest, and there is a hush as if the wood stops breathing for a moment, perhaps to smell you, sense your fear or ecstasy, as occurs in Blackwood's "The Man Whom the Trees Loved" (1912).

THE CANADIAN STORIES

Blackwood's Canadian tales vary in quality. In "The Wendigo" he creates an atmosphere of slowly gathering dread. As Joshi suggests, the story takes us into another world, or rather it transforms our view of the world.[40] Ashley argues that Blackwood's 1898 moose-hunting expedition in Canada inspired this story.[41] "The Wendigo" conjures a sense of an awful grandeur that is unbearable and brings death. According to Gardiner, the story is "the call of the wild personified."[42] It is frequently anthologized and considered one of Blackwood's premier stories. It is set in the Lake of the Woods area of northern Ontario, near Kenora (Rat Portage was its pre-1905 name).

It is a tale of men in the vast outdoors confronting the unknown. The characters include moose hunters: Dr. Cathcart and his nephew Simpson, a divinity student. There are a couple of guides: a Quebecois, Joseph Défago, who knows the woods, is a storyteller, and is captive of that "singular spell . . . [of] the wilderness" (158), and Hank Davis, a tough guy. There is also an aboriginal cook, Punk. They are a small party in a great wilderness, and "the silence of the vast listening forest stole forward and enveloped them" (160). They are "in the jaws of the wilderness" (163), which seems a sentient being. Their hunting has been poor so far, and they decide to break out from their base camp in pairs in search of game. Blackwood paints a sinister picture of their small, fragile camp in the midst of the wilds. Throughout the tale the sense of smell (perhaps a sense of the primitive) plays a role in evoking the allure of camping along with the danger of the wild. There is the comforting "fragrance of the wood-fire" (163) and the "odours of coffee and fried bacon" (165). But Punk at the base camp moves through the darkness and sniffs "the keen air" and catches a "thin odour of something that seemed unfamiliar—utterly unknown" (164).

Leaving base camp, Cathcart and Davis head in one direction and Simpson and Défago in another. Simpson may be characterized as a greenhorn of the woods; he and Défago set up a campsite on Fifty Island Water. On one side they are confronted by "silver-birch and maple, spear-like and slender, against the immense stems of spruce and hemlock" and on the other, "blackened stumps, savage and desolate" (168), as if they were two sides of Nature. A rose and saffron sky spreads over the wilderness, with its "indifference to human life, the merciless spirit of desolation which took no note of man" (169). Joshi suggests that this is when "the cosmic insignificance of human beings becomes a source of acute terror," and that this is a hallmark of Blackwood's horror tales in contrast to his tales of awe.[43] At their camp, Défago shows signs of increasing wariness and suddenly jumps up and "sniffed the air, like a dog scenting game" (171).

At night, Simpson wakes to find Défago quaking with fear. Outside the tent there is a soft roaring voice that seems to be calling for Défago, who runs out of the tent away into the forest. Continuing with the key sense of smell, Simpson breathes a "strange perfume"; it is a "penetrating, all-pervading odour"; it is the "odour of a lion" (180). For Simpson it is like the odor of a big forest. In the story the forest seems the main character, the most power-fully described. It is sentient as it "stood waiting, listening, watching so to see what" (183) Simpson would do, as if the hunter and the hunted had changed places. Looking for Défago, Simpson finds tracks in the snow: "They were ominous signs—these mysterious writings left in the snow by the unknown creature . . . by something nameless" (183–84), alongside which are Défago's. Soon Défago's tracks begin to resemble those of the other and then both vanish.

Blackwood describes the utter sense of panic in the dark forests with only a "dark ruin" (187) of thoughts howling in Simpson's head. Somehow Simp-son makes it back to his fellow hunters and they return to hunt for Défago, but the tracks are hidden, covered by snow. As the three men huddle around a campfire near the lake they talk of the Wendigo—they talk to keep away "silence"; they talk "against darkness, against the invasion of panic" (197). However, Blackwood has the main character strike again, "for the wilderness had already the advantage of first attack—and of a hostage" (197). Défago seems to scream from the sky. Something falls and they hear crunching through the snow toward them. The "darkness brought forth" a thing that appeared like Défago, but the three men "saw across the frontiers of normal vision into the Unknown" (199). Then "the darkness" (203) takes Défago away "into untold space and silence" (204).

Blackwood was trying to "describe the indescribable" (201) experience of panic in the woods. When the hunting party arrives at home camp, they find the "true" Défago, though his mind is gone. He survives only a few weeks, a broken person, no longer whole but a fragment, for the forest now has his soul. Throughout the tale the monster is only known by its effects; the Wen-digo never comes onstage. This contributes to the unease of the story. The Wendigo itself represents the otherness of the landscape—the estrangement of humans from Nature. It is the great spirit of the wilderness, the keeper of its secrets. And it may erase memory because to unite with Nature may mean losing your personal self. Penzoldt concluded that "Blackwood's spirits . . . are nature herself, nature surprised, as it were, in her deepest secrets."[44]

The Wendigo is a persistent image in Canada. Colombo has collected written and visual artifacts in *Windigo: An Anthology of Fact and Fantastic Fiction*. At times it is depicted as a cannibalistic creature, at other times as a reification of the starving that was a natural part of winter in cold climes, and yet again as a symbol for "going bush," that is, to go feral, to lose one's mind and go crazy in the wilds. In a way it is a shape-shifter, appearing differently to different peoples at different times. Colombo notes that originally the Windigo (to use his spelling) was nameless or the name was not to be spoken, a taboo word that could conjure up the beast. Early in "The Wendigo" Défago mentions the Wendigo as he and Simpson prepare to rest for the night; both seem near panic, and the very word seems to unsettle the darkness. Margaret Atwood points out the various images and incarnations of Wendigo. She suggests the real danger was in becoming a Wendigo, of releasing an internal monster: "It's what you might turn into if you don't watch out."[45] For Blackwood, the Wendigo is an image for a spirit of the forest, a wilderness that can appropriate the souls of people. In the woods of Blackwood everything is sentient, "even the wind," as Jack Sullivan argues.[46]

"A Haunted Island" is one of Blackwood's first stories. By setting his Canadian stories in the forest, he presents his human characters as diminished or overawed by the natural setting. In this tale, he places a human abode within the wilds, and it is no safer than a tent. Ashley suggests that the story arose from Blackwood's time in the Muskoka region of Ontario.[47] The narrator is alone on an island in a two-story cottage to read for the law. He finds the forest so close to the cottage that a light wind inspires the "branches to scrape the roof and tap the wooden walls."[48] The surrounding lake and forest and the night darkness conspire to trap him.

A dominant sense in this story is sound; Sullivan notes that Blackwood delivered "a sonorous range of natural and 'psychical' sounds" in the tale.[49] But the story also has fine supernatural images. The narrator finds the island silent after the summer of noise but early on he hears "a shout or a cry" (22). Then he hears "innumerable footsteps, shufflings, the rustle of skirts and a constant undertone of whispering" (23) in the cottage. There are the loud strokes of a clock. He is startled at the "sound of a big tree falling . . . like the first guns of a distant night attack" (27–28). The boards of the cottage creak. But perhaps the worst sound is "the ominous and overwhelming silence" (25) foretelling a storm. He spies a canoe with two aboriginal men paddling by his dock and then landing. They approach the cottage, and the narrator freezes against a wall. Their journey is portrayed by sounds (a soft step on the verandah, a rattling of the doorknob) and by sights (a dark face pressed against a window, a shadow that "swayed to and fro like a bent tree" [32]), as if Nature herself is the attacker. The specters stealthily enter the cottage, where the narrator is paralyzed with terror against a wall. As if in slow motion, the pair move across the room toward the stair, passing within inches of the narrator. While the phantoms are upstairs, "there was silence," a quiet "before the birth of sound," torn apart by a "shriek of terror" (35) from above. The intruders thud down the stairs with a heavy burden and as they pass before the narrator, he sees it is a body, his body, dead. He reaches out in anger for the aboriginal man and touches nothing. In the atmosphere of the story, his senses are heightened by the counterpoint of silence and sound. But is the image really of him? Is he dreaming at the end? As he flees the island he sees the phantom aboriginal men in their canoe again circling the island. Is this a repetitive cinematic experience? What is it he has really seen or experienced? The story induces a sense of the strange and the sense of a person invading a space that belongs to another. And it may be that the house is the center of the haunting and not the narrator. The cottage is out of place in the wilderness.

"Running Wolf" has moments of authenticity and is not just an ordinary ghost story. It is set in the Quebec woods. Here Malcolm Hyde, hotel clerk and white fisher on holiday, goes to Medicine Lake, "lying there in the vast Canadian backwoods."[50] He travels through an "immense world of forests that stretched for hundreds of miles . . . strange to any echo of human tread . . . a deserted and primeval wilderness" (54). He ignores warnings and camps on the east side of the lake; a similar dismissal of warnings occurs in "The Willows" (1907). He enjoys great success fishing. It is like an Eden for the hotel clerk. But he soon feels he is not alone but being watched as "unreasoning terror gripped him" (58) like the panic of the forest. He no longer feels exhilarated but wary; and at night "the darkness of the forest lay like an impenetrable wall" (60) all around him, as if he is now trapped in the woods. The forest has been transformed from a space of beauty and serenity into a Gothic space of terror. Soon he discovers the presence of a gigantic timber wolf, first seeing its green eyes glowing in the darkness. The wolf stalks him and even sits at his campfire, "as a man might sit" (66). As the wolf stares at him, Hyde experiences a paralysis, "transfixed with that nameless terror that is said to attack human beings who suddenly face the dead" (67). But then the feeling shifts and Hyde establishes a sort of communication with the beast, as if "the gulf betwixt animal and human seemed in an instant bridged" (67). Hyde eventually follows the wolf through the woods and unearths a skeleton of an indigenous person. As if prompted by the wolf, "he wrapped the bones in bark; he laid the tomahawk beside the skull; he lit the circular fire round the pyre" (72); he buries the dead man. Then the wolf is gone. Hyde has released the indigenous man, named Running Wolf, trapped in the body of a spirit wolf, doomed to haunt the east side of the lake until a man of another race buried him. A white man rescues an indigenous ghost.

Slavoj Žižek argues that dead return because "they were not properly buried" and they return as "collectors of some unpaid symbolic debt."[51] In this story the wolf is the symbolic representation of the dead, who will not stay dead. And the wolf has appropriated one side of the lake, which is abandoned by the living for the dead. It is a haunted space, where the forlorn beast wanders alone until Hyde arrives and responds to the performance of the wolf as human. In a sense, the wolf is the totem of a symbolic rite to ensure the dead are ushered properly into the long night of darkness. Running Wolf, who broke a taboo of his people by killing a wolf, cannot be buried by his own but must await the other to atone for him. Running Wolf is "the body that is present without being dead on the symbolic level";[52] he is a living corpse in the shape of a wolf. The rite of burial is symbolic of reverence for the dead, and this does not take place until an outsider enters the haunted ground and performs the needed symbolic atonement. For Running Wolf's destiny is out of his hands, or paws, as the wolf cannot dig up the dispersed bones. And he cannot change the meaning or significance of his life, which was one of disrepute. But it can be changed by one of the living.

"The Valley of the Beasts" is set in "Snow River country"[53] somewhere in the northwest of Canada, a sort of mythic warm spot in the North, another Eden. The Englishman, Grimwood (a nice touch in naming by Blackwood), the hunter, and his guide, Tooshalli, are tracking "the biggest moose in the world" (115). Tooshalli refuses to venture into the valley where the tracks lead. The land belongs to Ishtot (a supposed aboriginal hunting god). Tooshalli is repaid with a brutal fist to the face. Seemingly ready to kill, Grimwood is hit suddenly with a "sense of awe," as the "lonely wilderness" puts an "inexplicable chill on his raging blood" (121). He stops. Nature here is a calming force.

The guide leaves, and the hunter ventures into the valley alone. Here, as in "Running Wolf," the "air was like wine" (123), intoxicating to the hunter. Grimwood senses a deep comfort in the forest, an overwhelming beauty, and he "felt safe, at home in it" (124). In the valley Grimwood experiences a transformation as he stares into the eyes of the great moose and throws away his rifle. He seems to become animal, as he fears fire and laps water and joins in a sharing circle of animals, like "some magical homecoming . . . where he was natural" (131). Is this the wondrous land where a wolf licks gently at the injured shoulder of a bull moose, where all are one? But Grimwood is awakened from his union with Nature or reverie by the touch of the totem left by his guide—or is the totem a symbol of his reawakening awareness of self? He had not given up his self-identity. And then the animals turn on him. But his guide shows up at the right moment and kills a gigantic bear about to attack him. Punter raises a question: "What would our relations with the animals, the forests, the ghosts be like if we were constantly aware of their fears, their awareness of danger and mortality?"[54] Grimwood forswears hunting, but Tooshalli appears estranged from his heritage, for he has violated the taboo as well, and he becomes a kept pet of Grimwood.

"First Hate" is an old-style frame tale, where the telling takes place in an English club. Ashley suggests that Blackwood wrote this story to explore the innate drive to violence and revenge in humans.[55] It is a twist on Christopher Marlowe's line on love at first sight. Here it is hate at first sight. It may be characterized also as a doppelgänger story. The action takes place in the Campbell River area and on the Pacific Coast of Vancouver Island, British Columbia. Fates or obsessions intersect in a "god-forsaken bit of wilderness"[56] where Ericssen kills Hazel, although it was Hazel who fired the first shot. The forest is more a backdrop than an impetus in the story, a place for fishing, hunting, and killing. In a "lonely valley, where only the noises of wind and water were audible" (93), Ericssen chances upon his fated other. Hazel is Ericssen's demonic double, whom he must kill to live himself. Ericssen also kills Hazel's guide, as the punch line for the story.

"Skeleton Lake: An Episode in Camp" tells of an ill-fated moose-hunting expedition set in "the Quebec backwoods" on the "utter loneliness" of a lake with a "lugubrious atmosphere that haunted its shores and islands."[57] The hunters camp in an area of deep forests shimmering with their gold and crimson leaves of autumn. The telling event is the appearance of Rushton, who along with Jake the Swede, his guide, has made camp on Beaver Lake, fifty miles from the narrator's camp. Rushton tells a story of capsizing their canoe. He was fortunate to swim to an island, but Jake failed in his efforts. But "something moved secretly between his words" (195), the narrator reveals. That secret was that Rushton had killed Jake, and the truth emerges as the story cracks under its changes and contradictions. It's as if guilt will always speak out.

As with "First Hate," this is a story of white men killing white men in the Canadian wilderness. Perhaps it is a tale about the falsity in stories. Our language is a veil through which we try to see the world, and it is false. What we tell each other about the world may be a vapor of lies. However, even in this slim story, Blackwood calls forth the atmosphere of the outdoors, as "forest odours floated . . . on the autumn air" and the "cedar fire smelt sweet" and the hunters could hear "the gentle wash of tiny waves along the shore" (200). Blackwood has the power to paint being in the forests and experiencing their many moods, some of rapture, some of terror.

STORIES WITH TRACES OF CANADA

Many of Blackwood's short stories explore terrain similar to that of his Canadian stories. "The Camp of the Dog" (1908) is set in Scandinavia but, as Joshi suggests, "clearly echoes Blackwood's camping trips in Canada."[58] Colombo contends that the "tale of possession and projection pivots on the 'Red Indian ancestry' of Peter Sangree."[59] Hubbard, Dr. Silence's associate, narrates this story of a camping excursion on a lonely island, among many islands, featuring "pine-woods that came down to the water's edge and led the eye through unknown depths of shadow and mystery into the very heart of primitive forest" (172). Blackwood delivers wonderful descriptions of the sights, sounds, and scents of the wilderness in this story. The forest seems conscious as the "trees crowded down to the shore to hear us pass . . . their fine dark heads, bowed low" (181). Even the weather seems sentient as "the advance guard of the fog was creeping lowly among the trees, like white arms feeling their way" (217).

A clergyman, Timothy Maloney, his wife, their daughter Joan, and a young Canadian, Peter Sangree, accompany Hubbard on the camping trip. On the uninhabited island they encounter a strange sequence of events, including dog/wolf tracks, a torn tent, and an attack by a large animal. But in the beginning the campers experience the joy and healing of Nature. Then "a sense of wonder, of poignant distress, and of trepidation" (199) creeps over them. The terror is lycanthropy, and Dr. Silence expounds on it after his entrance about halfway through the story, which is the weakest portion, as both fear and awe seem to dissipate slowly.

Most of all, "The Camp of the Dog" is a story about the liberation in Nature of human sexual desire camouflaged as a werewolf tale. The image of the overpowering passion of Sangree is very effective. Dr. Silence and Hubbard observe a "dark mass of 'something' on four legs . . . and the . . . gleam of fiery eyes and white fangs" (222) circling Sangree. It is a beast with fur and the face of a wolf or wild dog, but it also has "the face of Sangree" (223). Its wail is a "broken human voice, mingling with the savage howl of the brute beast" (224), as if human and the wild merge. And Joan answers with "a singular wild sweetness" (225). It is a love match in the wilderness, which seems to have unleashed the restraints civilization places on desire between men and women.

"The Man Whom the Trees Loved" (1912) is another story centered on the wonder and the terror of the forest. David Bittacy is a forester who has devoted his life to trees. He feels a "dim, vast living" in trees, especially "in India; and in Canadian woods"; he loves the "Forest Personality."[60] And he finds it again in England in the New Forest, with its "great encircling mass of gloom" (214) around his cottage. In it there is a "slumbering monster" (215) that will eventually take him. Trees are described as sentient in the story. The forest is a great consciousness with a sense of safety, with "purpose" (213), with a voice. A voice of many moods: a "roaring," or a "murmur," or a whispering "with ten thousand soft lips of green" (237). Even individual trees in villages seem alive; they "longed and prayed to enter the great Peace of the Forest" (216).

Early in the story, Sophia Bittacy, David's wife, feels the forest coming dangerously toward the cottage, but Mr. Bittacy and his guest, the painter Sanderson, yearn for it. She feels the menacing aspect of the forest while Mr. Bittacy is entranced by its majesty and splendor. Perhaps in this couple the tension between the dual aspects of Nature is displayed. There are two perceptions: Mrs. Bittacy sees the forest as ghastly and threatening, while Mr. Bittacy finds solace—the "forest made him happy and at peace; it nursed and fed and soothed his deepest moods" (247). Mr. Bittacy finds another lover. Throughout the story, Mrs. Bittacy feels the dangerous power of trees and their hunger for Mr. Bittacy. She tries to fend them off, to take up battle for her husband, but she loses in the end. Mr. Bittacy patronizes her throughout the story and dismisses her concerns or any of her thoughts. For him the forest is rapture. He begins to smell like "the earth and forest" (256), as the trees ensnare him or he embraces them.

Mrs. Bittacy challenges the forest by entering it to fight the trees. In the middle of the forest, the trees "shouted at her in the silence" and stared at her, but she sees "so little" (259) of them. And then she glimpses her husband moving in the forest, "a man, like a tree, walking" (260), and she knows "he was gone" (261). Finally, the forest invades their bedroom, and she has lost all. He knows the beauty and awe of the forest but not her. In the end she seems to give up, resigned to her fate. The forest, vampire-like, takes her personality, draining it away, sucking away her life, killing her slowly. The forest takes her husband alive; his voice becomes part of the roaring of the forest. David Bittacy is taken in a way similar to Défago, in that he is dehumanized; like Défago, he is "but a shell, half emptied" (273). Mrs. Bittacy is a heroine fighting against the dense darkness of the forest and its hunger for her husband.

H. P. Lovecraft assessed Blackwood a "master of weird atmosphere."[61] He revered "The Willows" as perhaps the finest supernatural tale in all literature. E. F. Bleiler concludes that the suspense of the story "is hard to match anywhere."[62] The narrator and his companion are canoeing down the Danube. The companion is referred to as the Swede throughout the tale and is compared to a "red Indian" for his prowess in steering the canoe[63] and in mending their torn tent (41), one of several attacks on their island encampment. The Swede is playing a role similar to that played by indigenous people in Blackwood's Canadian tales. Beyond the cities and towns they enter "the wilderness . . . the land of the willows." It is "the land of desolation." But it is also a "kingdom of wonder and magic" (18), similar to what is expressed in "The Wendigo." Right away the landscape is animate with "the shouting willows" (19). The river seems to sing and laugh. From their Canadian canoe they spy wildlife on the banks of the river, very much like in his Canadian stories. In a way "The Willows" is a companion piece to those stories, with the natural environment even more distant, even more uninterested in the lives of humans. The grandeur seems more menacing. Roger B. Salomon argues the "wonders are awful, the magic black"[64] in the story. But there is "awe and wonder" (32) as the narrator is enraptured by huge columns of figures flowing from the island into the sky, like animated aurora.

At first the narrator feels the healing of Nature; he lies "peaceful in the bath of the elements—water, wind, sand and the great fire of the sun" (19). However, the island, "untrodden by man" (28), turns out to be "an alien world" (24) where the campers "are interlopers" (29). They have passed a frontier into a "beyond region" (50) of "disorder, disintegration, destruction"

(48). The island of willows is not like a forest. The narrator ruminates: "the mystery of great forests exercises a spell peculiarly its own. . . . They tend on the whole to exalt" (24). The willows are different, the awe is infused with terror; the willows are like "silver spears" (29), and they seem to crowd closer, purposefully, toward their tent. And this terror creeps closer throughout the story. So much so that the narrator fears being "drawn across the frontier into *their* world" (50). This other world is called forth through a series of impressions. There is a sound like a "gong" (47) or "the whirring of wings" or "muffled humming" (48) or "a swarm of invisible bees" (59), all seemingly like an attempt to describe the indescribable.

The marsh, the deadly willows, and odd sand-funnels set the stage for an encounter. The men see something moving. The impressions are different for the two campers. The narrator sees it "through a veil," and it seems like "several large animals grouped together." The Swede sees it "like a clump of willow bushes" and "coiling itself like smoke" (56–57). They are groping for a reality within an unreal environment. Lovecraft noted the artistic craft in the "manner in which certain footprints tell certain unbelievable things"[65] in "The Wendigo." But these enigmatic footprints are transformed in "The Willows" into titanic impressions of nameless things from an unknown, perhaps unknowable world.

Hibbert in "The Glamour of the Snow" (1911) feels most of his being belongs to the "world of Nature" yet understands that it does have "a savage domain."[66] The "spell of Nature" calls to him during his sojourn in the Valais Alps. It is something "'twixt terror and wonder" that calls his "pagan soul" (194). The tale centers on his enchantment by a strange young woman, whom he first encounters skating at night. Her hand has a "softness of that cold and delicate softness" (197) of snow, and her voice calls to mind his mother and the woman he had loved. She is like a dream. He is entranced yet wary. He seems in tension with Nature, with an "unexplained uneasiness and disquieting joy" along with a sense of "dread" (199), focused on the mysterious beauty. She gradually tempts him further away from safety, high into the mountains, just keeping ahead as if teasing him. She lures him beyond the trees to where the snow rises in "mountainous terror and beauty" (205). She is another form of the Wendigo, beautiful, with "wintry kisses" (208) bringing paralysis in the cold and snow. The spell on Hibbert is broken by the cold crash of a snowdrift, and he skis at breakneck speed toward the "friendly forest far beneath" (209). The tension is explicit in this story, with the snow witch as a loving terror, creating a terrible comfort in the "oblivion of the covering snow" (208).

In "The Wolves of God" (1921), Jim Peace returns to Scotland from Canada after thirty years in a "loneliness of trees,"[67] working for the Hudson Bay Company. He is a nervous man, vexed by his past in Canada. Seemingly he is pursued by the "wolves of god," beings that avenge deadly wrongs, according to a supposed indigenous legend. They were "a sacred pack, a spirit pack" (17). During a windstorm the wolves besiege the house where Peace harbors with three other men, two of whom are swapping stories, one recalling the Wendigo. The howling of the wind is described as akin to a pack of wolves. Peace shouts a confession to murder and, with a mask of "mystical horror on his face" (25), flees the house out into the darkness of the storm. Was it the call of the wolves or his own guilt that drove him out into the windstorm to die? "Wolves" is used eleven times in the story and "wolves of god" five times, as if the voices of wolves themselves. The story seems haunted by Canada, as Blackwood seemed to be.

NATURE IS WONDROUS BUT PERILOUS

Algernon Blackwood's experiences in the Canadian forests influenced his supernatural fiction. He traveled by train across the country, lived in Toronto, and failed at a dairy business and a tavern business there, and his mining adventure turned out to be a flop. But in the woods he found a dangerous beauty and a frightening awe. Blackwood described the Canadian wilderness with a grand sweep of language, as if he were in love. Nature gave "a sense of rapture, of ecstasy."[68] And whenever a human love would appeal to him, Nature worked her spell on him with "a sound of rain, a certain colour in the sky, the scent of a wood-fire smoke, the lovely cry of some singing wind,"[69] and the feeling would languish. His true love was Nature. In "The Camp of the Dog," "two 'wild' lovers" (228) are united finally after a struggle, something that Blackwood seemed to have yearned for himself with Nature. In some of his short stories the forest is more beautifully described and seems more alive and sentient than the human characters.

Perhaps all is connected in Nature. In "The Wendigo," a passing breath of wind lifts one leaf and lands it softly down with no other effect: "It seemed as if a million invisible causes had combined to produce that single visible effect" (171). And such a gentle effect it seems. This is reminiscent of William Blake, who in "Auguries of Innocence" sang, "To see the world in a grain of sand, / And heaven in a wild flower, / Hold infinity in the palm of your hand / And eternity in an hour."[70] But Nature is not always so serene, and Blackwood knew it; he seems no sentimentalist in his tales of terror.

Part of the essential uneasiness of his stories is that Blackwood taps a deep well of the unknown in us, who "are still close enough to primitive days with [our] terror of the dark,"[71] as he expressed it. There is a deep fear of the wild as it takes us back to the primitive, to the cave, and the howling of the wild. The great sweeping beauty of Nature holds a terror. In "The Transfer" (1911), there is an ugly patch of ground, "a bald, sore place . . . where green lizards shot their fire in passing . . . a centre of disease."[72] The barren ground seems alive as it "lay there waiting" (234), as it "scented its prey" (235). The black spot of earth is symbolic of a great maw of Nature, hungry and fearsome.

Blackwood expressed his rapture in Nature in *Episodes before Thirty*. It was "by far the strongest influence"[73] in his life. For him, Nature was sentient, "some kind of consciousness struggled through every form."[74] He went to Nature for solace and celebration. At times of crisis, "it was to Nature"[75] that he turned. While in Toronto it was "a pine forest beyond Rosedale,"[76] and later a "fairyland of peace and loveliness amid the Muskoka lakes."[77] The Muskoka experience stayed with Blackwood as a "sparkling, radiant memory . . . set against a background of primeval forests that stretched without break for six hundred miles of lonely and untrodden beauty."[78] Later, after leaving the Rainy River area, he found the same soothing Nature, "the air perfumed beyond belief," and above in the "blue-black bed of naked space"[79] the moon in splendor. Blackwood felt healed in the forest. "From hours spent alone with Nature . . . I returned refreshed and invigorated."[80]

But there is a tension in the stories. Philip Challinor sees "the monstrous and the magnificent"[81] expressed together in "A Descent into Egypt" (1914). It is not easy to commune with Nature, and not all are apt. In "The Touch of Pan" (1917), Heber and Elspeth are united with Nature and all its joys, and are welcomed by Pan himself. But others at a manor house party are artificial and degenerate in their talk, love, and actions. A man and woman leave the manor for a tryst in the garden, but the woman seems nervous in Nature and the man vexed. After the couple vacate the garden, Nature herself comes

> through the wood as though to cleanse it, swept out the artificial scent and trace of shame, and brought back again the song, the laughter, and the happy revels. It roared across the park, it shook the windows of the house, and then sank away as quickly as it came. The trees stood motionless again, guarding their secret in the clean, sweet moonlight that held the world in dream until the dawn stole up and sunshine took the earth with joy.[82]

Blackwood created a new field of the Gothic, according to Penzoldt, with "his stories on the hidden mysterious aspects of nature."[83] His Canadian stories of the haunted wood arouse both the wonder and terror of those mysteries. They give voice to our estrangement from, hunger for, and fright and awe in the wilderness. Blackwood's Gothic sense in these stories is of an alienation from the grandeur of Nature. The vastness of the Canadian forest represents an unknown Nature that is beyond our ken. The horror is in our loneliness, loss, and separation. Blackwood's stories are not nostalgic about Nature but rather express its power and terror, yet also express a yearning for rapture. Nature is wondrous but perilous.

NOTES

1. Dates of Algernon Blackwood's works are of first publication from Mike Ashley's *Algernon Blackwood: A Bio-Bibliography* (Westport, CT: Greenwood Press, 1987).

2. Algernon Blackwood, "The Wendigo," in *Best Ghost Stories of Algernon Blackwood*, ed. E. F. Bleiler (New York: Dover, 1973), 188–89. Hereafter cited in the text.

3. S. T. Joshi contends that it was the departure of Blackwood from the forests of Canada to the brutal New York City that was the pivotal event in his life. Joshi, "Algernon Blackwood: The Expansion of Consciousness," in *The Weird Tale* (Austin: University of Texas Press, 1990), 91. In *Episodes before Thirty* (New York: Dutton, 1923), 269, Blackwood wrote: "The city life was killing something in me, something in the soul"; and "New York hell, the Backwoods heaven." Moreover, Blackwood also thought the horrors of his "New York experiences of crime and vice . . . emerged in story form." Blackwood, "Introduction to the 1938 Edition," in *Best Ghost Stories of Algernon Blackwood*, xiii.

4. John Robert Colombo, *Blackwood's Books: A Bibliography Devoted to Algernon Blackwood* (Toronto: Hounslow Press, 1981), 105.

5. John Robert Colombo, *Algernon Blackwood's Canadian Tales of Terror* (Shelburne, ON: Battered Silicon Dispatch Box, 2004), 198.

6. David Punter, "Pity: Reflections on Algernon Blackwood's Gothic," *English Language Notes* 48, no. 1 (2010): 129.

7. Greg Gatenby, *The Wild Is Always There: Canada through the Eyes of Foreign Writers* (Toronto: Knopf Canada, 1993), 21.

8. Jeff Gardiner, "Some Dark Ancestral Sense: Awe in the Work of Algernon Blackwood," *Wormwood* no. 5 (2005): 21.

9. Colombo, *Tales of Terror*, 201, claims the island is Bohemia Island, north of Port Carling, Ontario.

10. Blackwood, *Episodes before Thirty*, 272.

11. See Mike Ashley, *Algernon Blackwood: A Bio-Bibliography*, for a chronology of important dates in the life of Blackwood.

12. Joshi, "Algernon Blackwood: The Expansion of Consciousness," 87–132.

13. Blackwood, *Episodes before Thirty*, 39.

14. Blackwood, *Episodes before Thirty*, 40.

15. Blackwood, "The Camp of the Dog," in *The Complete John Silence Stories*, ed. S. T. Joshi (Mineola, NY: Dover, 1997), 262. Hereafter cited in the text.

16. William Blake, *The Poems of William Blake*, ed. R. H. Shepherd (London: Basil Montagu Pickering, 1874), 99.

17. Blackwood, *The Centaur* (London: Macmillan, 1911), 119.

18. Gatenby, *The Wild Is Always There*, 21.

19. Blackwood, *The Centaur*, 118.

20. Peter Penzoldt, *The Supernatural in Fiction* (Atlantic Highlands, NJ: Humanities Press, 1965), 236.

21. For example, Roger S. Ulrich, "View through a Window May Influence Recovery from Surgery," *Science*, New Series 224 (April 27, 1984): 420–21, found that views of nature sped up recovery from illness. Frances E. Kuo, "Coping with Poverty: Impacts of Environment and Attention in the Inner City," *Environment and Behavior* 33, no. 1 (2001): 5–34, discovered that nearby green space enhanced urban public housing residents' effectiveness by diminishing mental fatigue. Moreover, Andrea Faber Taylor, Frances E. Kuo, and William C. Sullivan, "Coping with ADD: The Surprising Connection to Green Play Settings," *Environment and Behavior* 33, no. 1 (2001): 54–77, found that children function better than usual after activities in green settings and that the more natural a child's play area, the less severe his or her attention deficit symptoms. In addition, Nancy M. Wells and Gary W. Evans, "Nearby Nature: A Buffer of Life Stress among Rural Children," *Environment and Behavior* 35, no. 3 (2003): 311–30, demonstrated that nearby nature moderated the effects of stressful life events on the psychological well-being of children.

22. Punter, "Pity," 130.

23. Karen Armstrong, *A Short History of Myth* (London: Cannongate, 2005), 4.

24. Blackwood, "Introduction to the 1938 Edition," xiv.

25. Joshi, "Algernon Blackwood: The Expansion of Consciousness," 87–132.

26. Blackwood also published several nonfiction pieces on Canada.

27. Ashley, *Algernon Blackwood: A Bio-Bibliography*. Ashley identifies another Canadian story, "How Garnier Broke the Log-Jam" (1904). This latter story was published in the *Boy's Own Paper* 18 (December 31, 1904): 216–20, a British publication aimed at youths, and will not be discussed here.

28. Blackwood, "Confession," in *The Wolves of God and Other Fey Stories* (London: Cassell and Company, 1921), 243–64.

29. Gatenby, *The Wild Is Always There*, xii.

30. Northrop Frye, "Conclusion to the First Edition of *Literary History of Canada*," in *The Collected Works of Northrop Frye: Northrop Frye on Canada*, ed. Jean O'Grady and David Staines (Toronto: University of Toronto Press, 2003), 350.

31. Frye, "Conclusion to the First Edition," 351.

32. Susanna Moodie, *Roughing It in the Bush* (Charleston, SC: BiblioBazaar, 2007 [1852]), 46.

33. Moodie, *Roughing It in the Bush*, 46.

34. Moodie, *Roughing It in the Bush*, 88.

35. Moodie, *Roughing It in the Bush*, 335.

36. Margaret Atwood, *Strange Things: The Malevolent North in Canadian Literature* (Oxford: Oxford University Press, 1995), 9.

37. Margot Northey, *The Haunted Wilderness: The Gothic and Grotesque in Canadian Fiction* (Toronto: University of Toronto Press, 1976), 30.

38. Justin D. Edwards, *Gothic Canada: Reading the Spectre of a National Literature* (Edmonton: University of Alberta Press, 2005), xxviii.

39. Steve Duffy, "'They've Got Him! In the Woods!' M. R. James and Sylvan Dread," in *Warnings to the Curious: A Sheaf of Criticism on M. R. James*, ed. S. T. Joshi and Rosemary Pardoe (New York: Hippocampus Press, 2007), 177.

40. Joshi, "Algernon Blackwood: The Expansion of Consciousness," 118.

41. Mike Ashley, *Algernon Blackwood: An Extraordinary Life* (New York: Carroll & Graf, 2001), 97–98. This trip to Canada is evoked in Blackwood's nonfiction article: "'Mid the Haunts of the Moose," *Blackwood's Magazine* 168, no. 1 (July 1900): 58–72.

42. Gardiner, "Some Dark Ancestral Sense," 23.

43. Joshi, "Algernon Blackwood: The Expansion of Consciousness," 106.

44. Penzoldt, *The Supernatural in Fiction*, 233.

45. Atwood, *Strange Things*, 69.

46. Jack Sullivan, *Elegant Nightmares: The English Ghost Story from LeFanu to Blackwood* (Athens: Ohio University Press, 1978), 115.

47. Ashley, *Algernon Blackwood: An Extraordinary Life*, 90.

48. Blackwood, "A Haunted Island," in *The Empty House and Other Ghost Stories* (Kelly Bray, UK: House of Stratus, 2008), 22–23. Hereafter cited in the text.

49. Jack Sullivan, ed., *Lost Souls* (Athens: Ohio University Press, 1983), 297.

50. Blackwood, "Running Wolf," in *The Wolves of God and Other Fey Stories*, 53. Hereafter cited in the text.

51. Slavoj Žižek, *Looking Awry: An Introduction to Jacques Lacan through Popular Culture* (Cambridge, MA: MIT Press, 1992), 23.

52. Žižek, *Looking Awry*, 27.

53. Blackwood, "The Valley of the Beasts," in *The Wolves of God and Other Fey Stories*, 115.

54. Punter, "Pity," 137.

55. Ashley, *Algernon Blackwood: An Extraordinary Life*, 232.

56. Blackwood, "First Hate," in *The Wolves of God and Other Fey Stories*, 83. Hereafter cited in the text.

57. Blackwood, "Skeleton Lake," in *The Empty House and Other Ghost Stories*, 193. Hereafter cited in the text.

58. S. T. Joshi, introduction to *Ancient Sorceries and Other Weird Stories*, by Algernon Blackwood, ed. S. T. Joshi (New York: Penguin, 2002), viii.

59. Colombo, *Algernon Blackwood's Canadian Tales of Terror*, 205. At points, Blackwood suggests the aboriginal ancestry of Sangree as a locus of the intrusion of the wild in the story. Sangree has "an admixture of savage blood—of Red Indian Ancestry . . . the strain of the untamed wild-man on his blood," Blackwood, "The Camp of the Dog," 214. "Redskin" is a racist term originating with the European colonists to denigrate the indigenous people of North America. See Justin P. Grose, "Time to Bury the Tomahawk Chop: An Attempt to Reconcile the Differing Viewpoints of Native Americans and Sports Fans," *American Indian Law Review* 35, no. 2 (2010–2011): 695–728, for a comprehensive review of the term.

60. Blackwood, "The Man Whom the Trees Loved," in *Ancient Sorceries and Other Weird Tales*, 215. Hereafter cited in the text.

61. H. P. Lovecraft, *The Annotated Supernatural Horror in Literature*, rev. ed., ed. S. T. Joshi (New York: Hippocampus Press, 2012), 87.

62. E. F. Bleiler, introduction to *Best Ghost Stories of Algernon Blackwood*, ix.

63. Blackwood, "The Willows," in *Ancient Sorceries and Other Weird Tales*, 26. Hereafter cited in the text.

64. Roger B. Salomon, *Mazes of the Serpent* (Ithaca, NY: Cornell University Press, 2002), 13.

65. Lovecraft, *The Annotated Supernatural Horror*, 88.

66. Blackwood, "The Glamour of the Snow," in *Ancient Sorceries and Other Weird Tales*, 192. Hereafter cited in the text.

67. Blackwood, "The Wolves of God," in *The Wolves of God and Other Fey Stories*, 1. Hereafter cited in the text.

68. Blackwood, *Episodes before Thirty*, 40.

69. Blackwood, *Episodes before Thirty*, 39.

70. Blake, *The Poems of William Blake*, 145.

71. Blackwood, "Introduction to the 1938 Edition," xvii.

72. Blackwood, "The Transfer," in *Best Ghost Stories of Algernon Blackwood*, 230. Hereafter cited in the text.

73. Blackwood, *Episodes before Thirty*, 36.

74. Blackwood, *Episodes before Thirty*, 37.

75. Blackwood, *Episodes before Thirty*, 39.

76. Blackwood, *Episodes before Thirty*, 57.

77. Blackwood, *Episodes before Thirty*, 83.

78. Blackwood, *Episodes before Thirty*, 90.

79. Blackwood, *Episodes before Thirty*, 286.

80. Blackwood, *Episodes before Thirty*, 62.

81. Philip Challinor, "Over the Quiet Fall: On Algernon Blackwood's 'A Descent into Egypt,'" *Weird Fiction Review* 1 (2010): 89.

82. Blackwood, "The Touch of Pan," in *Day and Night Stories* (New York: E. P. Dutton, 1917), 40.

83. Penzoldt, *The Supernatural in Fiction*, 240.

Chapter Six

The Sickness unto Death in H. P. Lovecraft's "The Hound"

Mainstream literary critics have often condemned H. P. Lovecraft's stories for dreadful writing. Edmund Wilson called Lovecraft a writer of "bad taste and bad art."[1] When Lovecraft was included in the Library of America, Laura Miller[2] and Stephen Schwartz expressed outrage that Wilson was not in the Library at that time. Schwartz's indignation at Lovecraft's inclusion is reflected in the title of his review, "Infinitely Abysmal." He writes, "[Lovecraft's] stories always evince overwriting of a kind that disappeared with the pulp genre in which it flourished."[3] Schwartz calls Lovecraft's descriptions "absurd confabulations." Comparison with Borges, he says, "is ridiculous."[4] This is extreme literary elitism. Michael Dirda, on the other hand, contends that the Library of America volume helped Lovecraft reach "from beyond the grave to claim his rightful place as a grand master of visionary fiction."[5]

"The Hound" (1922), in particular, has been criticized as absurd and overwritten, suffering from the overuse of adjectives. Darrell Schweitzer suggests that the story gibbers from start to finish.[6] Even sympathetic criticism has characterized the story as a self-parody.[7] Steven J. Mariconda notes that Lovecraft himself referred to the story as a "dead dog," perhaps confirming the critical perspective.[8] The remark, however, may be ironic, similar to Mary Shelley calling *Frankenstein* (1818) her "hideous progeny."[9] Besides, Lovecraft depreciated much of his literary work.[10] Artists themselves are not always the best critics of their work; even so confident a writer as James Joyce expressed occasional self-doubts.[11]

Nonetheless, "The Hound" is a sound pillar supporting Lovecraft's literary status. The story is at the core of his art and shows him experimenting with form, style, plotting, and characterization. He marshals the common tools of horror stories, such as foreshadowing, building suspense through

97

mood, and returning characters to a disturbing place, as if he is using them up and squeezing what he can out of old techniques. What is more, he is also having fun—a bleak fun surely. This chapter explores the story through several intersecting lenses. As with much of Lovecraft, the story appeals in a fundamentally visceral manner, the way all true weird tales appeal as they evoke a primal sense of unwanted touching or being touched by an indefinite menacing something from a strange otherness. We find so much in "The Hound" about the experience of horror, about the language of horror stories creating mood and atmosphere (the language haunts readers more than the plot), and even about the American tradition of adventure stories. Lovecraft was beginning to cut the new wood of horror in this story. That is why some of the language seems crooked and the images splintered, but it is a gateway into his more mature body of work, where the themes are elaborated on a bigger stage. Still, the story unearths a sense of true dread.

The language itself is the fundamental gateway to understanding the story. It is the exemplar of the baroque language of horror—perhaps the only language to use in exploring the sickness unto death or in confronting authenticity in the experience of dread. That is the core bravery of the story: it is not fear but dread that Lovecraft confronts. And the message is that in the end even language cannot protect us. Eventually words fail in the story as they cannot describe phenomena, instead referring to "less explicable things," things of which "I must not speak,"[12] and that which is "utterly impossible to describe" (176). The odd sentence, "Bizarre manifestations were now too frequent to count" (176), is another example of the corroding and breakdown of language. By the last paragraph, language becomes confused, inarticulate, and chaotic, ending in a silent gunshot offstage.

A third way of exploring the story is through Søren Kierkegaard's concepts of dread and despair. The heroes suffer through the "sickness unto death." They experience the moral chaos of dread, the end of good and evil, where dread is ultimately a confrontation with a person's nothingness in the world. And the heroes fall prey to the sickness. But Lovecraft worked through this in his own life by revolting against dread. In a sense, Lovecraft is a metaphysical rebel as described by Albert Camus in *The Rebel* (1951). He rebels against the situation of life, against the world we inhabit. Michel Houellebecq argues that Lovecraft's art was a rebellion against realism, against the facts of existence.[13] Lovecraft "conquers his own existence"[14] by writing. Anne Lamott believes that "becoming a writer is about becoming conscious."[15] Lovecraft was heroic in an existential sense by knowing the anguish of life, yet persisting in the face of hopelessness through writing. In "The Myth of Sisyphus" (1955), Camus argues that the core philosophical question is whether to commit suicide or not in the face of the absurdity of life.[16] Maurice Lévy suggests that Lovecraft fought with suicide and survived at least in part through his dreams, which he later transformed into art.[17] In "The Hound," along with other stories, Lovecraft explores the idea of suicide as a response to knowledge of the world. The unnamed hero succumbs to the sickness unto death and takes his own life; Lovecraft soldiered onward.

In addition, it is helpful to read the story and the experience of dread through the perspective of the double. There are multiple layers of this theme in the characters, the action, and the act of reading itself. Throughout the story the reader is a double, as he or she is directly addressed by the narrator. We become co-conspirators in the crime of avoiding the truth of our existence in our very reading of the story if we become lost in the thickets of words. We are not just passive observers of the story's events but real agents in its creation as we respond or do not to the messages about dread. Lovecraft is an artist of substantial literary presence, and this chapter explores his talent in the writing of "The Hound."

The story starts with the unnamed narrator, hard gun in hand, fondly anticipating suicide after the killing of St. John, his companion. And death may be an ethical end for his sickness, reified as "the black, shapeless nemesis" (171). This is dread. This expression is similar to the "black seas of infinity" and that "dark terror which will never leave" in "The Call of Cthulhu"[18] (1926). In the poem "The Going," Thomas Hardy conveyed the same overwhelming dread: "in darkening darkness / The yawning blankness / Of that perspective sickens me."[19] Lovecraft is part of this tradition in literature: he wrote weird tales and poetry to express his anguish; Hardy wrote mainstream novels, stories, and poems. Lovecraft in pulp magazines and in his letters explored the same frontiers of thought. Massimo Berruti notes Lovecraft's use of obscurity as an image for "outsideness," which Berruti describes as "the pervasiveness of the horror and the ineluctability of its menace."[20] This is one way of apprehending the concept of dread. In "The Hound," this image of darkness is the real menace, for example, as the premonition of death, when "a large, opaque body darkened . . . [their] library window" (175). It is with the "blackest of apprehensions" (175) that they realize the language of the chattering outside their library door is Dutch. The narrator arrives at the scene of St. John's screams to "see a vague black cloudy thing silhouetted against the rising moon" (176). Later he witnesses "a black shape obscure one of the reflections of the lamps in the water" (177). In the last paragraph, the unnamed narrator speaks of the "night-black ruins of . . . Belial" (178). It is this overwhelming image of darkness—a symbol of dread—that engulfs his existence.

This presence of something that is almost not there but also everywhere arises from the tomb—the ghoul (underneath the ground, perhaps from hell); from the surface of the earth itself—the gigantic hound; and down from the sky—"the stealthy whirring and flapping of those accursed web-wings circles closer and closer" (178). There is no escape; it is everywhere. It is a suffocating, smothering atmosphere; one is numbed by the thick beating of the reptilian wings, overcome by the "stenches of the uncovered grave" (172), deafened by the unrelenting baying, and blinded by the "black, shapeless Nemesis" (171).

Lovecraft attacks all our senses, although there is a special ringing reek to this story—roused by the repeating gong of the baying monster. The story attacks our ears unrelentingly. Moreover, there is that intense unease at the dead human body; no one, willingly, is going to touch the thing "covered with caked blood and shreds of alien flesh and hair" (178). And yet, perhaps the heroes would do so. In the story, Lovecraft alludes to their cannibalism of the dead when, on first opening the grave, the heroes "feasted" (174) and in the description of the corpse of St. John laid out like a chewed cut of beef. There is the core of traditional horror in the story, but it is the consuming cosmic nothingness that gives it the biting edge.

In *Supernatural Horror in Literature* (1927), Lovecraft writes that he wanted to evoke in readers "a profound sense of dread, and of contact with unknown spheres and powers, a subtle attitude of awed listening, as if for the beating of black wings or the scratching of outside shapes and entities on the known universe's utmost rim."[21] Those moments of "awed listening" are ones that we all avoid, turning away from the buzzing night forest by turning up the TV, drinking, or praying. In "The Hound," Lovecraft articulates this avoidance from the dark night of the soul, an avoidance that will ultimately fail.

It is the language of the story that sticks with people, language that is over the top. Indeed, some find the language annoying and childish, but it is also exhilarating and enchanting. And contrary to the claims of mainstream criticism, Steven J. Mariconda, in "H. P. Lovecraft: Consummate Prose Stylist," and Berruti have demonstrated that Lovecraft altered his style to suit the subject matter of his stories. S. T. Joshi argues Lovecraft "was almost always the master, rather than the slave, of his style."[22] The self-affected style of "The Hound" purposely draws attention to the un-naturalism of the story and the spoiled-brat heroes. The rhetorical excess reflects the excess of the protagonists. The language expressly shows itself through word flourishes and hyperbole. But there is more to the language than baroque extravagance. Lovecraft's language serves a clear purpose as the "purple prose" itself expresses the substance of the story. "The Hound" is packed with adjectives, replete with qualifiers as if there are not enough words to describe the experiences of the characters, abounding with repetitions like incantations against evil. Perhaps by writing enough, the dread will pass by. But it is not to be. You can feel Lovecraft combating with the form and substance of horror in "The Hound," in the full, exuberant flowering of words. In the story, the words and phrases are artifices, fortifications against the tenebrous hours of darkness.

Among other things, "The Hound" is a study in using rhetoric to cope with horror. The language is its glory. The language is appropriate to the hysterical situation and to the annoying main characters, who may strike readers as immature, naughty boys. All through his writing career Lovecraft struggled with symbols and shadow to express his dark insights. The repetitions are necessary, the allusions to the canon of weird tales are central, and the alliteration and formulaic phrasings invoke the muses of horror.[23] This story is a nightmare. It followed on a visit that Lovecraft and his friend Rheinhardt Kleiner made to a graveyard. Lovecraft stole away a small chunk of a gravestone that he promised to put under his pillow—a charm to rouse the muses or demons of sleep.

However, the artifices of rhetoric fail to keep the dread at bay. Lovecraft uses many such devices in the story. From the first paragraph, onomatopoeia ("whirring," "flapping," and "baying" [171]) and anaphora (repetition of the same word or phrase in successive clauses: "It is not a dream—it is not, I fear" [171]) are used to signal the deployment of rhetorical devices. Overall, the story is a prime example of synathroesmus (piling up of adjectives), although the paragraph describing the first visit to the grave of the ghoul is the highlight sequence, and pleonasm (a word or phrase that, if omitted, would not change the meaning). Other examples include hyperbaton (reversal of normal word order: "Statues and paintings there were" [172]); neologism (*"Necronomicon"* [174]); alliteration ("dripping death aside a Bacchanale of bats from the night-black ruins of buried temples of Belial" [178]); tautology ("unknown and unnamable drawings" [172]); oxymoron ("articulate chatter" [176]); and allusion ("I heard a knock at my chamber door" [175], alluding to "The Raven"). Yet rhetoric cannot keep the dread away.

An overwhelming sense of existential despair, disgust, and dread permeates the adventures of the heroes.[24] It is a case study of the sickness unto death spelled out by Kierkegaard. In *Either/Or* (1843) Kierkegaard describes two ways for humans to live, the aesthetic or the ethical. The aesthetic existence leads to hedonism, consisting of a search for gratification and a nurturing of mood. The aesthetic person must always seek novelty in an effort to stave off world-weariness and an all-pervading melancholy; but in the end he has only boredom and despair.[25] The heroes in "The Hound" live the aesthetic life and try to escape ennui by indulging in the grotesque and morbid, hoping to enliven their existence through a continuous spiral deeper into degradation and corruption as they hunt for satiation of their feeling of nothingness. They live in a sort of death-coma, as Kierkegaard might say. Although the heroes recognize dimly the emptiness of their aesthetic life, they cling desperately to it. Kierkegaard's argument is that this emptiness arises from the fact that we have within us something else, which will not be satisfied by a sensory life. This is the eternal. For Kierkegaard, we are a synthesis of body and spirit, of temporal and eternal, of necessity and freedom. The aesthetic life, however, emphasizes the corporeal, the temporal, and the finite. This leads to a desperate search for endless gratification. The aesthetic way of life leads to dread or angst. In contrast, the ethical life is based on adhering to moral codes and living in a spirit of fellow-feeling. It is possible to achieve the ethical life by following cultural moral precepts. There is also a third way of living, the true way, the religious way of life, when we make a leap of faith beyond despair by acknowledging our sin and embracing belief in God. But if we have felt dread, yet obstinately persist in an existence in the sensory sphere, we will end in despair.

Despair is the sickness unto death. The narrator seems to be moving toward the ethical life as he retells the adventure. He speaks of the moral failure of their exploits and calls to God.[26] However, the heroes confront dread, persist in their worldly adventures, and end in despair, in the death desire as described by Kierkegaard in *The Sickness unto Death* (1849). A way of thinking about this matter is to consider that people tend to deal with this anxiety by obsessively focusing on physical apparitions and fantasies rather than the dread itself. Dread is not like fear; it lacks any determinate object and is something we all feel. "There lives not one single man . . . in whose inmost parts there does not exist a disquietude, a perturbation, a discord, an anxious dread of an unknown something, or of a something he does not even dare to make acquaintance with."[27] No wonder—as it is so overwhelmingly awful, like a cold darkness spilling eternally into your bedroom, or night falling through your tall dark windows like coffins. We objectify dread[28] to escape the valley of existential loss as long as we can. Mistakenly, we displace the anxiety to an external object and hope that dread can be managed by getting rid of the object—but when this fails the fear reverts to the original dread. This is the horror of human existence that Lovecraft experienced and tried to dissolve in his writings.

The heroes objectify dread into a thing that seems like a gigantic hound, or at least the narrator does. However, it is more than a black dog barking in their heads. In the story, the quest for escape from ennui leads the heroes to grave-robbing. In this expedition, they find more than they bargain for, as out of their frenzied digging arises the monster, the objectification of dread, the false hope to transform it into fear. In a sense, they unearth the other and see their personal hell. The "sickness unto death" infects the entire story and erupts in many words and phrases: "soul-upheaving stenches of the uncovered grave" (172), "dissonances of exquisite morbidity and cacodaemnoniacal ghastliness" (172), "features . . . savouring at once of death, bestiality and malevolence" (174), "vexed and gnawed at the dead" (174), "wind moaned sad and wan" (175), "gibber out insane pleas" (178), "queer combination of rustling, tittering, and articulate chatter" (176), and "madness rides the starwind" (178). These strange phrases are attempts by the narrator to describe his illness and his dread.

In "The Uncanny" (1919), Freud describes an encounter with dread, where the known causes terror precisely because it is known, but somehow now twisted into the unfamiliar and disruptive of the normal. The uncanny is "that class of the terrifying which leads back to something long known and to us, once familiar."[29] The uncanny arises from the unclear boundaries between the living and the dead and the figure of the double. Both of these resonate throughout "The Hound." The narrator and St. John are old hands at the boundaries of life and death and know decay and corruption; indeed, that is their rapture. Even the icon of dread in the story, the amulet, "was not wholly unfamiliar" (174) to the pair. Alien to most but not to these two, who have read the *Necronomicon*. However, this does not protect them from a fiend of the grave. But more important is the notion of the double, for the narrator and St. John are doubles. St. John is the purported leader, but this is hard to believe as the narrator does not seem like the tag-along type. The double is one mode of the uncanny. It can be considered part of the longing for immortality. Freud thinks the notion of the double does not disappear with the "passing of the primary narcissism"[30] of childhood. The double, at that early stage, protects against the loss of the ego. Later, the double functions as the conscience. Otto Rank describes the various incarnations of the double and sees the double developing into an "opposing self" appearing "in the form of evil,"[31] that is, as the bringer of death. So the double becomes a "vision of terror," according to Freud, just as, after the collapse of a religion, "the gods took on daemonic shapes."[32]

In "The Hound," Lovecraft expresses the horror through the double; for who is St. John and who is the unnamed narrator but two of the same, partners in crime? A reader gains a vague notion of the narrator, but St. John is only a shadowy figure, befitting a double. And when the double dies, the original is sure to follow.

However, the real double is the "one buried for five centuries, who had himself been a ghoul in his time" (174). Lovecraft deploys the dislocating effect of the known transforming into a monstrous unknown, yet still familiar, presence in the story. Dirk W. Mosig explicates this disturbing effect of many of Lovecraft's stories. There are other layers of doubles in this weird tale. The protagonists are both predators and prey. The ghoul in the grave was a fellow despoiler of graves, who also "had stolen a potent thing from a mighty sepulchre" (173). The scene at the grave is repeated, explicitly representing the intrusion of the past into the present. Opening the grave opens the past and unleashes the horror; it is as if the monstrous events will occur eternally, for there is no salvation. The characters in the story are struck by dread, but the real cosmic dread is that we, as readers, are drawn into the same recurring horror story.

Reason collapses under the weight of dread. This is Lovecraft's philosophical perspective. There is a difference between the narrator of "The

Hound" and Lovecraft: the narrator gives up, but Lovecraft, in the grip of despair, persisted. Lovecraft saw the universe as awful, like Pascal, who, when thinking of the starlit night sky, wrote: "The eternal silence of these infinite spaces frightens me."[33] This is the universe Lovecraft experienced and tried to articulate in his writings. Indeed, in "The Call of Cthulhu," Thurston speaks in a tone similar to Pascal of the horrible possibility that knowledge "will open up . . . terrifying vistas of reality."[34] In "For the Time Being: A Christmas Oratorio," W. H. Auden also describes this alien landscape, where "We are afraid / Of pain but more afraid of silence; for no nightmare / Of hostile objects could be as terrible as this Void."[35] For Kierkegaard there is an escape with a leap of faith. This leap is awakened by our longing for and recognition of the essential need for religion. We can obliterate our dread and the manifestations of this dread in apparitions through God. Fear of nothingness and despair at our limitations can be overcome. But Lovecraft would not traffic with a God. Nietzsche had already broadcasted that "God is dead."[36] Moreover, the horrors of World War I had spotlighted the emptiness of the idea of a personal God. Nietzsche, of course, did not think there was a God to die, but he argued that the idea was bankrupt in a scientific world. In a sense, the concept of God had no meaningful explanatory role in the world. Talking about God was talking nonsense. It was time for humans to grow up and throw away the thoughts of children. Lovecraft does have some fun with the notion of appealing to God in the story. The second paragraph starts: "May heaven forgive the folly and morbidity which led us both to so monstrous a fate!" (171). Of the particularly noxious tomb-loot, the narrator exclaims, "thank God I had the courage to destroy it long before I thought of destroying myself!" (173). In the last scene at the ghoul's grave, when the narrator says, "I know not why I went thither unless to pray, or gibber out insane pleas" (178), Lovecraft compares praying to gibbering.

Maurice Lévy argues that Lovecraft gave up on religion knowing the bleak cosmos and tried in his writing to forge a meaningful life in spite of the fact of nothingness. Houellebecq writes that Lovecraft lived an "exemplary life," that his "only animus was literature and dreams."[37] He was a "man without hope," according to Lévy,[38] the true existential man, who felt always the absurdity of life. Lovecraft was authentic and expressed an understanding of himself in a hostile world. For Lovecraft, the unknown comes from within one's own head and the hostile universe we inhabit and try to ignore. The true weird tale needed more than a murder or clacking bones or ghostly forms—more than mere fear. Fear is, in a sense, composed of tangible things—like slasher movies, drooling zombies, or the fear of death. Dread, on the other hand, is more formidable because it has no objective source. There is not a sane method to overcome the sense, the feeling of nothingness.

In "The Hound" the unnamed narrator is trying to flee from everything, including the reader, and uses language to shape-shift and distort his story. Always he turns away from the real truth of dread, using words to keep the night at bay and to confuse us, the readers. But that is part of the agony he goes through, and perhaps it is so awful that none of us could stomach it— not the actual sense of cosmic loneliness. Lovecraft chronicles this objectification of dread and the hopelessness of doing so in "The Hound." But the objectification of dread in a fear object is a temporary measure. The emotions in the story move from ennui, to excitement, to fear, to horror, then to full-blown dread. And at the conclusion of the story, language breaks down entirely when the narrator faces the unexplainable despair elucidated by Kierkegaard. Finally, the narrator is engulfed and can no longer use the magic of words to keep it away. The fear object becomes more intense throughout the story, from the faint but mounting sounds of the beast; to marks left by the dead monster outside a door, underneath a window; to a savaged, mutilated, dead friend; to the dread object itself, characterized as some "dead, fleshless monstrosity" (178). In "The Hound," there are no mild-mannered black dogs of suburban depression but a real howling madness. No Zoloft will work here.

But Lovecraft does have fun with the story. It is a takeoff on the grand English tradition of tomb-looting and museum-building. This colossal social edifice of stealing the relics of the dead is turned on its head, or perhaps illuminated for what it really is. As Lovecraft always reminds us, cemeteries are not dead; malignant, decayed, abominable yes, but not dead; the heroes eventually learn this the hard way. In the story, their museum is a re-creation of the tomb, of death. They lug trophies from the dead back to their chamber of horrors in England. They savor their sordid Elgin Marbles "far, far underground" (172) like a tomb itself. And the narrator "cannot reveal the details of . . . [the] shocking expeditions, or catalogue even partly the worst of the trophies adorning the nameless museum" (172). This is a sick archaeology, a twisted science to know death. And as the heroes seem to have no means of supporting themselves, perhaps they are in the market of selling pilfered grave goods, literally living off the dead. The heroes suffer the sickness unto death, but do not evoke much sympathy from readers because they seem too wearisome, just bad little boys.

The heroes—are they brothers, twins, lovers? Doubles? The double seems the most likely. "The Hound" is a story of two men on an adventure, a common theme in American literature. Leslie Fiedler, in *Love and Death in the American Novel* (1960), suggests that much of American literature is focused on male bonding through adventure, often in undefiled nature, and that it is essentially a boys' literature.[39] Lovecraft's "The Hound" is a sick adventure of two men who sometimes seem like juveniles in a defiled world, and finally in this tale we find out where all that really ends. This is not a boy's tale of the wilderness but an adult's descent into sickness, madness, murder, and suicide. From the hairy earth, the heroes have dug up their own death. Lovecraft has dared to express the truth about this stream of American writing.

In this story the narrator dares not say his own name—but howls at the outrages of life, of the earth, of the universe.[40] At the end, the narrator recognizes his own sickness, his own sin, his own monstrousness; he has become another monster, "the unnamed," the double of the "unnamable" (178). Even language cannot ward off the ennui, the darkness, the awfulness of existence, and so there is really only one last act. He succumbs to sickness and death and is overwhelmed by the darkness of Belial.[41] The unnamed transforms into the unnamable, realizing the nightmare of the sickness. For ultimate dread really is unnamable. But perhaps he is redeemed, a little, by plugging himself; he refuses to go back to regular culture and conventional morality, for he has seen the truth, and he will not pray.

So what is "The Hound"? What is the hound itself? Only a silly garish undead, a feeble image of infantilism? No. It is the reification of dread. We hear the real anguish, the howls of dread from the hero; perhaps more than we really want to hear or understand. Yes, as a story it has faults, there may be more than we want in adjectives but also less than we want in the elaboration of the chilling cosmic terror that Lovecraft explores in his later work. The baroque language is perhaps too florid and it fails finally at the end—as it must. The heroes or doubles are silly schoolboys, playing with forces too big for them to handle. The narrator succumbs to the sickness unto death. The action is full of repetition. The literary allusions may be too obvious and overdone, particularly the ongoing references to the baying hound. Yet there is a power in the story that creates unease; we sense an undertow tugging at us, dragging us down into the night ocean of dread. Lovecraft captures us with his magic language and in doing so has portrayed an episode in the experience of dread. Kierkegaard wrote: "If there were no eternal consciousness in a man, if at the foundation of all there lay only a wild seething power . . . if a bottomless void never satiated lay hidden beneath all, what would life be but despair."[42] Lovecraft knew this to be the truth of existence, and there was no salvation through Christian rapture. In "The Hound," we have been blessed with a brief glimpse into the sickness and death that envelops us all. The "unnamable" is the sickness unto death, and Lovecraft has broken down the walls of infinity for a moment, allowing us an instant of awed listening.

NOTES

1. Edmund Wilson, "Tales of the Marvellous and the Ridiculous," in *Classics and Commercials: A Literary Chronicle of the Forties* (New York: Farrar, Straus, & Co. 1950), 287.

2. Laura Miller, "Master of Disgust," *Salon.com*, http://www.salon.com/books/feature/2005/02/12/lovecraft (accessed May 12, 2005).

3. Stephen Schwartz, "Infinitely Abysmal—Review of *Tales, H. P. Lovecraft*, Library of America," *New Criterion* (May 2005): 75.

4. Jorge Luis Borges's admiration for Lovecraft is attested by "There Are More Things," a story in the mode of and dedicated "To the memory of H. P. Lovecraft." In *Collected Fictions*, trans. Andrew Hurley (New York: Viking, 1998), 471.

5. Michael Dirda, "The Horror, the Horror! H. P. Lovecraft Enters the American Canon," *Weekly Standard* 10, no. 23 (March 7, 2005), http://www.theweeklystandard.com/Content/Public/Articles/000/000/005/285tmhfa.asp (accessed August 2005).

6. Darrell Schweitzer, "Lovecraft and Lord Dunsany," in *Discovering H. P. Lovecraft*, ed. Darrell Schweitzer (Holicong, PA: Wildside Press, 2001), 86.

7. S. T. Joshi, in *H. P. Lovecraft: A Life* (West Warwick, RI: Necronomicon Press, 1996), 285, and elsewhere, has argued for the perspective of self-parody, or at least parody of blood and guts horror. It is true, I think, that Lovecraft is having fun in the story, but I am not convinced that Lovecraft would mock his own style this early in his "professional" writing career. There is parody, I think, for example, to the habit of literary allusion. But more important is the undertow of despair that finally takes the story into the depths of real horror, into dread.

8. Steven J. Mariconda, "'The Hound'—A Dead Dog?" in *On the Emergence of "Cthulhu" and Other Observations* (West Warwick, RI: Necronomicon Press, 1995), 45. Mariconda calls the story a literary joke and parody.

9. Mary Shelley, *Frankenstein* (London: Folio Society, 2004), xxv.

10. Mariconda in "'The Hound'—A Dead Dog?" traces Lovecraft's increasing dissatisfaction with the story. Peter Cannon, *H. P. Lovecraft* (Boston: Twayne, 1989), 33, also notes Lovecraft's dismissal of this story, but thinks the story has some merit due to "its vivacity alone."

11. Joyce writes "is there one who understands me?" toward the end of *Finnegans Wake* (New York: Viking, 1939), 627. And in a letter to Viscount Carlow, *Selected Letters of James Joyce*, ed. Richard Ellmann (London: Faber & Faber, 1978), 395, Joyce wrote of *Finnegans Wake*, "I think I can see some lofty thinkers and noble livers turning away from it with a look of pained displeasure."

12. Lovecraft, "The Hound," in *Dagon and Other Macabre Tales*, ed. S. T. Joshi (Sauk City, WI: Arkham House, 1986), 173. Hereafter cited in the text.

13. Michel Houellebecq, *H. P. Lovecraft: Against the World, Against Life*, trans. Dorna Khazeni (San Francisco: Believers Books, 2005).

14. Albert Camus, *The Rebel*, trans. Anthony Bower (New York: Vintage, 1956), 103.

15. Anne Lamott, *Bird by Bird: Some Instructions on Writing and Life* (New York: Anchor, 1995), 225.

16. Camus, "The Myth of Sisyphus," in *The Myth of Sisyphus and Other Essays*, trans. Justin O'Brien (New York: Vintage, 1955), 3.

17. Maurice Lévy, *Lovecraft: A Study in the Fantastic*, trans. S. T. Joshi (Detroit, MI: Wayne State University, 1988), 32.

18. Lovecraft, "The Call of Cthulhu," in *The Dunwich Horror and Others*, ed. S. T. Joshi (Sauk City, WI: Arkham House, 1984), 125 and 149.

19. Thomas Hardy, *A Selection of His Finest Poems* (Oxford: Oxford University Press, 1994), 80.

20. Massimo Berruti, "H. P. Lovecraft and the Anatomy of the Nothingness: The Cthulhu Mythos," *Semiotica* no. 150 (2004): 372. The concept of "outsideness" is not exactly the same as the concept of "dread" elucidated by Kierkegaard, although there are intersections. Outsideness is similar to alienation, where we feel separated from the world and it evades our limited understanding and does not respond to our needs. Perhaps it is the unutterable and indescribable. Berruti writes that the experience is that "of the limit, of the threshold: on the edge, along the razor blade, one hovers between life and death, between sanity and madness" (382). It brings one to the edge of suicide. The story "Facts concerning the Late Arthur Jermyn and His Family" begins: "Life is a hideous thing" (*Dagon and Other Macabre Tales*, 73). There the

outsideness is embedded in a sordid evolutionary history where the link to apes is much closer than one would think. We are not made in the image of God but are adrift in an alien universe.

21. H. P. Lovecraft, *The Annotated Supernatural Horror in Literature*, rev. ed., ed. S. T. Joshi (New York: Hippocampus Press, 2012), 28.

22. S. T. Joshi, introduction to *The Call of Cthulhu and Other Weird Stories*, by H. P. Lovecraft (New York: Penguin, 1999), xix.

23. The phrase "baying of some gigantic hound" and its component words are used in a traditionally oral manner where key phrases and words are used as mnemonics. "Hound" is used eight times, "baying" fourteen times, and the phrase "some gigantic hound" five times. Some of the words in the story, such as "baying," "flapping," and "gigantic hound," function as a soundtrack does in horror movies to pump up the tension.

24. This feeling of existential loneliness infuses other stories, particularly "The Outsider" and *At the Mountains of Madness*. In both of these tales the sense of separation from others and from the universe is intense. The heroes inhabit a space of solitude and unbearable loss—they are exiles, as perhaps we all are.

25. Søren Kierkegaard, *Either/Or*, in *A Kierkegaard Anthology*, ed. Robert Bretall, trans. David F. Swenson, Lillian Marvin Swenson, and Walter Lowrie (New York: Modern Library, 1946), 19–108.

26. S. T. Joshi, in *H. P. Lovecraft: The Decline of the West* (Mercer Island, WA: Starmont House, 1990), 96, details the change in the narrator's ethical posture.

27. Søren Kierkegaard, *Fear and Trembling and The Sickness unto Death*, ed. and trans. Walter Lowrie (Garden City, NY: Doubleday, 1954), 155.

28. Kierkegaard's concept of dread is confusing, complex, and manifold. A key element is that dread or angst is a feeling that has no definite object; it is different from the fear that comes from an objective threat (for example, a mugger, a grizzly bear in the wilds). In a sense, dread is a sign that we have the eternal or the desire for the eternal within us, but something is missing. Kierkegaard suggests the solution to dread is finding a connection to the power that established us as humans, namely with God. By truly linking with the source of everything in the universe, we can be fully realized. Dread is a sin when we do not connect with God, which we do through faith. Of course, there is no rational basis for this, and Kierkegaard glories in it.

29. Sigmund Freud, "The Uncanny," in *Collected Papers*, vol. 4, ed. Ernest Jones (London: Hogarth Press, 1950), 369–70.

30. Freud, "The Uncanny," 387.

31. Otto Rank, "The Double as Immortal Self," in *Beyond Psychology* (New York: Dover, 1958), 82.

32. Freud, "The Uncanny," 389.

33. Blaise Pascal, *Pensées*, in *The Provincial Letters, Pensées, and Scientific Treatises*, ed. Robert Maynard Hutchins, trans. W. F. Trotter (Chicago: Encyclopedia Britannica Great Books, 1952), 211.

34. Lovecraft, "The Call of Cthulhu," 125.

35. W. H. Auden, "For the Time Being: A Christmas Oratorio," in *Collected Poems*, ed. Edward Mendelson (New York: Vintage, 1991), 352.

36. Freidrich Nietzsche, *Thus Spake Zarathustra*, trans. Thomas Common, rev. and ed. H. James Birx (Amherst, NY: Prometheus, 1993), 35.

37. Houellebecq, *H. P. Lovecraft*, 89.

38. Lévy, *Lovecraft: A Study in the Fantastic*, 31.

39. Leslie Fiedler, *Love and Death in the American Novel* (New York: Criterion, 1960), xxiv.

40. As the power and impotence of language are themes in this story, it seems appropriate that the narrator's name is not revealed. It is as if there is a disembodied voice crying out against the terror of life, not sure if there will be listeners.

41. Joshi pointed this out in his notes to "The Hound" in *The Call of Cthulhu and Other Weird Stories*. Belial is described in II Corinthians, 6:15, as akin to darkness: "what communion hath light with darkness? And what concord hath Christ with Belial?" In the Dead Sea Scrolls Belial leads the hordes of darkness against the army of light, "his rule is in Darkness": Geza Vermes, *The Dead Sea Scrolls* (London: Folio Society, 2000), 136. In *The Jewish Ency-*

clopedia, the meaning of the word is elucidated, and one of the references is as "the spirit of darkness": JewishEncyclopedia.com, "Belial," http://www.jewishencyclopedia.com/articles/2805-belial (accessed July 22, 2013). In a sense Belial is darkness. This speaks again to the real dread in the story—not the "hound" but the overwhelming universe expressed as darkness.

42. Kierkegaard, *Fear and Trembling*, 30.

Chapter Seven

What Is "The Unnamable"?

H. P. Lovecraft and the Problem of Evil

"The Unnamable" (1923) is not customarily considered one of H. P. Love-craft's classic stories. Peter Cannon calls it "stagey and static."[1] S. T. Joshi says it is "a very slight tale,"[2] although he thinks it can be read as a treatise on the aesthetics of supernatural horror fiction. Two recent studies suggest the story has more merit.

Massimo Berruti sees Lovecraft connecting thoughts on the limits of language with ideas on writing supernatural fiction in the story. Lovecraft's use of such words as "unnamable," "unmentionable," "unnamed," and "nameless" reflect his concern with the perimeters within which language works, and thus the limits of rationality. The conflict between rationality and the supernatural can be resolved "by the way of the 'unnamable,'"[3] which is, in a sense, the writing of supernatural fiction. This imaginative activity un-binds language and defies the limits of rationality. Lovecraft achieves this by deploying key words to signal where our language fails and our epistemology ends. In the story, reason is not so much argued away (which seems contradictory in any case) but dramatized away.

James Kneale sees the story as exemplifying Lovecraft's fiction as it explores the "paradox of representing entities, things and places that are beyond representation."[4] "The Unnamable" specifically attempts to resolve the problem of naming and knowing what is outside of normal experience. But as language is the tool we are trapped in, it illuminates the indeterminacy in using it to represent things or spaces of an undetermined nature. For Kneale, the textual geography of the story performs a key role in illustrating this indeterminacy and the problems of expressing the "unnamable." The graveyard is a threshold between the known and unknown, and it is the

111

pivotal ground in the plot. Kneale argues that Lovecraft represents thresholds (that is, change) as threats, and that is why monsters arise from them; and, moreover, they represent the essentially reactionary aspect of Lovecraft's fiction as a struggle against change.

Of course, cemeteries in Lovecraft are at the edge of reality, serving as gateways to horror, opening up tunnels from the past; they are places to surface the unknown, as Maurice Lévy has argued,[5] or as landscapes to reveal evil. But it is not a threshold; it is "a cavernous rift"[6] in the settled experience of things that this story is getting at. Here the setting is a clue to readers that Lovecraft is engaged in an archaeology of horror fiction. He is mining below the surface of appearances to reveal an artistic response to a metaphysics of chaos. We are "upon the riven tomb by the deserted house" (202) to see what is always before us but ignored, to face the problem of evil.

John P. Langan calls Lovecraft's use of such words as "unnamable" and "nameless" part of his "approximate language" that is essential to his fictional works. Langan focuses on "nameless," which refers to the failure of language to account for something; the nameless is "a blank spot."[7] Our failure to comprehend the truly alien is mirrored by the language in the stories failing to describe the other. According to Langan, Lovecraft writes a "fiction about the attempt to construct knowledge, often crucial knowledge, through language, an attempt that is hindered, often fatally, by lack of adequate linguistic and therefore representational resources."[8] Lovecraft's work is about the failure to attain meaning and, in a sense, the failure of any epistemology. Donald R. Burleson also focuses on "nameless" in his deconstruction of "The Nameless City" (1921). The word "nameless"[9] is also found across Lovecraft's work. For Burleson, "nameless" is a contradictory word, both naming and denying that it names.[10] My intent is to focus on "the unnamable."

In a way both Berruti and Kneale, along with Langan, see the story as confronting epistemological questions, and the use of terminology like "the unnamable" speaks to the limits of human knowledge. This also articulates an anxiety about the impotence of language generally and more particularly the impotence of fiction writing to tell us anything meaningful.[11]

In a letter to Clark Ashton Smith in November 1931, Lovecraft stated he was experimenting with an idea for a new story, that is, "The Shadow over Innsmouth" (1931), by "writing it out in different manners, one after the other, in an effort to determine the mood and tempo best suited to the theme."[12] In the same spirit, this chapter is a series of field experiments toward understanding what the unnamable means. That is, I will explore "The Unnamable" from several angles, in a broad sense similar to mixed methods in qualitative research, in order to comprehend the meanings. As a beginning hypothesis, I think the story and the language deployed in the telling of the story, as well as in others, are really all about metaphysical issues in the end. Indeed, a reading of "The Unnamable" is an introduction to the overall fiction of the unnamable in the Lovecraft canon.

Metaphysics is the philosophical enterprise to make sense of the world. It is a search for the fundamental principles of the world. At its core, metaphysics attempts to answer the question: What is? In addition, a core activity is to clarify the ideas or language that we use in our efforts to understand the world and our place in it. In this chapter, it is particularly the challenge to make sense of a world where there is evil. The fictions of Lovecraft seem to be saying that the only metaphysics that makes sense is one founded on dread and the horror of existence. Is the unnamable then shorthand for a metaphysics of dread and nothingness, a philosophy of death and negation—the only way to make sense of our blood-stained time? We live in an absurd universe that is not congruent with Hegel's dictum, "when we look at the world rationally, the world looks rationally back."[13] There is really only irrational silence. The lack of intelligibility of the world is not a failure of epistemology but a failure of any first principles. Everything is fabrication; we have our being in a matrix of falsehoods. The visceral power of Lovecraft's works arises from the way he uses language to illuminate that there are no truths, nothing is as it seems; everything rests on the quicksand of metaphysical incomprehension, highlighting the fear we all experience when such an unintelligible world is revealed. That is because the core of this unintelligibility is, to use an old turn of phrase, the evil in creation.

There are several contrasting and intersecting themes at work in the story: the revivification of the past and its chaos overwhelming the present, the limits of science and the illusion of certainty, the instability of language at its core, and the anarchy with no meaningful metaphysics.

UN-DEFINITION

To begin, what does it mean to say something is unnamable? Surely not that something is simply unnamed, without a name yet, say like K2. Nor that the name is waiting to be discovered, or the name is hidden, or secret or forbidden to be told. In *The Golden Bough* (1890), Sir James George Frazer illustrates the powerful taboos surrounding names and concomitant need to conceal them. "Taboos are applied not only to acts and objects but also to words, and to none more than to names"[14] in many societies. This ban is especially held for the names of sacred kings and priests. Sometimes individuals have two names, one of which is kept secret, as the knowledge of a name may give power to another, who may bring harm. That is so because in "primitive thought, the name of a person is not merely an appellation but denotes what he is to the world outside of himself."[15]

In a more imaginative and poetic manner, Robert Graves also explores the power of names and the ancient tradition of secret or unknown names and the danger of revealing names in *The White Goddess* (1948). Graves traces the history of the holy unspeakable name of God. In the Jewish tradition, the name of God is sacred and not to be articulated; the Tetragrammaton is the name for the Hebrew symbols that only represent God's name.[16] The hidden or unspeakable name of God is directly related to the essentially unknowable nature of God in religious and philosophical contexts. For example, Benedict de Spinoza argues that the ultimate nature of God is unknowable, although for Spinoza the terms God, Nature, and Substance are equivalent. Spinoza was criticized for atheism, even though he was born into a Jewish family that fled to Amsterdam from the Inquisition. He argues that God, or Nature or Substance, is that without which nothing could be, and hence is necessary, and the scope of existence is unknowable.[17]

However, the mystical nature of hidden names or secret names is not what is going on in the story. In the fiction of Lovecraft many narrators are unnamed, suggesting hidden identities for readers, or perhaps the unreliability of the narrators as witnesses to the events of the stories, or the need for a cover because of their knowledge. It is also true that the past casts a shadow over the story. And, to be sure, the past is an element in an aesthetics of dread. Horror art calls up what is buried away, reveals what is hidden, unearths, as the New York police detective Thomas F. Malone finds in "The Horror at Red Hook" (1925), "secrets more terrible than any of the sins."[18] But the story is not centered on name hiding or name fear, or on the mysteries of religion. This is not to say that these human traditions have nothing to tell us as they speak to the fact that naming (let us say to our and the world's identity) is caught up within the web of language.

Lovecraft uses the word "unnamable" in several stories. In some it is paired with "unnamed," which may seem redundant, but the two words do differ in meaning and perhaps together emphasize the impossibility of rational explanation in the presence of the unknown, of the other, of evil, as will be explored in this chapter. I searched a selection of the stories of Lovecraft and found the word used in several. As a first approximation toward understanding this terminology, in the following stories the word is used to indicate the absence of descriptive power: "The Colour Out of Space" (1927): "breath from regions unnamed and unnameable";[19] "The Lurking Fear" (1922): "throngs of natives shrieked and whined of the unnamable horror"[20] and "forests of monstrous over-nourished oaks with serpent roots twisting and sucking unnamable juices" (199); "The Rats in the Walls" (1923): "peopled by unnamable fancies";[21] "The Dunwich Horror" (1928): "deeds of almost unnamable violence and perversity";[22] "The Crawling Chaos" (1921; with Winifred V. Jackson): "a curse unnamed and unnamable lowering over all";[23] "Through the Gates of the Silver Key" (1933; with E. Hoffmann

Price): "*HE WHO will guide the rash one beyond all the worlds into the Abyss of unnamable devourers*";[24] *At the Mountains of Madness* (1931): "the responsibility for unnamable and perhaps immeasurable evils";[25] "The Shadow over Innsmouth" (1931): "unnamable abysses of blackness and alienage";[26] and one of two instances from *The Case of Charles Dexter Ward* (1927): "A stench unnamable now rose up from below,"[27] and one of two from "The Hound" (1922): "held certain unknown and unnamable drawings."[28]

Another reference in *The Case of Charles Dexter Ward* is more complex, I believe, and adds to a deeper appreciation of the nuances Lovecraft is trying to articulate with such words. The sentence reads:

> It is hard to explain just how a single sight of a tangible object with measurable dimensions could so shake and change a man; and we may only say that there is about certain outlines and entities a power of symbolism and suggestion which acts frightfully on a sensitive thinker's perspective and whispers terrible hints of obscure cosmic relationships and unnamable realities behind the protective illusions of common vision. (207)

Although used as an adjective, the complete thought contextualizes the phrase within a perspective of metaphysical incomprehension. A second use in "The Hound"—"I shall seek with my revolver the oblivion which is my only refuge from the unnamed and unnameable"[29]—is as a noun. In "The Hound," the unnamable seems to be really shorthand for the experience of true dread, the sickness unto death as elucidated by Søren Kierkegaard. It is also interesting to note that the term was used in stories as early as 1922 and as late as 1933, in well-regarded tales and those less well-regarded, and in sole authorships and collaborations. It was embedded in Lovecraft's lexicon.

"The Unnamable" opens with two friends, Randolph Carter[30] and Joel Manton, "speculating about the unnamable" (201). They are in a graveyard, literally reposing on the past, with the vast hosts of the dead stacked underneath them, at the frontier of life and death, textually digging up the primitive as a form of confronting the unknown or confronting fear or revivifying evil. Interestingly, the miasma arising from the ancient burying ground seems to have a gradual intoxicating effect on the characters and on the language as the story progresses.

The protagonists are part of a tradition of two males on an adventure in American literature, a common theme in mainstream literature and in Lovecraft, who distorts and reframes the theme.[31] But here, this adventure is not in unspoiled nature but in the land of the dead, while arguing about spooks in the dark night. The plot of the story is, in one sense, an urban legend meant to scare Manton into agreeing with Carter's argument; and it works. When describing the bones and skull he found in the aged house, Carter felt "a real shiver run through Manton, who had moved very near" (206).

Theirs is a debate in isolation and desolation. It is almost as if they inhabit two solitudes early in the story as they debate. And the landscape is one of death. This is because horror fiction is outside of conventionality, in the personal space of its protagonists and its landscapes of experience. Carter and Manton argue as night creeps over them. In the story, Carter tries to convince Manton that the unnamable is genuine:

> Since spirit, in order to cause all the manifestations attributed to it, cannot be limited by any of the laws of matter, why is it extravagant to imagine psychically living dead things in shapes—or absences of shapes—which must for human spectators be utterly and appallingly "unnamable"? "Common sense" in reflecting on these subjects, I assured my friend with some warmth, is merely a stupid absence of imagination and mental flexibility. (202)

They continue their debate in "utter blackness" seemingly under the surveillance "of a tottering, deserted seventeenth-century house" (202). The story is stylized, in part, as notes on an academic debate. Lovecraft deploys a traditional scholarly point-counterpoint argument style at first, but this is transformed into a duel between the "objectification" of the commonsense view and the mythology of horror fiction, manifested through an increasingly baroque language. Early in the story, Carter says:

> Sensitive students shudder at the Puritan age in Massachusetts. So little is known of what went on beneath the surface—so little, yet such a ghastly festering as it bubbles up putrescently in occasional ghoulish glimpses. . . . And inside that rusted iron straitjacket lurked gibbering hideousness, perversion, and diabolism. Here, truly, was the apotheosis of the unnamable. (203)

Later, Carter exclaims:

> If the psychic emanations of human creatures be grotesque distortions, what coherent representation could express or portray so gibbous and infamous a nebulosity as the specter of a malign, chaotic perversion, itself a morbid blasphemy against nature? Moulded by the dead brain of a hybrid nightmare, would not such a vaporous terror constitute in all loathsome truth the exquisitely, the shriekingly unnamable? (205)

Always, Manton argues as an idealized rationalist, actually as a religious logical positivist. Carter deploys several strategies, including references to Cotton Mather's writing, to a diary of an ancestor, and to his own fiction writing, nearly like citations in a scholarly article; and he also uses his own direct experience with the "bones up under the eaves" (205) of the house. This strategy blurs the distinctions between journalistic or realistic writing and fiction writing. It acts to disrupt or breach the boundary dividing "reporting" from "speculating" on the universe within which we live and have our being.

In the story itself, the word "unnamable" is used nine times. Carter uses it four times, three as a noun, while Manton, when they are arguing, uses it as an adjective, but at the end he uses it as a noun. "The unnamable" is reified, objectified, and Manton has been converted; he is now a believer.

Lovecraft is not alone is using such words or phrases. Edgar Allan Poe says that *The Narrative of Arthur Gordon Pym of Nantucket* (1837–38) is "a story of disaster the most unspeakable."[32] It is like violating a terrible taboo, as horror fiction is generally considered to be outside of literary writing in the United States. Poe used the phrase "Tekeli-li!" as a neologism to express unknown horror. Lovecraft followed suit in *At the Mountains of Madness*,[33] a sort of cover of the *Narrative*. In *The Heart of Darkness* (1899), Joseph Conrad uses similar language as Marlow confronts the horror of darkness at the edge of the unknown, embodied in Kurtz's indulgence in "unspeakable rites"[34] and in Kurtz's "vast grave of unspeakable secrets."[35] In "Mr. Jones" (1928), Edith Wharton writes of the "unspeakable horror"[36] expressed by the eyes of the dead housekeeper, killed by the ghost of Mr. Jones. We are at the boundary of expression and are limited by our language. This has a long history. In *Oedipus Rex* (429 BCE), when blinded Oedipus is led in, his eyes are flowing with blood; Sophocles has the chorus speak but also say that they cannot speak:

> What madness came upon you, what daemon / Leaped on your life with heavier / Punishment than a mortal man can bear? / No: I cannot even / Look at you, poor ruined one. / And I would speak, question, ponder, / If I were able. No. / You make me shudder.[37]

The language of the unnamable is not simply misrepresentation; it is the confrontation with the irrational. And irrational impulses arise in us as we experience the world. Poe in the "Imp of the Perverse" (1845) writes about standing at the edge of an abyss; as we stare down we grow sick but do not run away, and by "slow degrees our sickness and dizziness and horror become merged in a cloud of unnamable feeling."[38] That feeling takes shape as "the idea of what would be our sensations during the sweeping precipitancy of a fall from such a height."[39] This is the urge to death at the critical moment in the experience of the absurdity of the human condition. A similar image is to be found in Lovecraft, Søren Kierkegaard, and Albert Camus.

At least part of the point seems to be that whatever the unnamable is, it is not possible to describe it or place it in a category familiar to human experience. The unnamable cannot be denoted or you cannot link a signifier to such an un-signified. Knowing, in part, is denoting, naming things.[40] In a sense it is grasping the world through categories of language. Ludwig Wittgenstein promulgates: "The limits of my language mean the limits of my world."[41] But the unnamable is outside of experience. It is unknown; at least, it is not known in the traditional ways of knowing. Noël Carroll argues that the real issue of horror is to "disclose, and manifest that which is . . . unknown and unknowable."[42]

In a way, whatever the thing, experience, or event is, it is not part of our understanding of the world. It is inexpressible, indefinable, infandous.[43] "Infandous" is an archaic term defined as "unspeakable," and according to Roger B. Salomon, horror literature's essential aim is to "remind us of the unspeakable."[44]

But using synonyms is not really helpful in moving our understanding forward about "the unnamable" as used by Lovecraft. In the story, one of the keys is that the unnamable is used as a noun, not an adjective; it is, in a sense, not a descriptive but the thing, or un-thing, its un-self. Not to name a person, animal, place, thing, or abstract idea, but to unname. Moreover, using the definitive article usually means a noun is a special sort of noun, which normally refers to a shared knowledge or something unique. In the story Lovecraft is illustrating writing fiction, so perhaps the unnamable is a way of stating that the monster in the Gothic and horror tradition is always a textual fabrication, as it must be, but also that all our ways of knowing the world are fabrications because the world is hideous at its core. And this core is mostly kept at a distance by a "slender gulf that is mercifully fixed between . . . [us] and the Outer World."[45]

FOREST AS SYMBOL

The story[46] is a fictional exposition on the writing of horror fiction. It is a fictionalized "In Defense of Dagon" (1921), where Lovecraft argues that weird fiction is imaginative literature, akin to realism in psychology and emotion but different in confronting the unknown and different in evoking fear. In "Notes on Writing Weird Fiction" (1933), Lovecraft says his stories "emphasise the element of horror because fear is our deepest and strongest emotion. . . . It is hard to create a convincing picture of shattered natural law or cosmic alienage or 'outsideness' without laying stress on the emotion of fear."[47] In *Supernatural Horror in Literature* (1927), Lovecraft articulates in finer detail this fear when he writes that in an effective weird tale "a certain atmosphere of breathless and unexplainable dread of outer, unknown forces must be present," and there should be an expression of "a malign and particular suspension or defeat of those fixed laws of Nature which are our only safeguard against the assaults of chaos and the daemons of unplumbed space."[48] The story says that artists (here a writer) speak about the unspeakable, arising from an apprehension of the world different from the commonsense view, similar to what Poe writes in "Alone": "I have not seen / as others saw" but am enthralled by "the mystery which binds me still" away from the world of ordinary sight to see things as "of a demon in my view."[49] The story is then a sort of exercise (perhaps a primer) in writing horror fiction, and the act of writing is art critiquing the accepted norms of understanding, representing, or apprehending the world. Horror writing, at its best, opens a fissure in our customary and comfortable living, to expose fear, to illuminate dread, and to give voice to the repressed, the hidden, and the locked away.

It is a space where few venture directly in their art. Roberto Calasso says that Kafka delimited his work to a "zone of the nameable"[50] because the world was turning back into a primeval forest, full of power, dangers, and apparitions. A world of "absolute atrocity,"[51] as Fielder writes—a world where mass death is nearly commonplace.[52] Kafka, particularly in *The Castle* (1926), describes the human experience within walls, within a perimeter of confusion, away from the dark forest—perhaps the forest where the raven "in the shadow of the silent night, doth shake contagion from her sable wings."[53] It is "the dismal wood"[54] of contagion, as expressed in *Beowulf.* Lovecraft goes far into this "antediluvian forest darkness" ("The Lurking Fear," 190), forest of fear, "nighted woods."[55] This journey into the "primal wood"[56] is not just literal, as "Forests may fall, but not the dusk they shield."[57] It is the force of this nightfall that Lovecraft illustrates.

In "The Great God Pan" (1890), Arthur Machen expresses it this way: "Such forces cannot be named, cannot be spoken, cannot be imagined except under a veil and a symbol, a symbol to the most of us appearing a quaint, poetic fancy, to some a foolish tale."[58] The heart of this is the fear of the vast nothingness all around us, yet which we want to unveil; when we do, it tears apart our perceptions and may drive us mad, as happens to many of Lovecraft's heroes.

The fiction of the unnamable is a trip into this dusk, a dusk of dread—for authentic apprehension of a cosmos of indifference at best, but also a cosmos with malevolence toward humankind, a cosmos of terror, dread, and hideousness. The arguments in the story start with a remark by Carter on "the giant willow in the centre of the cemetery, whose trunk had nearly engulfed an ancient, illegible slab" (200) and whose roots fed on the dead. Manton mocks this remark and the debate is on.

Horror literature, at its apex, is at the nexus of the metaphysical paradox regarding humans' quest for meaning in a "world of atrocity" and only finding displacement and the feebleness of any and all principles of comprehension constructed by us about the world. And the forest is both a metaphor of the experience of otherness and descriptive of an actual experience of an individual in a real woods, away from the battlements of home. Both uses suggest uncharted territory, a place where it only makes sense to say, "Here there be dragons."

In his best fiction, Lovecraft evokes that feeling of being in the woods alone, as related by Steve Duffy,[59] away from civilization, where panic grips one, where there are only dark spaces, where the evil breathes. It is where you may be "caught by the goblin touch of the willows."[60] And this space is located geographically and psychologically, as when the Nurse in Robinson Jeffers's adaptation of Medea dreads "where . . . evil stalks in the forest of her dark mind."[61] Later in the play evil is sighted "through the dark wood . . . at the end of the tangled forest."[62]

Carter and Manton argue in the dark, on a tomb, watched over by a tree and in the shade of a crumbling vestige of civilization, the deserted seventeenth-century house—a house that appears early in the story and returns later as a portent of the appearance of the unnamable. The house models in a way the emptiness of the arguments of science and religion and the monsters in our heads. There are things in our minds that we do not know. In Lovecraft, houses are almost always dangerous. Houses are desecrated, unholy, desolate, full of old festering sin and death. It is a place not for comfort or protection but for defilement. Here it is vacant of human life; it is the past that we think is dead, but sinister things persist. Homes are not safe from the woods. A house is a symbol of the past, of the forgotten past, of the loss of memory and impossibility of burying the monstrous, even in our heads. It also represents the intellect of humans, an intellect that in the end is empty, aside from the monstrous deeds of our ancestors. And the beasts infect every floor from basement to attic, representing the depravity in all spheres of the mind. Everything is in chaos, in disorder. Our reason produces monsters as dramatized in the film *Forbidden Planet* (1956).[63]

THE ETERNAL RETURN OF THE PAST

The story illustrates a longing for the past, perhaps a longing for death, perhaps for a dead lover. Yet it also seems to say that such an act only results in guilt and shame as the protagonists must be punished. This story, along with others in the Lovecraft canon, connects us "face to face with the ancient world of terror and devotion"[64] as expressed by Albert Camus in "On the Future of Tragedy" (1955). Revenants of the past come through the fissure because "beneath the ruination . . . of older powers is really a deathly chaos"[65] —a chaos where it makes no sense to name and where there are no identities. This is a worldview reviled by science—yet a world that we still inhabit. It is a dangerous world as the heroes of the story discover, a world of terror and revulsion and contagion: the closer we get to it the more likely we are to be infected, especially morally.

As Carter remarks of the "unmentionable nourishment which the colossal roots [of the willow] must be sucking in from the charnel earth" (200) in the cemetery, so the roots of horror are nourished by a nostalgia for the haunted past, the archaic and atavistic that continue to trouble us. There is a mood of longing for the past by Carter, perhaps best expressed in "The Silver Key" (1926), where he knows "he must go into the past and merge himself with old things."[66] The ancient lore is not dead yet: it still hints at the malignant powers surrounding us and shut away in our attics but yet alive and ready to feast on our fears. In Lovecraft, the monsters harken back to the pagan gods of myth who, as Karen Armstrong writes, brought pain, sorrow, and death. In *At the Mountains of Madness*, upon the discovery of Old Ones found in the ice, the scientist Lake notes: "Important discovery . . . found monstrous barrel-shaped fossil of wholly unknown nature. . . . Arrangement reminds one of certain monsters of primal myth, especially fabled Elder Things in *Necronomicon*" (20). These fossils return to life and bring death to those who unearthed them. So the return of the past, the primitive, is code for unexplainable evil.

During the argument, Carter delves into the psychic underworld to drag out of the past facts that science and religion now shun. He is a journalist of the haunting, indeed the possession, of the present by the past. The past is populated by the dead and is an arena of dread. It is where everything is corrupted and vestigial—a locale of unspeakable acts in the darkness of memory. For Lovecraft, "The past is *real*—it is *all there is*."[67] This is not a salutary past, as it holds a "shocking and primordial tradition" with "ceremonies older than mankind."[68] Part of the aesthetic expressed in the story is an aesthetic of passivity in the rapture of the past, and it is also an aesthetic of a heroic struggle to express the monstrous fear and darkness that envelops us from the past and elsewhere. Out of the vast camps of loneliness, destruction, and atrocity that define our world, part of the character of Carter tries to express the consuming howl of anguish of past generations along with the awful power of that howl to capture us and hold us fast. Through the adoration of the past his "soul has become a ruin."[69]

SCIENCE AND ART

Writing a story is not a science; it is "to relate events without analysing causes."[70] There is no formula for art in fiction, although there are formulaic writers and formulaic stories, which are entertainments and divert attention from the imperative to express the unnamable.

Science and progress are not unequivocal; the unnamable "undermines ordered notions of civilized humanity and rational progress."[71] The common sense of order is not completed and assured. In fact, horror is everywhere and horror fiction, at its best, is meant to bare these facts, which are concealed. The language used in this hopeless endeavor must necessarily be twisted and bizarre. Maurice Lévy noted that the "unintelligible is necessary hideous."[72] The unnamable is, in a sense, a "psychic intervention," as described by E. R. Dodds, when consciousness is disturbed and jolted out of normality, as Agamemnon was by "Erinys who walks in darkness."[73] It is a force that impels behavior and actions and comes from outside conventional human experience. In a sense, it is the inevitable intrusion of the irrational in our experience. This is the world within which we live, a world of fear and trembling that we often ignore or shun. This necessitates inverting the norms of the aesthetics of beauty. As with Albert Camus, Lovecraft might say, "Beauty is unbearable, drives us to despair, offering us for a minute the glimpse of an eternity that we should like to stretch out over the whole time."[74] Lovecraft says that "My reason for writing stories is to give myself the satisfaction of visualising . . . impressions of wonder, beauty and adventurous expectancy."[75] And fear sometimes becomes "so mixed with wonder and alluring grotesqueness, that it was almost a pleasant sensation" ("The Lurking Fear" 195). In the end the beautiful is awful. Camus admits that "At the heart of all beauty lies something inhuman, and these hills, the softness of the sky, the outline of these trees at this very minute lose the illusory meaning with which we had clothed them, henceforth more remote than a lost paradise . . . that denseness and that strangeness of the world is absurd."[76] To write horror fiction is to display that strangeness, which is often hideous.

The story interrogates science and religion (although religion virtually only in passing) on their claims as the true ways of knowledge. Lovecraft compares and contrasts art and science as ways of understanding the world. Supposedly, science is the exemplar of truth, with its rigorous methodology, instrumentality, and its defined language, while writing (and art generally) is "lowly" (200).[77] The tale speaks to the limits and distortions of scientific knowledge but also about the dangers of artistically venturing into the unknown, of venturing to the frontier of the unknown, that is, of being conscious of the world of dread—of awakening the destructive force that erodes our normalized awareness, and that leads to self-destruction as a normalized response, which is what happens to many of Lovecraft's heroes.

Moreover, in doing this Lovecraft illuminates the horror of modern times and elucidates "a poetics of annihilation and nullity,"[78] as expressed by Salomon. It is an aesthetic of dread that embraces hideousness, for beauty is not rapture but agony, and an aesthetic that, in the end, embraces evil as a necessary fact of human existence in an absurd world.

The story plays off a theme of Edgar Allan Poe, expressed most concisely in the poem "Sonnet—To Science." In this poem, Poe does not so much mock science as describe its usefulness and its limits. It has demolished the old gods, any gods really, and cleansed the mind of the folly of silly "summer dreams" in the arms of loving gods. Science helps us grow up, but it is not the truth as it "alterest all things with . . . peering eyes."[79] It misrepresents. Poe contrasts the magic of his words and his imaginary worlds with the barren, "dull realities" of the world of science. A true artist casts aside any interest in the findings of science and, as Richard Wilbur suggests, constructs "visionary gropings towards imaginary realms."[80] Poe accepts and glories in the fact that the artist has been driven deep into the past or to "some happier star."[81]

Lovecraft did not dismiss science but expressed similar sentiments about the power of aesthetics. Indeed, perhaps his fiction enshrines a counter-myth to the narrow view of logico-empiricism about the world and our experience in it. His use of language exemplifies this—especially in his evocative descriptions of the unknown where the language itself seems to come alive as bizarre and ugly. The story challenges the stance that science is the only truth about the human experience of nature. Imaginative literature is a way of knowing or describing the world, scientific inquiry is another. Aesthetics is as significant and as meaningful as scientific methodology.[82] This story is about the dangerous fissures between the rational and the irrational and the role of art in moving us through into the perilous wilderness beyond. It is not just that scientific explanation is not the only way of apprehending the world; there is also artistic imagination. But it is that any authentic apprehension of the world necessarily is full of dread.

In "Facts concerning the Late Arthur Jermyn and His Family" (1921), Lovecraft paints a violent perspective:

> Life is a hideous thing, and from the background behind what we know of it peer daemoniacal hints of truth which make it sometimes a thousandfold more hideous. Science, already oppressive with its shocking revelations, will perhaps be the ultimate exterminator of our human species—if separate species we be—for its reserve of unguessed horrors could never be borne by mortal brains if loosed upon the world. If we knew what we are, we should do as Sir Arthur Jermyn did; and Arthur Jermyn soaked himself in oil and set fire to his clothing one night.[83]

Jermyn's suicide is of a particularly gruesome kind.

Camus says: "There is but one truly serious philosophical problem, and that is suicide. Judging whether life is or is not worth living amounts to answering the fundamental question of philosophy."[84] For Camus, an unintelligible world empty of eternal truths or values is still worth enduring even in the face of an awareness of nothingness. "A world which can be explained, even with bad reasons is a familiar world. But, on the other hand, in a universe suddenly divested of illusions and lights, man feels an alien, a stranger."[85] It is the clear bracing air of awareness of the indifferent universe within which we live. Yet, for Camus, it does not lead to the negation of life but to an affirmation of living in revolt while not masking our absurd condition, our world without hope. Matthew Hamilton Bowker argues that "the philosophy of the absurd offers both a grounding for moral and political thinking and an appeal for a unique kind of psychological, moral, and political maturity."[86] This is right, but for Bowker the absurd is a psychological experience that demands a morally mature response, and this is what Camus meant. I think that the absurd for Camus is more than a psychological state; it does demand a moral response, but it is a response to humans' metaphysical condition in the universe. Camus experienced the absurd in a real, visceral manner, not in the abstract. The moral response is only real in action, not just in words.

THE UNREADABLE

In the story the phrase "illegible slab" (200, 205) is used twice to suggest the flip side of the unnamable. That is, a corollary of texts addressing the unnamable is that they should be forbidden, banned, unread. Or they are unreadable, as of the book Poe says "that does not permit itself to be read,"[87] which Lovecraft quotes in "The Horror at Red Hook." On a deeper level it may be that true horror cuts off language, obliterates thinking, and ends witnessing. The use of phrases like "unnamable," "inexpressible," and "unmentionable" signals that there are experiences beyond our human ability to endure, comprehend, perhaps even imagine.

In attempting to understand the relation between Hebrew literature and the *Shoah*, Gershon Shaked asked, almost despairingly: "What is, therefore, the way writers choose to express the fundamentally indescribable?"[88] Witness writers of the Holocaust like Elie Wiesel and Primo Levi lived the true horror of the twentieth century. They faced the real evil and wrote about it. The first version of Wiesel's *Night* (1960) was written in Yiddish as *Und di Velt Hot Geshvign* (1955), which translates as *And the World Remained Silent*. *Night* is a book of moral honesty about a time of the complete failure of all values, including the terrible silence that fell across the world about the Nazis and their engineering of the Holocaust.

But perhaps, in times of such personal and community horror, words work to kill memory, as W. G. Sebald argues in *On the Natural History of Destruction* (1999).[89] In the face of horror, there is a conspiracy of silence; we are mute, terrified, like stone. Of course, we want to escape with our wits intact. Some events, experiences, things are too disturbing. What is the authenticity of an experience when words fail because of its terror? How can the truly terrible be expressed, even be stored in our heads, without madness? Does survival depend on forgetting, as Sebald wonders, or is his argument merely a cover-up or an excuse for silence by perpetrators after so many victims have been brutally silenced? However, Daniel R. Schwarz, writing about Holocaust narratives, says: "Were the victims to remain numb and mute, they would remain *material* without soul as well as participate in an amnesia that protected the culprits."[90] Lovecraft writes of "that chief of torments—inarticulateness."[91]

The fiction of the unnamable is saying that in art there must be a revealing of the hideous, even when we want to look away. That is why so many of Lovecraft's stories are filled with references to virtually unreadable texts. The silent cosmos is unreadable, yet we are impelled to read. The use of the unnamable expresses the paradox that there are some things and experiences beyond expression but yet which we must talk about. The best in horror fiction goes where to speak is to be in danger, to be with the alien; where to be articulate is to be a stranger, shunned by society, to be outside the norms of society away from established ways of getting around the world, away from common sense. Manton in the story represents the commonplace with which the world abounds. Carter speaks about the extremes of otherness—an otherness that surrounds us and comes from inside and outside. The point of his argument is, in part, not to be silenced about that world, which is different from the ordinary world of everyday experience.

Conventional arguments speak from a view of the world that "behold[s], without perceiving."[92] And Manton's critical argument is: "even the most morbid perversion of Nature need not be *unnamable* or scientifically indescribable" (205). At this point, Carter does not argue logically; rather, his endgame is to unleash florid language about "monstrous apparitions more frightful than anything organic could be; apparitions of gigantic bestial forms sometimes visible and sometimes only tangible, which floated about on moonless nights and haunted the old house, the crypt behind it, and the grave where a sapling had sprouted beside an illegible slab" (205). And Carter now reveals that the nearby house is the locus of the beast and where he had found the disturbing bones.

Manton's argument is founded on logico-positivism, a school of philosophical thought modeled after scientific inquiry, or so believed by its adherents, who wanted to have a philosophy like a science. For logical positivists, statements are only meaningful if they are verifiable. Statements are verifiable in two ways. There are empirical statements, including scientific theories, that are verified by experiment and evidence; and there are analytic truths, statements that are true or false by definition. But even science is circumscribed by our confrontation with the world through the perception of appearances and our inability to know what is really behind those appearances, except by conjecture. In a sense we are captives of appearances. Logical positivists thought that the scientific method was the only way of knowledge and the only true way of apprehending the world. This was how to make the world intelligible. This is still true of a core of modern analytical philosophy. This viewpoint is expressed by Manton, except that he also believes in the word of God as expressing the truth about the world.

Wittgenstein writes, "What we cannot speak about, we must pass over in silence."[93] So ended the *Tractatus Logico-Philosophicus* (1922). Wittgenstein recognizes here the vast unnamable and urges that we must be silent even though there is a world beyond our current powers of expression. He is arguing for the inadequacy of language and the irrationality of going beyond it.

Marlowe has Faustus express the power of words to reveal too much, when he says, "Be silent, then, for danger is in words."[94] If we say too much, perhaps the real power of darkness will be unleashed, as happens in "The Unnamable" when Manton's "odd cry" (206) is answered horribly. This may be the other side of Wittgenstein's admonition. If we venture too far away from ordinary discourse, we will discover things or have experiences that will destroy us. And once experienced we are forever changed. This break between speaking out and keeping quiet is the fissure we must go through to overcome our fear. It is the crack, from an aesthetic perspective, that must be penetrated to achieve the expression of the unnamable, to reveal that which is buried, ignored, shamefaced.

The story relies upon old tales, "spectral legends" (205), myths to move the action forward, a strategy used by Lovecraft in other stories. Karen Armstrong says that myth "looks into the heart of a great silence."[95] The so-called Cthulhu Mythos reflects the interconnections of several of Lovecraft's stories, which seem to arise from a common font of anxiety or reflect an attempt to speak to a deep despair and unconscious chaos. Myth is a way to persist in the inscrutable, silent world.

The aesthetic imperative to overcome silence is also a task in mainstream literature, as the unnamed hero in Samuel Beckett's *The Unnamable* (1953) enters the same space: "I shall have to speak of things of which I cannot speak." He "is obliged to speak . . . never be silent. Never."[96] As readers we are not sure in that novel who or what is speaking and what the narrator is speaking about, and whether to believe anything because all that is said can "be invalidated as uttered, sooner or later."[97] This is the condition of the unnamable. As with the Lovecraft story, there is an attempt to find grounding outside language, to go beyond our normalized experience conditioned by state, religion, family, and culture.

But what is beyond our accepted or customary ways of speaking, writing, or representing experience? It does not seem to make any sense. Language is our conscious means of understanding the world, even as it reveals and distorts things. Words are normally the carriers of meaning, but in this story words are distorting; in the end, are they empty of significance? But silence is anathema; we must not be like Cotton Mather, who did not tell all: "Perhaps he did not know. Or perhaps he knew but did not dare to tell. Others knew, but did not dare to tell" (204). In *At the Mountains of Madness* the narrator declares, "I am forced into speech because men of science have refused to follow my advice without knowing why" (3). But his partner refuses to witness all: "Danforth is closer mouthed than I: for he saw, or thinks he saw, one thing he will not tell even me" (33).

The conclusion of "The Unnamable" calls up the other, the disfigured one, the dead one, to evoke expression; or rather, the unnamable itself attempts to speak at the end. Manton is found with "two malignant wounds in the chest and less severe cuts or gougings in the back" (207). Carter "was covered with welts and contusions of the most bewildering character" (207). This is the unnamable, itself, attempting to verbalize, leaving a message, but it is illegible, unreadable, illustrating the instability of all texts, of all understanding, of all metaphysics. What we are supposed not to speak about are the most important things, as even Wittgenstein came to believe later in his life.

THE PROBLEM OF EVIL

The traditional problem of evil is how evil can exist in a world created by an all-knowing, all-loving, all-powerful God; simply, how can God allow evil? Even in this world of contingency, how can evil be reconciled with God? Much has been written on this matter, and many have attempted to reconcile a God with evil through arguments about free will or this being the best of all possible worlds. These are attempts to overcome the problem through reason; others simply rely on faith. The arguments based on reason seem to have been demolished by David Hume, especially in the *Dialogues concerning Natural Religion*, published in 1779, three years after his death. But even in the *Enquiry concerning Human Understanding*, published in 1748, he notes all the hard work we do "to save the honour of the gods; while we must acknowledge the reality of that evil and disorder, with which the world so much abounds."[98] And the real issue is that reason itself seems not only impotent but "in pain" in the face of evil.[99] Acknowledging the fact of evil, in the precise manner of Hume, results in realizing that we cannot simply explain it away.

For purposes of clarification, let us say that evil as a noun means something like undeserved harm, or a wicked or morally wrong act or thing or event, or a force that governs and brings about wickedness. For Mary Midgley, the problem of evil is a human problem and "wickedness" means "intentionally doing acts that are wrong."[100] Susan Neiman says the problem of evil is really about the intelligibility of nature. It goes to our ability to understand the cosmos and ourselves. She argues that the fact of evil works to freeze our attempts to make sense of the world, that is, to make sense of our place in the world; yet it is also the key to understanding.

In the grand tradition, philosophy's purpose was to make sense of the world. And Neiman argues that the problem of evil is the driving force of philosophical inquiry. It might be helpful to review Leibniz's distinctions of evil.[101] Natural evil is like a hurricane that causes widespread suffering, destruction, and death. Moral evil is sin against God, according to Leibniz, but from a secular point of view it is a deed or act or failure to act that causes undeserved harm. Then there is metaphysical evil, the imperfection of creation that infects everything. Ari Hirvonen argues that the problem of evil must be disconnected from religion: "from the perspective and standpoint of our own time, we have to start again and again to deconstruct evil, to take responsibility for the problem of evil, and to be sensitive to new forms of the phenomena of evil."[102] The terrors of the twentieth and twenty-first centuries are the driving force for Hirvonen's argument for a secular rethinking of evil, with humans at the center of evil. He says evil must be brought back into law. It is not a theological matter but a human matter for response even in a world of metaphysical chaos.

There are some events so horrible that all would call them evil, such as the Holocaust. Such a hideous thing can only be called evil. How does such an organized, almost industrialized, evil killing for the sake of complete annihilation make any sense? David B. Levy notes Emil Fackenheim's assertion that it can be nothing but radical evil when children were thrown into the ovens alive to save money on Zyklon-B gas, and their screams could be heard echoing throughout the death camps.[103] How do we make sense of a human world of such irreducible horror, rationally planned, executed, and recorded? Kant writes of a natural propensity to evil, which he calls a radical innate evil in human nature. He says: "This evil is radical, because it corrupts the grounds of all maxims; it is, moreover, as a natural propensity, inextirpable by human powers, since extirpation could occur only through good maxims, and can not take place when the ultimate subjective ground of all maxims is postulated as corrupt."[104] This means that there is an evil that is a natural predisposition in humans, and Kant believed that this was brought upon humans by themselves, as they are free. The word "radical" signifies that we are "corrupted"[105] fundamentally and there is a "foul taint in our race."[106] Although perhaps not the standard interpretation of Kant's notion, this speaks to the contagion or infection of evil that affects humans and that seemingly is a part of nature. Does this help us understand how supposedly ordinary people become torturers and mass murderers, committing heinous crimes, engaging in hideous cruelty and atrocities? The suffering of the innocent conforms to no logic.[107] Modern times, indeed, perhaps all times, have been evil times.

We are near a disturbing aspect of Lovecraft's work in horror. Fiedler wrote that literary criticism is "an act of total moral engagement."[108] It is obvious that what one tries to say about literature arises from one's own experience in a particular time. And the truth of what one writes is mirrored by one's personal authenticity and commitment to understanding the texts one reads. There is something offensive in many of Lovecraft's stories; not the raw, grating, baroque style, not the sometimes loose plots and the over-the-top monsters. It is the elitism, the overt racism, the social reactionary-ism,[109] and the fascination with fascism (especially the linkage between anti-democratic political systems and racism) that infects some of the fiction and that is clear in his letters and other writings. The elitism is reflected in even minor comments such as Lovecraft writing that his paternal side is of "un-mixed English gentry."[110]

In "The Shadow Out of Time" (1934–35), the political system of the four divisions of the Great Race is described as "a sort of fascistic socialism, with major resources rationally distributed, and power delegated to a small governing board elected by the votes of all able to pass certain educational and psychological tests."[111] This is an echo of "Some Repetitions on the Times" (1933), where Lovecraft argues that a fascistic, non-democratic government would be best for the United States for economic recovery during the 1930s.

There is a fetish for the Nordic and the superiority of a certain class of people.[112] Lovecraft expresses support for the actions of Mussolini[113] and even writes favorably about Hitler in a letter dated September 23, 1933, to J. Vernon Shea. In the letter he refers to the "rabble-catering equalitarian columnists of the Jew-York papers."[114] Adolf Hitler became chancellor on January 30, 1933. The Reichstag building was burned on February 27, 1933, and on February 28 the German government suspended basic rights. In March the Nazi-controlled Reichstag passed the Enabling Act, which, combined with the suspension of freedoms as a result of the Reichstag fire, made Hitler's government into a dictatorship. In April, Hitler's boycott of Jewish shops was proclaimed. Lovecraft's entire letter (and others) is filled with racial slurs, directed at blacks[115] and Jews mostly, and expressions of support for the actions of Hitler and admiration for the German people in supporting him. Joshi[116] argues that Lovecraft's expressions of support modified over time and that his attitude toward fascism was not of the Nazi type. In a letter to Robert E. Howard in 1936, Lovecraft does say that "the most repellent and exasperating of the great powers are Soviet Russia and Nazi Germany,"[117] although he goes on to say that these countries had many points of superiority. It seems clear that Lovecraft's examples of fascism are governments led by an elite, who are in some sense superior to others, and the state is nationalistic with a strong unity of control and development (with economic and social regimentation) and with individuals subordinated to the state. Although the governmental system of the Old Ones in *At the Mountains of*

Madness is called socialism, the culture is founded upon an underclass of slaves.

Lovecraft's racism has been self-documented in his fiction and in his letters. Michael Houellebecq argues that Lovecraft's power arises in part from racism, which can be found in such stories as "The Shadow over Innsmouth," "The Horror at Red Hook," "He," and "Herbert West—Reanimator,"[118] not to mention his letters, which Houellebecq quotes with relish, such as the vile letter to Frank Belknap Long, wherein Lovecraft writes about the inhabitants of New York slums:

> The organic things—Italo-Semitico-Mongoloid—inhabiting that awful cesspool could not by any stretch of the imagination be call'd human. They were monstrous and nebulous adumbrations of the pithecanthropoid and amoebal; vaguely moulded from some stinking viscous slime of earth's corruption, and slithering and oozing in and on the filthy streets or in and out of windows and doorways in a fashion suggestive of nothing but infesting worms or deep-sea unnamabilities.[119]

Houellebecq goes on to assert that the works of Lovecraft proclaim the "universal presence of evil."[120] Indeed, they insist that "life is itself evil."[121]

Lovecraft throws lit gasoline on the problem of evil. The barrage of calamities, of senseless sorrow, of atrocity, of continuous violence that engulfs humans and is perpetuated by humans, is in his stories just a fact and simply that. Predominantly, there is no hidden thing that will survive and prosper; no hope of escape; rather, the hidden thing, if there is one, is even more monstrous and destructive. The visceral, raw power of Lovecraft's best work arises from the reader colliding with metaphysical evil—that is, whether the world is truly intelligible, worth living in, surrounded as we are by endless cruelty and atrocity, for that is the core of the problem of evil.

TWO FACES OF MANTON

The action in the graveyard may be understood as an initiation rite of Joel Manton: defilement is necessary to go through the fissure; experiencing the unnamable is to expose oneself to the unholy. Manton, who has been subject to sleep deprivation, incessant interrogation, and shock, finally collapses and "actually cried out with a sort of gulping gasp" (206), as if waterboarded. Afterwards, Manton is changed; he has lost his identity and becomes someone else. His words are like blasphemies, like chants from a savage time. It is the return of the primitive similar to Malone's contemplations in Red Hook:

> that modern people under lawless conditions tend uncannily to repeat the darkest instinctive patterns of primitive half-ape savagery in their daily life and ritual observances; and he had often viewed with an anthropologist's shud-

der the chanting, cursing processions of blear-eyed and pockmarked young men which wound their way along in the dark small hours of morning . . . he seemed to see in them some monstrous thread of secret continuity; some fiendish, cryptical, and ancient pattern utterly beyond and below the sordid mass of facts and habits and haunts. [122]

This theme is explored in several stories and is explicit in "The Rats in the Walls," where the civilized American regresses to cannibalism. As expressed in "The Horror at Red Hook," Carter has lured Manton to where "the beast is omnipresent and triumphant." [123]

In the beginning of the story Manton is vigorous and active. At the end he is passive in the face of horror. It is like a paralysis induced by Carter. Menaced, Manton submits; he now accepts the propagandistic story line of Carter. The language used by Carter is meant to distort reality, disrupt thinking, and convert. It works. In a way, Manton gives in to the forces of oppression; the terror world wins, and it is as if fascism marches triumphant.

Of the real nature of the final defilement there must be silence or lies; that is why Manton (who now has the mark of the beast or bears the scars of torture or is an unreadable text) ends the story with a story about a bull. The witness here lies to the world as if it is a story that is ineffable, that should not be told. It is like another story made up for reporting to the masses while the truth is buried. Or is this really just false witnessing? Or is all "bull"? That is, bullshit, horror writing is just nonsense. Lovecraft does have a sense of humor.

The unnamable is the instability of any apprehension of the world, including art rooted in our fears. The unnamable speaks about the "beyondness" of certain experiences of "utter remoteness, separation, desolation, and aeon long death" (*At the Mountains of Madness*, 29). It is a confrontation with the abnormal that disrupts our comfort with the everyday accepted ways of ignoring the vastness of the nothingness within which we live. Speaking of the unnamable is an attempt to contextualize the problem of the human response to the fact of evil. Part of the context is the absurd experience of the indifferent world, but also it is the reality of humankind's steel savagery of bullets, bombs, and torture, where science and technology are used to engineer malevolence.

Hannah Arendt compares evil to a fungus or an infection that has no intentions but may work according to some unknown law of nature. [124] This is the metaphysics of evil of the unnamable. Metaphysics states what we hold to be self-evident and even possible; it is the foundation of our understanding of the world. It is the fundamental principles of our worldview that are not themselves explained. The metaphysics of "the unnamable" is disorder as the norm; the world is a "blasted heath" [125] as described in "The Colour Out of Space."

Within this world of dread and despair, there is no salvation in a Lovecraftian universe. We are separate from and meaningless in the universe. Within such an absurd environment, Kierkegaard believes the only overcoming is by a leap to faith founded on belief that only a God makes sense in an awful universe, because we have within us a vision of the truly beautiful and beneficent. Kierkegaard argues that the absurd is that which is contradictory to reason itself, but resignation and belief will deliver an individual to God. For him, this makes faith courageous in a world of uncertainty, a world that is unknowable. Rationality and logic have gaping holes and fail to account for our experience in the world. The leap to faith is over a chasm of uncertainty, and the flight is propelled by fear and trembling over the bottomless void.

For Camus, the condition of humans is also absurd; we live in solitude and separation. Our unattainable desire for a communion with and in nature results in the sense of the absurd, which is heightened by our glimpses of beauty. Simply, the absurd is the human condition. There is no religious salvation in Camus, but humans rebel and persist without hope within the danger zone. "The danger . . . lies in the subtle instant that precedes the leap. Being able to remain on that dizzying crest—that is integrity and the rest is subterfuge."[126] Camus repudiates Kierkegaard's religious leap. The authentic act of humans is to be aware of the absurd and yet not accept a false god and not commit suicide. Camus links this absurd rebellion to creativity and the creative process. For him, "art is the activity that exalts and denies simultaneously. . . . Artistic creation is a demand for unity and a rejection of the world."[127]

Samuel Beckett ended *The Unnamable* with, "I can't go on, I'll go on."[128] It is persistence in the face of nothingness, and it is akin to writing your name on the walls of time, knowing they will erode and vanish. This seems true of Lovecraft himself, for, as Lévy writes, he was "a man without hope."[129]

Of course, there is no hope in a Lovecraftian universe. In "The Call of Cthulhu" Thurston says, "I have looked upon all that the universe has to hold of horror, and even the skies of spring and the flowers of summer must ever afterward be poison to me."[130] This is the bitter taste of beauty overthrown. Lovecraft's characterization of the danger zone, of being poised on the perilous crest of life, is different from Kierkegaard's and Camus's. In a number of stories the characters choose death; none seem to choose religion. Moreover, the fiction implies that there is nothing in common human resistance or rebellion, or fellow-feeling or community solidarity. In the fiction of the unnamable, "it is a relief and even a delight to shriek wildly and throw oneself voluntarily along with the hideous vortex of dream-doom into whatever bottomless gulf may yawn" ("The Lurking Fear," 195).

THE PIT—THE MAELSTROM—THE ULTIMATE ABOMINATION

At the end of "The Unnamable," Manton exclaims: "It was the pit—the maelstrom—the ultimate abomination. Carter, it was the unnamable!" (207). Here, Lovecraft pays homage to his master, Poe; the references to "The Pit and the Pendulum" (1841) and "A Descent into the Maelström" (1841) are clear. But why these two stories? Both of them take their narrators to the brink of death in an abyss. In these stories the narrators initially react rationally to the chaos within which they find themselves, by measuring the dungeon and timing the maelstrom; this is akin to Manton's initial response to Carter's speculations. Then they realize they are in an irrational world, but the bedlam appears wonderful; for example, the unnamed narrator sees the descending blade "somewhat in fear, but more in wonder."[131] Gerard M. Sweeney argues this is the first step toward salvation, but really deliverance is only possible by entering or embracing the horror event. The sailor in "The Descent into the Maelström" throws himself into the water, embracing the chaos, entering the abyss. And the prisoner of "The Pit and the Pendulum" escapes the blade by embracing "the irrationality and absurdity of the dungeon-world, by inviting the rats to his ropes and his lips."[132] It is by recognizing and acknowledging the irrational that one becomes free. But there is a difference between the stories. The pit is a monstrous torture chamber created by humans. The gigantic whirlpool exemplifies the essential irrationality of our experience in nature. The sailor/narrator realizes the futility of any attempt to define it. Sweeney points this out, noting that the sailor concludes his naming of the surrounding islands with: "These are the true names of the places—but why it has been thought necessary to name them at all, is more than either you or I can understand."[133] This is the absurdity of naming and reflects the powerlessness of our language in the face of the anarchic and baleful power of the world.

The first word of the final phrase "ultimate abomination" may also arise from Poe. In "The Pit and the Pendulum" the narrator says the pit is "typical of hell, and regarded by rumor as the Ultima Thule of all their [Spanish Inquisition] punishments."[134] That is, it is final realization or epitome of delivering pain and terror. The phrase is also found in "Dream-Land":

By a route obscure and lonely,
Haunted by ill angels only,
Where an Eidolon, named NIGHT,
On a black throne reigns upright,
I have reached these lands but newly
From an ultimate dim Thule—
From a wild clime that lieth, sublime,
Out of SPACE—out of TIME.[135]

Ultima Thule is thought of as the extreme limit of discovery and sometimes as an ultimate ideal or exemplar; Thule was the northernmost limit of exploration. Clearly this poem influenced Lovecraft, as he uses the final words in two important stories; his admiration for Poe runs deep. So perhaps the final phrase is saying that at the limit of rationality we encounter the abomination.

The word "abomination" is derived from the Latin *abominatus*, past participle of *abominari*, which means to denounce as an ill omen. "Abomination" signifies something that is exceptionally loathsome, hateful, vile, or wicked. It is something that should be avoided; perhaps it is taboo as it spreads pollution or is contagious, and it should not be touched. It is a source of dread. It is evil. In "The Lurking Fear," the narrator, again in a sinister house, upon seeing the shadow of the "death-demon," can only describe it as "a blasphemous abnormality from hell's nethermost craters; a nameless, shapeless abomination which no mind could fully grasp and no pen even partly describe" (184).

The three phrases are fossil traces in the Lovecraftian fiction of the unnamable about three types of evil: natural evil, so called by humans, for natural events or things, such as a maelstrom that causes destruction and death; moral evil or human wickedness against humans, such as the pit of inquisitorial cruelty and death; and the overwhelming evil that seems to infect everything in the world we experience, ultimate metaphysical incomprehension.

Lovecraft uses these images in other stories. The pit is best exemplified in *The Case of Charles Dexter Ward*. Dr. Willett explores the "black pit" (201) beneath the old bungalow of Joseph Curwen. This is a story of the possessive power of the past, the revivification of the dead, the allure of torture, and the glorification of a deathly chaos. Joseph Curwen rediscovered an ancient process to bring the dead back using their decomposed remains. He then tortured and killed them, perhaps repeatedly. The force of evil is forever. In exploring the vile underground chambers, Dr. Willett witnesses the harrowing outcomes of Curwen's experiments. The dungeon is like a Nazi prison. Surveying a vast open space, Dr. Willett spies "a large carved altar" and turns away from the "dark stains which discoloured the upper surface and had spread down the sides in occasional thin lines" (205–6). Casting a flashlight on the distant wall, he sees it is "perforated by occasional black doorways and indented by a myriad of shallow cells with iron gratings and wrist and ankle bonds on chains fastened to the stone of the concave rear masonry" (206). The whole subterranean abyss sounds of wailing, yelps, and screams, and is filled with "a stench unnamable" (206). Narrow cylindrical cells are sunk deeply down below the slimy stone floor. Within the shafts, Dr. Willett sees something that could only be hinted at: "unnamable realities behind the protective illusions of common vision" (207). This is the environment of evil brought back from the past, built by humans where identity is erased, and suffering and cruelty are everlasting. Unlike Poe's pit, there is no real escape for the inmates from Lovecraft's pit.

In "The Dreams in the Witch House" (1932), Walter Gilman is sucked into an abyss of evil. "On the morning of the twenty-ninth Gilman awaked into a maelstrom of horror."[136] The witch house is another dangerous house located in Arkham. Gilman's room in the house has odd dimensions and appears to be geometrically awry, with its slanting wall and ceiling. The horror arises from the realization of the import of the muddy marks in his room as evidence that Gilman's dream—where he joins the ancient witch Keziah Mason and her rat-bodied, human-faced companion Brown Jenkin in the kidnapping of a child—is real. Gilman dreams that he stops Keziah from killing the child but does not save the child from Brown Jenkin. But he does not escape as the sailor narrator does in Poe's story. Later Gilman is found dead in his room. Keziah returns from the past and shows the horror delivered by the "Sheeted Memories of the Past."[137] There is no salvation from the maelstrom in Lovecraft.

"The Colour Out of Space" (1927) is a story from the view of yet another unnamed narrator, a surveyor for a new reservoir, who finds the "blasted heath," a wasteland. It is a zone of death where a prosperous farm once existed, run by the Gardner family. The story is a sinister retelling of the Gawain Grail legend. The sickness of Nahum Gardner is a reshaping of the sickness of the Fisher King, and this has spread to the land. It is an area of complete desolation and nothing lives. The king is now dead and the surveyor is like Gawain, who Jessie L. Weston says came to "restore the waters"[138] and bring the land back to life, although in Lovecraft's tale it is to flood the area. To end the waste of the land in the original Gawain legend, it is critical to ask the right questions. The surveyor also asks about the wasteland. He is told that a mysterious presence or color from the meteorite seemingly had infected the family, leading to illness, insanity, and horror. The presence spreads across the property, killing all living things. It is like a "maelstrom of horror," a natural contagion that comes out of space and may or may not be a conscious alien. The presence appears to be unknowable, another manifestation of the unnamable. From the story it does not seem to have any intentionality; it is like a blind infection. It is like Arendt's image of evil as a fungus. In this story, Lovecraft writes a tale that dramatizes this sense of evil, an evil that sucks all life away.

The real meaning of abomination is expressed in *At the Mountains of Madness*. This story evokes a vast feeling of existential despair and loneliness. Reading the story is like experiencing a deep loss; this mood is pervasive. The survivors of the Miskatonic expedition are bewildered as they explore the cold desolation, the odd geography, and sense terror everywhere. They are in an alien landscape beyond the edge of the known world. The story tells of the brutal slaughter of expedition members by the Old Ones dug

up from the ice,[139] and the strange city built by the Old Ones, which has long
been abandoned but is still plagued by monsters. Beyond the mountains, the
ultimate evil strikes Danforth dumb when he sees it (that is, becomes fully
aware that evil is omnipresent).

Flying into the heart of the Antarctic, upon first sight of the "jagged line
of witchlike cones and pinnacles" (28), Dyer says:

> I could not help feeling that they were evil things—mountains of madness
> whose farther slopes looked out over some accursed ultimate abyss. That
> seething, half-luminous cloud background held ineffable suggestions of a
> vague, ethereal beyondness far more than terrestrially spatial, and gave appall-
> ing reminders of the utter remoteness, separateness, desolation, and aeon-long
> death of this untrodden and unfathomed austral world. (29)

Later, beyond the "cube-barnacled peaks" (105), Dyer and Danforth discover
a strange stone city of odd volumes and cones and star-shapes, a nightmare
city. Interestingly, there is a deliberate blurring of the distinction between
made and natural landscapes in the description of the mountains, as, in the
end, evil pervades both landscapes. The two explore the alien environment
and eventually enter "the black inner world" (77). They find the remnants of
the exploration party's camp and the bodies of decapitated Old Ones, mutilated by the shoggoths, who once were "ideal slaves to perform the heavy
work of the community" (62). But these protoplasmic beings eventually revolted against their masters.

Deep in the cavern the two explorers hear a monstrous shuffling and
whistling, and they turn and run away back to their airplane. Danforth apparently sees something that cripples part of his intellect. And this is com-
pounded on the flight out, where Danforth has "a single fantastic, demoniac
glimpse, among the churning zenith clouds, of what lay back of those other
violet westward mountains which the Old Ones had shunned and feared"
(105). Danforth cannot speak about it, the final picture of evil. The scene
represents dread and despair in the face of a world incomprehensible to
humans and anathema for humans. The setting for *At the Mountains of Madness* is the Ultima Thule of metaphysical evil.

INNOMINATE

At the end of "The Unnamable" there are only sentence fragments, like
verbal shrapnel. These broken phrases, askew words, are akin to incoherent
stammers as language is powerless, a mere figment of human egoism; it is
incommensurate with our experience of the world. There is cacophony here
as not only language but our place in the world is in chaos. Manton's final
words seem like a bestial cry after the embrace from the unnamable. It is an

expression of moral chaos. What response is meaningful while confronting the fact of evil in the world? In "The Shadow over Innsmouth," it seems that in the end the only possible act other than death (and perhaps it is really another form of death) is to join evil, enlist in the army of death. That is the only "salvation."

On the other hand, "The Shunned House" (1924) gives us a different perspective on the problem, a sense of the moral commitments we have to our fellow humans. It is unusual in the Lovecraft canon in that the protagonist overcomes the monster and seemingly lives on, while fully aware of the "tenacious existence of certain forces of great power and, so far as the human point of view is concerned, exceptional malignancy."[140] In the story the explanation for the monster hinges on a sort of scientific rationale (as Manton might give):

> Such a thing was surely not a physical or biochemical impossibility in the light of a newer science which includes the theories of relativity and intra-atomic action. One might easily imagine an alien nucleus of substance or energy, formless or otherwise, kept alive by imperceptible or immaterial subtractions from the life-force or bodily tissue and fluids of other and more palpably living things into which it penetrates and with whose fabric it sometimes completely merges itself. (252)

The narrator flees from the terror of the basement, to "where tall buildings seemed to guard me as modern material things guard the world from ancient and unwholesome wonder" (259). A reader suspects that the hero does not really believe in the guarding power of the tall buildings but soldiers on anyway. The narrator extirpates the alien thing, the intruder, the monster, as a "duty with every man not an enemy of the world's life, health and sanity" (252). One can see Manton in that noble role before he is contaminated by Carter, before he hits the wall of the unnamable, before he is infected by the world of nothingness and alienation, before he fails to witness and try to read the message left on his body. "The Shunned House" is a story of a human trying to live in a world of evil and working to eradicate it, doomed surely, as the story suggests, but still continuing the effort. That is because the important thing is a common social purpose, a common moral purpose even in metaphysical chaos.

More congruent with the fiction of the unnamable is "The Shadow over Innsmouth," a story that chronicles the descent into and the embrace of evil. Evil is characterized as coming from the sea and drawing humans back into the sea, as deformed beings in a deformed world, but where they "shall dwell amidst wonder and glory forever";[141] that is, they are converted to the culture of Innsmouth, where "some cryptic, evil movement was afoot on a large scale."[142] It is like an infection spreading across a populace, but a disease gladly embraced by some, including the protagonist, who discovers his

Innsmouth look and accepts the call of Cthulhu, the call to evil. It is more than an acceptance of the fact of evil; it is an overwhelming loss of ethics, as if a lover forgoes humanity and ethics to carry out the vile orders of the beloved, or the terror orders of a dictator. It is akin to the loss of identity as one joins in the death march of fascism, a return to chaos, an adoration of atrocity.

The fiction of the unnamable expresses this corruption as if it is an infection. It is dangerous, as Sir Thomas Browne writes: "tempt not contagion by proximity, and hazard not thyself in the shadow of corruption."[143]

In the fiction of Lovecraft, there are contradictions, of course. And this is not a weakness but a strength. These works are not trivial entertainments. Lovecraft mined the true vein of horror. The original spring of the Gothic was to question the legitimacy of the sovereignty of state and religion and to reveal the duplicity of societal bonds among classes. It revealed the decadent social edifice for what it really was: built on the bones of the working class, violent in maintaining a rigid social order, and full of horror against the poor, women, and outsiders. The fiction of the unnamable asserts the sovereignty of dread and the metaphysics of incomprehension within a world of fear and the insoluble problem of evil. It reveals the duplicity of language, science, and the human intellectual enterprise generally. There is a loss of all humanity. In doing so the fiction illuminates the fact of evil in the universe and humankind; it is a place where we lose our identities; we are all captives on a death march. There is a rawness in his stories—a savage, stammering, disturbingly familiar strangeness. Something awful hits you when you read his words—as if you have stepped into a propeller. Franz Kafka, in a letter to Max Brod, says writing is a "descent toward the dark powers . . . [an] unchaining of spirits that are naturally kept bound."[144] More than others, Lovecraft unchains the spirits of dread. At his best you begin to feel those awful, diabolical spirits disgustingly touch you. Sometimes it is as if Lovecraft is retelling something you have tried to forget, forcing you to listen. And ultimate meaning is not the point of the tales; rather, it is the effect. Clear meaning is incompatible with art anyway. For Lovecraft the power or effect is to incite fear, and that is through the dramatization of the metaphysics of evil. Poe saw art as a way to escape from mundane consciousness into a world of beauty and wonder; for Lovecraft the escape leads to more terror.

"The Unnamable" is a foundational story in Lovecraft's canon of work, wrestling with the problem of our place in an unintelligible world. Although the story does not have the sustained brilliance of some stories, it is a sketch of the power of dread and is the start of a journey into the fiction of the unnamable. Even on the surface, it is important, as it uses Arkham as a fictional site for the full story, deploys the serial character Carter, and is Lovecraft's fictional treatise on the poetics of horror writing. But most importantly, it is an early story in the fiction of the unnamable and provides a gateway into the major texts. In short form, it explores the human condition in an irrational world and the metaphysical incomprehension of being in an unreadable world of evil.

NOTES

1. Peter Cannon, *H. P. Lovecraft* (Boston: Twayne, 1989), 41–42.

2. S. T. Joshi, *A Subtler Magick: The Writings and Philosophy of H. P. Lovecraft* (Mercer Island, WA: Starmont House, 1996), 99.

3. Massimo Berruti, "The Unnamable in Lovecraft and the Limits of Rationality" (paper presented at research seminar, University of Helsinki, 2005), http://lucite.org/lucite/archive/fiction_-_lovecraft/6380270-the-unnamable-in-lovecraft-and-the-limits-of-rationality.pdf (accessed December 16, 2013), 2.

4. James Kneale, "From Beyond: H. P. Lovecraft and the Place of Horror," *Cultural Geographies* 13 (2006): 106.

5. Maurice Lévy, *Lovecraft: A Study in the Fantastic,* trans. S. T. Joshi (Detroit, MI: Wayne State University, 1988), 40.

6. H. P. Lovecraft, "The Unnamable," in *Dagon and Other Macabre Tales*, ed. S. T. Joshi (Sauk City, WI: Arkham House, 1986), 202. Hereafter cited in the text.

7. John P. Langan, "Naming the Nameless: Lovecraft's Grammatology," *Lovecraft Studies* no. 41 (Spring 1999): 27.

8. Langan, "Naming the Nameless," 41.

9. Rhys Hughes treats such language in a sardonic manner in "A Languid Elagabalus of the Tombs," in *Stories from a Lost Anthology* (Leyburn, UK: Tartarus Press, 2002), 184–208. This title is derived from Lovecraft's "Herbert West—Reanimator," in *Dagon and Other Macabre Tales*, 155. The story verges on a parody of "The Unnamable." In the story Mr. Delves says "Definition is the foe of horror!" (197) Delves goes through the synonyms of the word and views namelessness as "the key to the bloody lock on the wormy door which led to the slimy dungeon of total horror" (199). In part, the story is about Delves's search for and eventual discovery of a room of nameless and hidden textbooks of unspeakable horror. Delves solves the problem of namelessness by writing titles and text for what turns out to be unused college ledgers. It is a fun story and is a form of homage to Lovecraft in the Rhys Hughes style.

10. Donald R. Burleson, *Lovecraft: Disturbing the Universe* (Lexington: University Press of Kentucky, 1990), 49–57.

11. The unnamable could be interpreted as a confrontation with the "Real": a notion of Lacan used by Eric Savoy in his discussion of the American Gothic. Eric Savoy, "The Rise of American Gothic," in *The Cambridge Companion to Gothic Fiction*, ed. Jerrold E. Hogel (Cambridge: Cambridge University Press, 2002), 167–88. The "Real" is meant to characterize all those things or experiences that are beyond our current knowledge, beyond our current science, beyond representation that yet haunt us and keep demanding attention.

12. Lovecraft, *Selected Letters*, ed. August Derleth, Donald Wandrei, and James Turner (Sauk City, WI: Arkham House, 1965–1976), 3.435.

13. Hegel, quoted in Susan Neiman, *Evil in Modern Thought: An Alternative History of Philosophy* (Princeton, NJ: Princeton University Press, 2002), 313.

14. Sir James George Frazer, *The New Golden Bough*, ed. Theodor H. Gaster (New York: Criterion, 1959), 187.

15. Frazer, *The New Golden Bough*, 219.

16. Robert Graves, *The White Goddess* (London: Faber & Faber, 1961).

17. See Benedict de Spinoza, *Selections*, ed. John Wild (New York: Scribners, 1930), 94–143.

18. Lovecraft, "The Horror at Red Hook," in *Dagon and Other Macabre Tales*, 248.

19. Lovecraft, "The Colour Out of Space," in *The Dunwich Horror and Others*, ed. S. T. Joshi (Sauk City, WI: Arkham House, 1984), 67.

20. Lovecraft, "The Lurking Fear," in *Dagon and Other Macabre Tales*, 181. Hereafter cited in the text.

21. Lovecraft, "The Rats in the Walls," in *The Dunwich Horror and Others*, 44.

22. Lovecraft, "The Dunwich Horror," in *The Dunwich Horror and Others*, 157.

23. Lovecraft and Winifred V. Jackson, "The Crawling Chaos," in *The Horror in the Museum and Other Revisions*, ed. S. T. Joshi (Sauk City, WI: Arkham House, 1989), 12.

24. Lovecraft and E. Hoffmann Price, "Through the Gates of the Silver Key," in *At the Mountains of Madness and Other Novels*," ed. S. T. Joshi (Sauk City, WI: Arkham House, 1985), 431.

25. Lovecraft, *At the Mountains of Madness*, in *At the Mountains of Madness and Other Novels*, 40. Hereafter cited in the text.

26. Lovecraft, "The Shadow over Innsmouth," in *The Dunwich Horror and Others*, 366.

27. Lovecraft, *The Case of Charles Dexter Ward*, in *At the Mountains of Madness*, 206. Hereafter cited in the text.

28. Lovecraft, "The Hound," in *Dagon and Other Macabre Tales*, 172.

29. Lovecraft, "The Hound," 178.

30. This experience of Randolph Carter is summarized in "The Silver Key," in *At the Mountains of Madness*: "[H]e went back to Arkham, the terrible witch-haunted old town of his forefathers in New England, and had experiences in the dark, amidst the hoary willows and tottering gambrel roofs, which made him seal forever certain pages in the diary of a wild-minded ancestor" (413).

31. Based on the work of Fiedler, Cannon briefly explores this theme in Lovecraft. Peter Cannon, "Lovecraft and Classic American Literature," in *"Sunset Terrace Imagery in Lovecraft" and Other Essays* (West Warwick, RI: Necronomicon Press, 1990).

32. Edgar Allan Poe, *The Narrative of Arthur Gordon Pym of Nantucket, and Related Tales*, ed. J. Gerald Kennedy (Oxford: Oxford University Press, 1998), 30.

33. Lovecraft takes the use of the neologism to its awful logical conclusion. It is "that eldritch, mocking cry—'*Tekeli-li! Tekeli-li!*'" of the "demoniac shoggoths—given life, thought, and plastic organ patterns solely by the Old Ones, and having no language save that which the dot groups expressed—had likewise no voice *save the imitated accents of their bygone masters*." *At the Mountains of Madness*, 101. This is the cry that haunted the narrator and Danforth on their searches for the source of the horror in the Antarctic. When Danforth is witness to the ultimate abomination, his "shrieks were confined to the repetition of a single, mad word of all too obvious source: '*Tekeli-li! Tekeli-li!*'" (106). Danforth becomes inarticulate.

34. Joseph Conrad, *The Heart of Darkness and Two Other Stories* (London: Folio Society, 1998), 123.

35. Conrad, *The Heart of Darkness*, 139.

36. Edith Wharton, "Mr. Jones," in *The Ghost Stories of Edith Wharton* (New York: Scribners, 1973), 195.

37. Sophocles, *Oedipus Rex*, in *The Oedipus Cycle: An English Version*, trans. Dudley Fitts and Robert Fitzgerald (New York: Houghton Mifflin Harcourt, 2002), 70–71.

38. Edgar Allan Poe, "The Imp of the Perverse," in *Tales and Sketches*, ed. Thomas Ollive Mabbott (Cambridge, MA: Harvard University Press, 1978), 2.1222.

39. Poe, "The Imp of the Perverse," 2.1223.

40. Very young children frequently ask: "What's the name of it?" about things. It is a way of making the world familiar and known.

41. Ludwig Wittgenstein, *Tractatus Logico-Philosophicus*, trans. D. F. Pears and B. F. McGuiness (London: Routledge Classics, 2001), 68.

42. Noël Carroll, *The Philosophy of Horror or Paradoxes of the Heart* (New York: Routledge, 1990), 127.

43. "Unwholesome recollections of things in the *Necronomicon* and the Black Book welled up, and he found himself swaying to infandous rhythms said to pertain to the blackest ceremonies of the Sabbat and to have an origin outside the time and space we comprehend." Lovecraft, "The Dreams in the Witch House," in *At the Mountains of Madness*, 290.

44. Roger B. Salomon, *Mazes of the Serpent: An Anatomy of Horror Narrative* (Ithaca, NY: Cornell University Press, 2002), 15.

45. Algernon Blackwood, *John Silence—Physician Extraordinary* (Boston: John W. Luce, 1909), 31.

46. "The Unnamable" is a modernist story in that the how of writing is as important as the what of writing.

47. Lovecraft, *Collected Essays, Volume 2: Literary Criticism*, ed. S. T. Joshi (New York: Hippocampus Press, 2004), 176.

48. Lovecraft, *The Annotated Supernatural Horror in Literature*, rev. ed., ed. S. T. Joshi (New York: Hippocampus Press, 2012), 28.

49. Edgar Allan Poe, *Poe: The Complete Poems*, ed. Richard Wilbur (New York: Dell, 1959), 73–74.

50. Roberto Calasso, *K* (New York: Alfred Knopf, 2005), 3.

51. The early twentieth century was a time of mass charges to death, the terror of mustard gas, endless artillery bombardments, horror in the trenches, ever more armaments, and piles of the dead. This turned out to be only a prelude to the killing fields history of the twentieth century. There are so many that any listing cannot be defended. The Holocaust is beyond thought; in Auschwitz alone, more than one million Jews died in gas chambers, by forced labor, by starvation, and by torture; overall six million were killed by the Nazi regime. Then there are the Armenian massacres, the Gulag, the Ukraine famine, the Khmer Rouge regime of terror in Cambodia, and more recently Rwanda and Darfur. Of course, mass societal murders and the deliberate distortions of history are nothing new. W. M. Denevan, "The Pristine Myth: The Landscape of the Americas in 1492," *Annals of the Association of American Geographers* 82 (1992): 369–85; and Richard Wright, *Stolen Continents: The Americas through Indian Eyes since 1492* (Boston: Houghton Mifflin, 1992) speak to the effects of the European invasions into North and South America killing tens of millions of the indigenous peoples.

52. Leslie Fielder, *Love and Death in the American Novel* (New York: Criterion, 1960), 115.

53. Christopher Marlowe, *The Jew of Malta*, in *The Plays and Poems of Christopher Marlowe* (London: George Newnes, 1905), 241.

54. *Beowulf. A New Verse Translation*, trans. Seamus Heaney (New York: Norton, 2001), 99.

55. Lovecraft, "The Call of Cthulhu," *The Dunwich Horror*, 137.

56. Lovecraft, "The Wood," in *The Ancient Track: The Complete Poetical Works of H. P. Lovecraft*, ed. S. T. Joshi (San Francisco: Night Shade, 2001), 60.

57. Lovecraft, *The Ancient Track*, 60.

58. Arthur Machen, "The Great God Pan," in *Tales of Horror and the Supernatural* (New York: Pinnacle, 1983), 44.

59. Steve Duffy, "They've Got Him! In the Trees! M. R. James and Sylvan Dread," in *Warnings to the Curious: A Sheaf of Criticism on M. R. James*, ed. S. T. Joshi and Rosemary Pardoe (New York: Hippocampus Press, 2007), 177–83.

60. Algernon Blackwood, "The Dammed," in *Tales of the Mysterious and Macabre* (London: Spring, 1967), 156.

61. Robinson Jeffers, *Medea: Freely Adapted from the "Medea" of Euripides* (London: Samuel French, 1976), 11.

62. Jeffers, *Medea*, 28.

63. *Forbidden Planet*, DVD, directed by Fred M. Wilcox (1956; Burbank, CA: Warner Home Video, 2010).

64. Albert Camus, "On the Future of Tragedy," in *Lyrical and Critical Essays*, trans. Ellen Conroy Kennedy, ed. Philip Thody (New York: Knopf, 1968), 297.

65. Jerrold E. Hogle, introduction to *The Cambridge Companion to Gothic Fiction*, 5.

66. Lovecraft, "The Silver Key," in *At the Mountains of Madness*, 414–15.

67. Lovecraft, *Selected Letters*, 3.31.

68. Lovecraft, "The Horror at Red Hook," in *Dagon and Other Macabre Tales*, 249.

69. Edgar Allan Poe, "MS. Found in a Bottle," in *Tales and Sketches*, 1.145.

70. Lovecraft, "The Tomb," in *Dagon and Other Macabre Tales*, 4.

71. Fred Botting, "Aftergothic: Consumption, Machines and Black Holes," in *The Cambridge Companion to Gothic Fiction*, 279.

72. Maurice Lévy, *Lovecraft: A Study in the Fantastic*, trans. S. T. Joshi (Detroit, MI: Wayne State University, 1988), 88.

73. E. R. Dodds, *The Greeks and the Irrational* (Berkeley: University of California Press, 1951), 6.

74. Albert Camus, *Notebooks 1935–1942*, trans. Philip Thody (New York: Modern Library, 1965), 10.

75. Lovecraft, "Notes on Writing Weird Fiction," 175.

76. Albert Camus, "The Myth of Sisyphus," in *The Myth of Sisyphus and Other Essays*, trans. Justin O'Brien (New York: Vintage, 1995), 11.

77. Counter to this, consider that in "The Call of Cthulhu" the strange dreams do not inform average people, or scientific men, but "It was from the artists and poets that the pertinent answers came" (131). And more tellingly, later archaeologists cannot "form the least notion" of the "linguistic kinship" (134) of the characters on the base of the strange figure found by Legrasse. Scientists in "The Colour Out of Space" can make no sense of the wasteland. These speak to the failure of rationality in the face of the unknown.

78. Salomon, *Mazes of the Serpent*, 124.

79. Poe, "Sonnet—To Science," in *Poe: The Complete Poems*, 58.

80. Richard Wilbur, introduction to *Poe: The Complete Poems*, 9.

81. Wilbur, introduction, 9.

82. Bruce Aune, *Knowledge, Mind, and Nature* (New York: Random House, 1967) argues that the way we view and experience the world is dependent on our conceptual scheme, which is informed and expressed through our language. But our language is not cast in stone. Science is engaged in fundamental criticisms of our worldview, that is, our language (which it can be argued determines the manner in which we as language-users characterize the world, indeed experience the world). In a sense science disrupts our interactions with the outside and changes the way we control and manipulate the world. It may be argued that literature is doing something similar. The language employed in *Finnegans Wake*, for example, is radically different from our ordinary discourse, and if we were able to adopt this language one could give fundamentally different descriptions of the world legitimately.

83. Lovecraft, "Facts concerning the Late Arthur Jermyn and His Family," in *Dagon and Other Macabre Tales*, 73.

84. Camus, "Myth of Sisyphus," 3.

85. Camus, "Myth of Sisyphus," 5.

86. Matthew Hamiliton Bowker, "Albert Camus and the Political Philosophy of the Absurd" (Ph.D. diss., University of Maryland, 2008), 22.

87. Poe, "The Man of the Crowd," in *Tales and Sketches*, 1.506.

88. Gershon Shaked, "Afterword," in *Facing the Holocaust: Selected Israeli Fiction*, ed. Gila Ramras-Rauch and Joseph Michman-Melkman (Philadelphia: Jewish Publication Society, 1985), 275.

89. W. G. Sebald, *On the Natural History of Destruction*, trans. Anthea Bell (New York: Random House, 2003).

90. Daniel R. Schwarz, *Imagining the Holocaust* (New York: St. Martin's Press, 1999), 37.

91. Lovecraft, "Hypnos," in *Dagon and Other Macabre Tales*, 166.

92. Thomas Hardy, "To Sincerity," in *Collected Poems* (New York: Macmillan, 1926), 262.

93. Wittgenstein, *Tractatus*, 89.

94. Christopher Marlowe, *The Tragical History of Doctor Faustus*, in *The Plays and Poems of Christopher Marlowe*, 157.

95. Karen Armstrong, *A Short History of Myth* (London: Cannongate, 2005), 4.

96. Samuel Beckett, *The Unnamable*, in *Three Novels by Samuel Beckett* (New York: Grove Press, 1965), 291.

97. Beckett, *The Unnamable*, 293.

98. David Hume, *An Enquiry concerning Human Understanding: A Critical Edition*, ed. Tom L. Beauchamp (Oxford: Oxford University Press, 2000), 104.

99. Neiman, *Evil in Modern Thought*, 168.

100. Mary Midgley, *Wickedness: A Philosophical Essay* (London: Routledge Classics, 2001), vii.

101. Gottfried Wilhelm Leibniz, *Theodicy: Essays on the Goodness of God, the Freedom of Man, and the Origin of Evil*, trans. E. M. Huggard (London: Routledge & Kegan Paul, 1951).

102. Ari Hirvonen, "The Problem of Evil Revisited," *No Foundations: Journal of Extreme Legal Positivism* no. 4 (October 2007): 48.

103. David B. Levy, review of *The Banality of Evil: Hannah Arendt and "The Final Solution,"* by Bernard J. Bergen (H-Holocaust, H-Net Reviews, August 1999), http://www.h-net.org/reviews/showrev.php?id=3372 (accessed January 27, 2009).

104. Immanuel Kant, *Religion within the Limits of Reason Alone*, in *Readings on Human Nature*, ed. Peter Loptson (Peterborough, ON: Broadview Press, 1997), 108.

105. Kant, *Religion within the Limits of Reason Alone*, 104.

106. Kant, *Religion within the Limits of Reason Alone*, 109.

107. In *The Brothers Karamazov*, Ivan Karamazov speaks about the evil of the suffering of innocent children. No god can be worshipped with the knowledge of the facts of children suffering horrible fates and brutal deaths. He knows the evil in the world and rebels and remains unforgiving: "It is not worth one little tear of that tortured little girl who beat herself on the breast and prayed to her 'dear, kind Lord' in the stinking privy with her unexpiated tears. It is not worth it, because her tears remain unexpiated." Fyodor Dostoevsky, *The Brothers Karamazov* (New York: Penguin, 1979), 286. There is no possible explanation or sense in such suffering.

108. Fielder, *Love and Death in the American Novel*, xiv.

109. In 1933, Lovecraft in a letter says: "No settled & homogenous nation ought (a) to admit enough of a decidedly alien race-stock to bring about an actual alteration in the dominant ethnic composition, or (b) tolerate the dilution of the culture-stream with emotional or intellectual elements alien to the original cultural impulse," *Selected Letters*, 4.249. These are the words of a social reactionary. Lovecraft says this logic shows that "Hitler's basic racial theory is *perfectly & irrefutably* sound," *Selected Letters*, 4.249. Where Hitler's race theory logic led was the Holocaust.

110. Lovecraft, *Selected Letters*, 1.296.

111. Lovecraft, "The Shadow Out of Time," *The Dunwich Horror and Others*, 399.

112. In a 1926 letter to Frank Belknap Long (*Selected Letters*, 2.68–69), Lovecraft expresses his admiration for the Nordic: "There are two Jew problems in America today—one national and cultural, and to be met by a firm resistance to all those vitiating ideas which parasitic subject-races engender; and another local and biological—the New York Mongoloid problem, to be met God only knows how, but with force rather than intellect."

113. Lovecraft, *Selected Letters*, 1.208.

114. Lovecraft, *Selected Letters*, 4.247. Lovecraft is not alone as a writer in his racism. Anthony Julius, *T. S. Eliot, Anti-Semitism and Literary Form*, rev. ed. (London: Thames & Hudson, 2003), details the anti-Semitism of T. S. Eliot. In *After Strange Gods: A Primer of Modern Heresy* (New York: Harcourt, Brace, 1934), Eliot writes that a well-formed society must "make any large numbers of free-thinking Jews undesirable" (20). In "Burbank with a Baedeker: Bleistein with a Cigar," Eliot writes: "The rats are underneath the piles / The Jew is underneath the lot" (Eliot, *Collected Poems 1909–1962* [London: Faber & Faber, 1974], 43). In "Gerontion" he writes: "My house is a decayed house, / And the Jew squats on the window sill, / the owner, / Spawned in some estaminet of Antwerp" (*Collected Poems*, 39). Like Lovecraft, Eliot has his defenders and apologists.

115. Lovecraft's invectives against African Americans are sharply contrasted by the efforts of Olivia Howard Dunbar, a writer of ghost stories in the early twentieth century, and her husband, the playwright Ridgely Torrance, in support of rights for blacks (Jessica Amanda Salmonson, introduction to *The Shell of Sense: Collected Ghost Stories of Olivia Howard Dunbar*, ed. Jessica Amanda Salmonson [Uncasville, CT: R. H. Fawcett, 1997], 3–11). Torrance published a collection of plays written specifically for black actors in 1917 and wrote a biography of the black educator John Hope. Dunbar published essays on a range of liberal issues, including the education of African Americans.

116. S. T. Joshi, *H. P. Lovecraft: A Life* (West Warwick, RI: Necronomicon Press, 1996).

117. Lovecraft, *Selected Letters*, 5.247.

118. As an example, consider Lovecraft's descriptions in "Herbert West—Reanimator" of Buck Robinson: "He was a loathsome, gorilla-like thing, with abnormally long arms that I could not help calling fore legs, and a face that conjured up thoughts of unspeakable Congo secrets and tom-tom poundings under an eerie moon. The body must have looked even worse in life—but the world holds many ugly things" (*Dagon and Other Macabre Tales*, 146). And yet, although Herbert West believes that the revivifying fluid failed on Robinson because it was devised with white specimens in mind, at the end of the episode we learn differently.

119. Lovecraft, *Selected Letters*, 1.333–34, and Michel Houellebecq, *H. P. Lovecraft: Against the World, Against Life*, trans. Dorna Khazeni (San Francisco: Believer, 2005), 106.

120. Houellebecq, *Lovecraft: Against the World*, 111.

121. Houellebecq, *Lovecraft: Against the World*, 113.

122. Lovecraft, "The Horror at Red Hook," 248.

123. Lovecraft, "The Horror at Red Hook," 265.

124. Hannah Arendt, *The Jew as Pariah: Jewish Identity and Politics in the Modern Age* (New York: Grove Press, 1978), 251.

125. Lovecraft, "The Colour Out of Space," in *The Dunwich Horror and Others*, 54.

126. Camus, "The Myth of Sisyphus," 37.

127. Albert Camus, *The Rebel: An Essay on Man in Revolt*, trans. A. Bower (New York: Vintage, 1956), 253.

128. Beckett, *The Unnamable*, 414.

129. Lévy, *Lovecraft: A Study in the Fantastic*, 115.

130. Lovecraft, "The Call of Cthulhu," 154.

131. Poe, "The Pit and the Pendulum," in *Tales and Sketches*, 1.689.

132. Gerald M. Sweeney, "Beauty and Truth: Poe's 'A Descent into the Maelström,'" *Poe Studies* 6, no. 1 (June 1973): 23.

133. Poe, "A Descent into the Maelström," in *Tales and Sketches*, 1.579.

134. Poe, "The Pit and the Pendulum," 1.690.

135. Poe, *Poe: The Complete Poems*, 90.

136. Lovecraft, "The Dreams in the Witch House," in *At the Mountains of Madness and Other Novels*, 287.

137. Poe, "Dream-Land," in *Poe: The Complete Poems*, 91.

138. Jessie L. Weston, *From Ritual to Romance* (Mineola, NY: Dover, 1997), 19.

139. This is the recurrent theme of digging up the past. The past haunts because, as Delmore Schwartz writes in "Personae," "Only the past is immortal." Delmore Schwartz, *Selected Poems (1938–1958): Summer Knowledge* (New York: New Directions, 1967), 65.

140. Lovecraft, "The Shunned House," in *At the Mountains of Madness*, 251. Hereafter cited in the text.

141. Lovecraft, "The Shadow over Innsmouth," in *The Dunwich Horror and Others*, 367.

142. Lovecraft, "The Shadow over Innsmouth," 345.

143. Sir Thomas Browne, "Christian Morals," in *The Voyce of the Worlds: Selected Writings of Sir Thomas Browne*, ed. Geoffrey Keynes (London: Folio Society, 1997), 252. Lovecraft's reaction to New York is expressed as a form of infection of a population: "the broad, phantasmal lineaments of the morbid soul of disintegration and decay . . . a yellow leering mask with sour, sticky, acid ichors oozing at eyes, ears, nose, and mouth, and abnormally bubbling from monstrous and unbelievable sores at every point," *Selected Letters*, 1.334.

144. Franz Kafka, quoted in Roberto Calasso, *K*, 111.

Chapter Eight

The Aboriginal in the Works of H. P. Lovecraft

More than 400 years ago, Francisco Vásquez de Coronado and his band of conquistadores ravaged the Southwest in their quest for gold. The Superstition Mountain just east of Phoenix, Arizona, was one of their targets. The Apache believe the area of Superstition Mountain is the home of the Thunder God; it is a sacred place, treated with reverence and honor, akin to a cathedral and not a place to plunder. Jill Pascoe writes that over hundreds of years countless people have vanished and died in this mysterious area, which continues to be fabled for lost gold.[1] The Spaniards were unable to coerce the Apache to help them scour for gold on Superstition Mountain, where many found only terror and death. The Spaniards viewed the Apache, along with all Amerindians, with distain, as primitives, perhaps with a touch of fear, but with a rapacious loathing.

In 1552, Bartolomé de las Casas documented the savagery of the Spaniards as they subjugated the Americas, where they tortured and murdered millions.[2] The extent of the "genocide" is virtually unimaginable, according to Tzvetan Todorov.[3] Estimating the population of the overall Americas before colonization is challenging, and there are huge variations. Russell Thornton and others show the decline of the American Indian population was a holocaust—precipitous, devastating, and dreadful.[4]

This devastation was founded on the notion of the inferiority of the indigenous people. Celia Brickman notes that the colonizing Europeans saw the American Indian as "the quintessential emblem of the first, primitive stage of human development."[5] Reneé L. Bergland suggests that the American "land is haunted because it is stolen."[6] Bergland argues that the source of the American uncanny lies in the history of "murders, looted graves, illegal land transfer and disruptions of sovereignty"[7] of the Native peoples and the landscape is now one of ghosts.

D. H. Lawrence writes: "The Aztec is gone, and the Incas. The Red Indian, the Sequim, the Patagonian are reduced to negligible numbers. . . . Not that the Red Indian will ever possess the broad lands of America. At least I presume not. But his ghost will."[8] Of course, American Indians were never completely gone and continue yet to protect and nurture their unique cultures and have not been swallowed up by Lawrence's "great white swamp."[9] But Lawrence does hit on the hauntedness of America and the impact of the American Indian on American literature. To paraphrase a line from Toni Morrison's *Beloved* (1987), there is no forest, prairie, valley, mountain, or town in the country not packed with some dead American Indian's grief,[10] and that is why the American landscape is haunted.

THE GHOSTS OF AMERICA

This haunting of the landscape, or geographic terror, is a key theme in the horror fiction of H. P. Lovecraft. That is because for Lovecraft the world in itself is sinister. Dread and horror are the nature of existence, and his textual topography makes this alive. In Lovecraft's ontology the fundamental elements are indifferently malevolent. His haunted landscape was primarily in New England but also in other locales, such as the American Southwest. And the haunting in his stories, in many cases, has a particularly American shape to it. The argument of this chapter is that the haunting in many stories finds its origin in the American Indian. In the fictional woods[11] of Lovecraft the aboriginal is defined as essentially inferior to white Europeans, as demonic or unclean, as savage, as primitive. American Indians are also removed, effaced, overwritten by a legion of monsters, who are portrayed as previous occupiers of the land. These even more aboriginal beings, however, are really the reanimated indigenous peoples, for in the fiction of Lovecraft the millions of dead American Indians are the "soul of the forest,"[12] who keep rising from the graves.

Of course, the fiction of Lovecraft is firmly in the mainstream of American literature on this. Joshua David Bellin argues that the presence and dispossession of American Indians in America have shaped American literature and that this must be understood in the reading of all the literature.[13] Charles L. Crow argues that to know American literature one must understand the Gothic, which he says is "the imaginative expression of the hidden fears and forbidden desires of Americans."[14] The American Gothic is pervasive in the mainstream, and in genre form. It is a counter-argument to American triumphalism and American perpetual progress toward the promised land. Crow argues that the Gothic "patrols the line between . . . the living and dead."[15] It is a literature at the frontier, which is especially relevant in the United States, with its long fable of striking out into the wild frontier. In distorted and threatening form, the Gothic liberates what is hidden, buried away, taboo, and unspoken within a society. In American Gothic literature the dreadful encounters with "monsters" reify fears and nightmares about the original inhabitants.

American Indians haunt the Gothic fiction of Lovecraft. But his mastery of the horror idiom opens new ground in understanding the foundation of the fear of the aboriginal. In the end, it is the loss of utopia, the realization that we cannot get ourselves back to the pristine garden (a garden we have destroyed), that there is no safe home; we will never really be homeward-bound. Marianna Torgovnick argues that the desire of going home is akin to going primitive.[16] It is a wish to return to origins and the familiar, in a way that perhaps comforts, that helps us overcome our alienation from our culture and our world and perhaps from ourselves. Lovecraft turns this on its head; there is only a hostile strangeness everywhere. Joyce Carol Oates notes a pervasive and profound existential loneliness in Lovecraft's work, an "elegiac poetry of loss."[17] Some things are gone forever.

The ancient alien realms in Lovecraft's fictions are dystopias; there are no sacred places, just nightmare haunts. And over the mountains there is always something even more hideous, as the Old Ones in *At the Mountains of Madness* (1936) knew and feared, and as Danforth glimpses as he flies away from the Old Ones' abandoned city, and thus is reduced to gibbering. In a universe of dread, there is no salvation. Enmeshed in these themes is the problematical nature of storytelling itself. For Lovecraft is really a modern in Gothic literature. In many of his stories the narrator is not sure of what he has experienced; often the voice is confused, leaving the reader unsure. The narrative is sometimes constructed from fragments, as if all is artifice. He deploys varying styles and narrative voices. Moreover, as readers, should we trust the narrators of the stories? Lovecraft's fiction raises questions about how narratives are constructed and the reliability of those narrations. With a Gothic twist he explores the randomness of life, the disruption of conventional beliefs. His stories often express the loneliness of being and evoke an awful sense of existential despair. There are no absolute truths, and what truths we may find are likely to be terrifying. Although his stories deploy realism as a way of establishing the suspension of disbelief, the stories disrupt reality and question what is real. His library of imaginary texts establishes an alternate reality with alternative authorities. In addition, Lovecraft also deforms and reshapes American Indian models and beliefs into modern Gothic narratives in a manner akin to James Joyce's reshaping of Greek myths in *Ulysses*. The past is recast to a modern Gothic form.

THE ABORIGINAL

What, then, is the aboriginal? Used as an adjective, "aboriginal" means being the first or earliest known of its kind present somewhere, having existed from the beginning, something in an earliest or original stage or state. The word is also indicative of or relating to the indigenous peoples of Australia. In Canada, the term is embedded in the Constitution Act of 1982, which says the "Aboriginal peoples of Canada" include "Indian, Inuit, and Métis peoples of Canada." The synonyms of "aboriginal" include native, indigenous, autochthonous, original, first, earliest, primordial, and primitive. Torgovnick explores the complex and shifting meanings of "primitive" across a variety of fields—art, psychology, anthropology, and literature. In early usage it referred to the original state of something, that is, the aboriginal. This usage has changed and now, in the usage of a controlling society, it seems to refer to "the other," who is defined in distinction from accepted behavior or thoughts in that society.[18] The primitive here is the uncivilized, the irrational, the uncultured, the unintelligent, the untamed, and the unrepressed. These words resonate with the sense of primary but also less advanced.

In Lovecraft's fiction there is often a loathing of the aboriginal or primitive and a pathological aversion to and fear of regression to a primitive state, sometimes expressed through a fear of miscegenation and sometimes in a fear of the regression of isolated populations or in the fear of finding out one's own origins. This is expressed in many stories. A sampling of these is provided here. In "Beyond the Wall of Sleep" (1919), Joe Slater is described as "one of those strange, repellent scions of a primitive peasant stock whose isolation . . . has caused them to sink to a kind of barbaric degeneracy."[19] The local population in "The Dunwich Horror" (1928) is "now repellently decadent, having gone far along that path of retrogression so common in many New England backwaters."[20]

In the remote Catskills, the location of "The Lurking Fear" (1922), there is "a degenerate squatter population inhabiting pitiful hamlets on isolated slopes" (180). These inhabitants of the Catskills, "having descended the evolutionary scale" (186), are "poor mongrels who sometimes leave their valleys to trade handwoven baskets for such primitive necessities as they cannot shoot, raise, or make" (180). Later in this story the unnamed narrator shoots one of the multitude of underground monsters, which are "the ultimate product of mammalian degeneration; the frightful outcome of isolated spawning, multiplication, and cannibal nutrition . . . the embodiment of all the snarling and chaos and grinning fear that lurk behind life" (199). It is a "dwarfed, deformed" (198), "filthy whitish gorilla thing" (199) that has descended from the Martenses, a once wealthy family.

This degeneracy can happen rapidly, as expressed in "The Horror at Red Hook" (1925), in which Detective Thomas Malone ruminates that "modern people under lawless conditions tend uncannily to repeat the darkest instinctive patterns of primitive half-ape savagery in their daily life and ritual observances."[21] Moreover, the story's language expresses much anguish and dread, as the primitive is "the root of a contagion destined to sicken and swallow cities, and engulf nations in the foetor of hybrid pestilence."[22]

"Facts concerning the Late Arthur Jermyn and his Family" (1920) evidences why Sir Arthur Jermyn soaked himself in oil to hasten his suicide. The story starts, "Life is a hideous thing,"[23] and then asks the question whether humans are a separate species—that is, are we really civilized, are we really distinct from animals (in this story's case, apes), and not from an eon-long evolutionary perspective? Here it is a white ape, spawn of the great apes and a "prehistoric white Congolese civilization" (74), which had fallen into the primal—the awful terror that many stories evoke. Arthur Jermyn "went out on the moor and burned himself" (73) after seeing the gift of the mummy of his great-great-great-grandmother—a white ape princess. Origins are not salutary in Lovecraft but awful.

For Lovecraft, "The past is *real*—it is *all there is*."[24] But in the end that past is dangerous, as is found in many of his stories. And finding your ancestors is often full of horror. A fondness for the past is, in a sense, akin to trying to get back home. But Lovecraft's fiction tells us it is a fool's mission.

ILLUMINATION AND DISTORTION

In *Supernatural Horror in Literature* (1927), Lovecraft identifies one of the sources of the weird fiction of American writers as "the strange and forbidding nature of the scene into which they were plunged. The vast and gloomy virgin forests in whose perpetual twilight all terrors might well lurk;[25] the hordes of coppery[26] Indians whose strange, saturnine visages and violent customs hinted strongly at traces of infernal origin."[27] He is on the mark with this assessment as a particular feature of the American Gothic. This demonization of American Indians started right away. Cotton Mather writes that witches call the devil the Black Man and that he resembles an Indian and that the Indians "used all their sorceries to molest the first planters."[28] John Smith states, in reference to the American Indian religion, that "their chiefe God they worship is the Devil."[29] Charles Brockden Brown in the preface to *Edgar Huntly* (1799) argues that "The incidents of Indian hostility, and the perils of the western wilderness"[30] are the appropriate material for American writers. Brown's Gothic is the haunted forest where American Indians are akin to animals and represent natural evil.

Nathaniel Hawthorne in "Young Goodman Brown" (1835) takes the hero deep into a gloomy forest, where he says to himself: "There may be a devilish Indian behind every tree."[31] As Goodman Brown goes deeper into the "haunted forest" he hears "the yell of Indians."[32] According to Teresa A. Goddu, Americans have long been taught from birth to see the Indian as a Gothic monster.[33] In Melville's *The Confidence Man* (1857), there is a chapter, "Containing the Metaphysics of Indian Hating." The preceding chapter recounts the exploits of the Indian-killer Colonel John Moredock, whose family was purportedly massacred by Indians. Moredock "seldom stirred without his rifle, and hated Indians like snakes,"[34] equating American Indians with demons in the Garden of Eden. Lovecraft elaborates this theme in "The Curse of Yig." Dirk Peters in Poe's *The Narrative of Arthur Gordon Pym of Nantucket* (1837–38) is almost bestial in appearance and the other to Pym. This dark companion is "the son of an Indian squaw[35] woman of the tribe of the Upsarokas."[36] This perspective[37] was a means of justifying the genocide of indigenous peoples and the continued violent expansion of Europeans across the Americas.

Leslie Fiedler writes that in the American tradition "the aristocratic villains of the European tale of terror are replaced by skulking primitives and the natural rather than the sophisticated is felt as a primal threat."[38] In the European Gothic, it is the power of church and state that is confronted, but in America it is nature and the indigenous people. In a sense, as Fielder argues, the American Gothic is conservative and thematically is about building new power structures over killed ones in the wilderness. This demonization infuses American literature and is the foundation of a unique American literature, which is, as Fielder writes, "almost essentially a Gothic one."[39]

DEPICTIONS OF AMERICAN INDIANS IN THE FICTION OF LOVECRAFT

Lovecraft's fiction is dense with images and themes of the primitive. There are also explicit mentions of American Indians and in most they are negatively portrayed, often referred to in derogatory language. For example, in *The Case of Charles Dexter Ward* (1927), Curwen's servants "were a sullen pair of aged Narragansett Indians; the husband dumb and curiously scarred, and the wife of a very repulsive cast of countenance, probably due to a mixture of negro blood."[40] They are presented as in league with the evil Joseph Curwen.

The story "He" (1925) takes place in New York City, where the narrator is shown around the secret places of the city by a stranger dressed in eighteenth-century garb. This stranger tells of an ancestor, the Squire, who learned of magical rituals by observing "sartain half-breed[41] red Indians" as "at full moon" they "stole over the wall" of his property and "performed sartain acts."[42] The Squire "sarved them monstrous bad rum" (272)[43] to kill them off. They were "mongrel salvages" (272). But they have their revenge. The stranger has the power to present vistas of different times. Upon seeing the future vista, the unnamed narrator screams and his shrieks seem to rouse something from the grave. The stranger, the Squire, admonishes the narrator, "The full moon—damn ye—ye . . . ye yelping dog—ye called 'em, and they've come for me! Moccasined feet—dead men—Gad sink ye, ye red devils" (274). In this story Lovecraft uses the images of American Indians as vengeful ghosts returning for payback, a theme that is featured in much of his fiction. They seem to be nowhere in the modern New York City of the story, as if they exist only in nightmares.

In "The Call of Cthulhu" (1926), a stone bas-relief of Cthulhu is reported-ly worshipped in Greenland by a "singular tribe or cult of degenerate Esqui-maux whose religion [was] a curious form of devil-worship." Moreover, "It was a faith of which other Esquimaux knew little, and which they mentioned only with shudders, saying that it had come down from horribly ancient aeons before ever the world was made."[44] In the new world, there are even more aboriginal beings.

In "The Transition of Juan Romero" (1919), Romero's facial features, although "plainly of the Red Indian type, were yet remarkable for their light colour and refined conformation, being vastly unlike those of the average 'greaser' or Piute of the locality."[45] Interestingly, this light color was due to "the ancient and noble Aztec" (338). But only his face was noble. "Ignorant and dirty, he was at home amongst the other brown-skinned" (338). In the story a great abyss is revealed after a dynamite blast at Norton Mine. The bottom seems lost in the depths: "the void below was infinite" (339). During the night, a great throbbing or drumming and chanting sound from the shaft awakens the unnamed narrator and Romero. They are drawn "irresistibly . . . to the gaping blackness of the mine" (341). As they descend, Romero quick-ens his pace and leaves the narrator behind, who hears a shift in Romero's language, as if he is returning to his ancestral roots. Romero cries, "Huitzilo-potchli" (339), the Aztec god of the sun and war. Romero returns to his ancient home and finds terror. The narrator catches a glimpse of Romero deep down in the chasm, but he dares not tell what he saw. It is a place that cannot be described. In the morning, Romero is dead in his bunk and it is said that neither of them left the bunkhouse at night—nightmares are real.

In "The Dunwich Horror," the megalithic monument on a hilltop is "at-tributed to the Indians . . . as once the burial-places of the Pocumtucks" (159). The horror in the story seems to have its essential source in the "unhal-lowed rites and conclaves of the Indians, amidst which they called forbidden shapes of shadow out of the great rounded hills, and made wild orgiastic prayers that were answered by loud crackings and rumblings from the ground below" (157–58). Later in the story the odor at the Whateleys' house is akin to that "near the Indian circles on the hills and could not come from anything sane or of this earth" (164).

"The Whisperer in Darkness" (1930) begins with the sightings of strange creatures floating in the Vermont rivers after a mighty flood. "The Indians had the most fantastic theories of all"[46] about the nature of the strange beings in the so-called Pennacook myth of the winged ones. Their belief that the beings were not native to earth and came to extract a certain ore turns out to be the most accurate. Standing stones are a geographical element in the landscape of the story, as in others. Such stones are sometimes used as a motif for American Indians and are a signal from the past and often mark a geographical entrance point for "monsters."

In "The Curse of Yig" (1928), Walker and Audrey Davis move from Arkansas to Oklahoma to start a new life in the former Indian Territory. Audrey has a "slight Indian admixture."[47] The story centers around Walker's fears of snakes, rising to a crescendo after he learns Audrey killed a den of newborn rattlesnakes. He tries to atone to the snake god, Yig, modeled on Quetzalcoatl, the Toltec and Aztec god portrayed as a feathered serpent. Walker visits the "Wichitas, and talked long with the old men and shamans about the snake-god and how to nullify his wrath. Charms were always ready in exchange for whiskey" (88). This all fails, and during one night of terror Audrey mistakenly axes Walker to death. She goes mad and dies in an asylum. But first she gives birth to a rhumba of things, only one of which survives and is housed in the asylum. The creature is a "crawling and wriggling" thing "emitting every now and then a weak and vacuous hiss." It bears "some remote resemblance to a human form laid flat on its belly" but is "subtly squamous in the dim, ghoulish light" (82) of its cell. This is another Gothic incarnation of the primitive, arising from the indigenous peoples.

"The Mound" (1929–30) is centered on a mysterious low tumulus or mound near Binger, Oklahoma. This mound turns out to mark an entranceway to the underground world of Xinaián or K'n-yan, which has seemingly existed for eons. The first narrator is an "American Indian ethnologist"[48] who recounts several tales of expeditions to the mound, most of which result in strange disappearances. He hazards a way into the mound and finds a curious cylinder containing a scroll written by Pánfilo de Zamacona y Nuñez, who was part of Coronado's band. Zamacona[49] descends to the K'n-yan world[50] and is welcomed, apparently because he is of a "higher-grade" (132) than the indigenous people of the area, referred to as "ignorant tribes of the plains" (137). After centuries, the underground society finds only the European to be welcomed into their cities, although Zamacona is not free to leave. The story refers to American Indians in derogatory terms, and the speech of the character Grey Eagle is a caricature. The sentinels on the mound seem to be biologically distorted images of American Indians, an embodiment of the American Indian terror hallucination haunting the white imagination.

Often Lovecraft's works have nearly a cinematic quality, including a soundtrack. For aboriginals, it is the sound of drums. The New Orleans police in "The Call of Cthulhu" track deep into the "terrible cypress woods" (136), getting closer to the "beat of tom-toms" (137), the auditory signal of the primitive in Lovecraft. In "The Curse of Yig" the "tom-toms . . . [of] the Pawnee, Wichita and Caddo country pounded endlessly" (83) to ward off the snake god. In "The Mound" the real danger of American Indian drumming is told: "There are old, old tribes with old, old memories there; and when the tom-toms beat ceaselessly over brooding plains in the autumn the spirits of men are brought dangerously close to primal, whispered things" (97).

These drums are the emblem of the wild primitive[51] and are a source of fear in a number of Lovecraft's works, as Leigh Blackmore illustrates.[52] It is found also in "Herbert West—Reanimator" (1921–22), where Buck Robinson's face "conjured up thoughts of unspeakable Congo secrets and tom-tom poundings under an eerie moon."[53] Other examples include *The Dream-Quest of Unknown Kadath* (1926–27), where "the muffled, maddening beating of vile drums"[54] accompanies Azathoth, and in the poem "The Elder Pharos," where "the last Elder One lives on alone / Talking to Chaos with the beat of drums."[55]

This deep aversion to drumming is expressed not only by Lovecraft. For example, the historian Douglas Edward Leach, on the first page of chapter 1 of *Flintlock and Tomahawk*, takes this fear back to "1697 [when] the ominous drumbeats of large-scale organized resistance were heard in Connecticut as the enraged Pequots rose up against the English Settlers."[56]

THE RETURN OF ABORIGINAL BEINGS

But Lovecraft is a master; many of his monsters and horrific entities can be seen as a transformation of the primitive, the aboriginal, of American Indians. Fictionally, he displaces American Indians and replaces them with older beings, twisted and deformed in the Gothic tradition. It is as if New England is cleansed fictionally of any remnant of the real original inhabitants. Joel Pace suggests that Lovecraft's invocations of pre–American Indian ruins are an attempt to snuff out the Indian presence in the landscape, to write the Indian away.[57] This is another common thread in America's fabric of dispossession of indigenous peoples. In 1788, Philip Freneau in "The Indian Burying-Ground" made the American Indian "a shade"[58] and tried to write them out of the real "to shadows;"[59] mere "delusions"[60] haunting the land.

In "The Colour Out of Space" (1927), Ammi Pierce says that the woods around the blasted heath were not generally feared before the meteorite fell except for a "small island in the Miskatonic where the devil held court beside a curious lone altar older than the Indians."[61] The unknown thing in the swamp of cypress woods and lagoons in "The Call of Cthulhu," "had been there before d'Iberville, before La Salle, before the Indians" (137). This is of a piece with the looting of American Indian artifacts and grave robbing that started with the first invasions. Bergland points out that in the first year of settlement at Plymouth in 1620, the English plundered a number of grave sites. This progressed as the frontier was pushed across the continent, abetted by the military and museums.

In "The Mound," the tumulus is patrolled by ghostly guardians, and early in the story they are reported as American Indians: a male during the day and a headless female, who carries a "blue ghost-light" (106) at night. The narrator doubts the male is an American Indian, as he "was certainly *not a savage. He was the product of a civilization*" (108). These beings turn out to be former denizens of the underground world, one a "discredited freeman," and the second, "T'la-yub who had planned and aided" (157) Zamacona's first attempt at escaping from the underground world and, after they had failed, was punished. Even the ghosts of American Indians are usurped.

But in this dispossession, what Lovecraft's fiction achieves is the return of American Indians in the form of original beings, in Gothic form. American Indians are never really absent in his fiction; but they are often transformed. In "The Thing on the Doorstep" (1933), after Upton rescues Derby from Chesuncook, Maine, Derby explains his strange behavior as arising in part from his exploration of "certain Indian relics in the north wood—standing stones."[62] This is the locale of "Cyclopean ruins in the heart of the Maine woods beneath which vast staircases led down to abysses of nighted secrets, of complex angles that led through invisible walls to other regions of space."[63] American Indians are the source of the hauntings and transformations that come from the depths, as if they are arising from their looted graves.

In "He," the monster is prefigured by the "gleam of a tomahawk as it cleft the rending wood," and it opens the way for "a colossal, shapeless influx of inky substance starred with shining, malevolent eyes" (275). This is the return of American Indians in a shape twisted by the Gothic vision of Lovecraft.

Meso-American Indian gods are blurred with Lovecraftian monsters into a mixed pantheon of beings in "The Electric Executioner" (1929). In this story, as Marc A. Beherec identifies, Lovecraft displays considerable knowledge of Meso-American myths and geography.[64] The story character, Feldon, who identifies strongly with Meso-Americans, intones the mixing of beings in his many chants. One goes: "In the mountains—in the mountains—Anahuac—Tenochtitlan—the old ones."[65] As Beherec notes, this melds the land, the city, and Lovecraft's Old Ones.[66] Another chant, in part, is: "Mictlanteuctli, Great Lord, a sign! A sign from within thy black cave! Iä! Tonatiuh-Metztli! Cthulhutl! Command, and I serve!"[67] The lord of the underworld and the sun and moon are united with Great Cthulhu.

Beherec also illuminates Lovecraft's use of Aztec mythology in "The Curse of Yig."[68] In the story Yig is said to be an "older and darker prototype" (81) of Quetzalcoatl. This is Kukulcan, the Mayan god, which Lovecraft knew. Yig appears also in "The Mound" as one of the gods in the K'n-yan pantheon. In this story the longevity of the possession of the Americas by indigenous peoples is acknowledged, although it is overwritten by the K'n-yan people, who are portrayed as a sort of pseudo-human alien population of long duration on earth. The mounds in the United States were long believed to be the work of some other agency than the indigenous people, as discussed by George Milner.[69] This story describes the mound as perhaps "a product of Nature" or "a burial-place or ceremonial dais constructed by prehistoric tribes" (98). It is really an entranceway to the underground society and is another example of an indigenous people's formation being usurped as the work of older beings. The story continues the narrative that any major structures or alterations[70] in the landscape could not have been accomplished by American Indians but must be due really to others. This is part of the appropriation of the North American landscape by Euro-Americans. However, there is a link with the indigenous people; in Zamacona's narrative the K'n-yan people "seemed to be Indians . . . [but] their faces had many subtle differences" (129). And their language has "an infinitely remote linkage with the Aztec" (131).

At the close of "The Dunwich Horror" professors from Miskatonic University kill off the invisible monster. In this story the locals are not capable of destroying the horror, only the white intellectuals are able to do so; the locals are powerless to repossess the land. The Miskatonic mission pulls down all the rings of standing stones on the hills, as if these are the source of the horror, whence the horror really arose, that is, from American Indian haunts. In this story, it is as if the force of the original inhabitants comes back in invisible form. The Dunwich horror, the twin of Wilbur Whateley, is the reification of the fear of the vengeful return of the American Indian. In the Lovecraftian forest, the dispossession of American Indians continues, but their ghosts keep on coming back.

DYSTOPIA

Lovecraft's fiction is replete with images of a fallen utopia. No utopia is to be found in the past, the present, or the future. It is a vain quest. In "He" the vision of the past of New York is an "unhealthy shimmer of a vast salt marsh" (272–73). "The Mound" is particularly insightful in its dissection of the vision of utopia. It paints a disturbing picture of the K'n-yan culture that is lost in acedia and overcome with ennui and moral collapse, where hedonism and torture are the only reasons for living. It is hedonism of sadomasochistic dimensions, but where there is a realization that all is pointless. The progress of development of the underground people has led to a society of decadence. They are seemingly immortal, control advanced technologies, and seem to have magical powers to dematerialize and to communicate their thoughts; all things seem within their reach. But the society is repellent to the ancient Spanish adventurer Zamacona. The society is founded on a deformed "half-human slave class" (118)—an especially disturbing slave class continuously engineered through biological deformations and tortured into grotesque forms, something the Nazis dreamed of. Some of the elements of cultural collapse are akin to the Roman orgies of coliseum mutilation and depravity. But much is a spinoff of a post-industrial society, where leisure means torture and disgust. As Leonard Cohen sings about in "The Future," it is murder. It is a civilization of savagery and cannibalism. Interestingly, there are several levels of this dystopia, a sort of circles of hell, with the known bottom ring of N'kai ruled by sluglike beings surging darkly as if liquefied excretions in gutters. The story hints that there may be even more subterranean rings with even more horrific entities.

In "He," Lovecraft displays a hellish image of the future New York, with drumming as the soundtrack. It is like a dark bestial beating heart:

> I saw the heavens verminous with strange flying things, and beneath them a hellish black city of giant stone terraces with impious pyramids flung savagely to the moon, and devil-lights burning from unnumbered windows. And swarming loathsomely on aerial galleries I saw the yellow, squint-eyed people of that city, robed horribly in orange and red, and dancing insanely to the pounding of fevered kettle-drums, the clatter of obscene crotala, and the maniacal moaning of muted horns whose ceaseless dirges rose and fell undulantly like the wave of an unhallowed ocean of bitumen. (273–74)

The more we know, the more horrific things are; the deeper underground or farther in space or distant in time we venture or the more homeward we go, the more we find dread.

THE ORIGINAL

Near the end of *At the Mountains of Madness*, Danforth raves "the original, the eternal, the undying."[71] Lovecraft's fiction re-creates American Indians, gothically transformed but powerful and fearsome, reifying fear as they arise from the deep memory. In a real way, his fiction tells the truth about America and its foundation on violence and dispossession and the ongoing fear of the aboriginal. America is founded and spread on violence. This violence, as Richard Slotkin argues, is a continuing impulse in American society and embedded in national historical and fictional narratives.[72] Historically,

Americans have not confronted the death and destruction that the country was founded on. It is forbidden, or unspeakable, or written away, or engulfed in a mythology of manifest destiny and always moving and conquering new frontiers where the inhabitants are inferior and have to be removed, in reality, in imagination, and in history. Lovecraft was an outsider himself in many ways, his work published in the pulps and excoriated frequently and viewed as amateur at best until relatively recently. From this outsider post, yet also a defender of the flag, Lovecraft created a new American Gothic clearly founded on its tradition of fear of the vanquished or enslaved. In his fictions they have returned in even more horrific form to terrify society. This theme is throughout the fiction—in early stories, mature fiction, and ghostwritten tales. The eon-old monsters that Lovecraft invents are yet aboriginal themselves. Origins cannot be escaped.

The American Gothic is all about the aboriginal. The European Gothic can be thought of as an expression of rebellion against the obscenities of perverse power. The American Gothic is all about the killing of the powers of the natural, of origins, of the very source of our being. Lovecraft captures that overwhelming sense of loss in the New England landscape, in the great expanse of the United States. He describes a familiar place changing into an alien place of ancient horror that cannot be escaped. And the horror cannot really be escaped because in the end it is not just in the landscape, it is inside us. His stories give voice to the American soul in torment, full of torture and anguish. The genocide of the indigenous population gave Euro-Americans their land, their wealth, their being. In Lovecraft, the dead original peoples of America keep coming back in colossal form to repossess their land. Lawrence writes of Americans as necessarily killers. Lovecraft's fiction rewrites this as self-killers in the end, as all homes are full of ghosts.

NOTES

1. Jill Pascoe, *Arizona's Haunted History* (Gilbert, AZ: Irongate Press, 2008), 112.

2. Bartolomé de las Casas, *The Devastation of the Indies: A Brief Account*, trans. Herma Briffault (Baltimore, MD: Johns Hopkins University Press, 1992).

3. Tzvetan Todorov, *The Conquest of America* (New York: Harper & Row, 1992), 33. Todorov asserts that in Mexico on the eve of Columbus's arrival there were 25 million Amerindians, but in 1600 only 1 million.

4. Russell Thornton, *American Indian Holocaust and Survival* (Norman: University of Oklahoma Press, 1990), 22–36, provides 1492 population estimates in the Western hemisphere as ranging from 8.4 million to 112.5 million. Thornton himself suggests 72+ million for the Western hemisphere and 7+ million north of the Rio Grande, with 5+ million in the United States and 2+ million in Canada. According to information from the US Census and the US Commissioner of Indian Affairs, the American Indian population of the United States for the decade 1890–1900 was 250,000. David Stannard, *American Holocaust: The Conquest of the New World* (New York: Oxford University Press, 1993), 268, says "informed scholars" estimate the overall population of the Americas pre-Columbus as from 75 to 100 million, with some suspecting the figure was even higher. Ronald Wright, *Stolen Continents: The Americas*

through Indian Eyes since 1492 (Boston: Houghton Mifflin, 1992), 4, says the Native American population was approximately 100 million in 1492.

5. Celia Brickman, *Aboriginal Populations in the Mind* (New York: Columbia University Press, 2003), 17.

6. Reneé Bergland, *The National Uncanny: Indian Ghosts and American Subjects* (Hanover, NH: University Press of New England, 2000), 9.

7. Bergland, *The National Uncanny: Indian Ghosts and American Subjects*, 8.

8. D. H. Lawrence, *Studies in Classic American Literature* (London: Martin Seeker, 1993), 39.

9. Lawrence, *Studies in Classic American Literature*, 40.

10. Toni Morrison, *Beloved* (New York: Knopf, 1987).

11. The terror of the forest pervades the works of Lovecraft. In "The Lurking Fear," the unnamed narrator wonders what has "rotted and festered in the antediluvian forest darkness" and will come out of the "accursed midnight forests and strew fear, madness, and death." *Dagon and Other Macabre Tales*, ed. S. T. Joshi (Sauk City, WI: Arkham House, 1986), 190 (hereafter cited in the text). This is within the continuing flow of American literature. It is as if we are all aliens in nature.

12. H. P. Lovecraft, "The Tomb," in *Dagon and Other Macabre Tales*, 5.

13. Joshua David Bellin, *The Demon of the Continent* (Philadelphia: University of Pennsylvania Press, 2001).

14. Charles L. Crow, *American Gothic* (Cardiff: University of Wales Press, 2009), 1.

15. Crow, *American Gothic*, 2.

16. Marianna Torgovnick, *Gone Primitive: Savage Intellects, Modern Lives* (Chicago: University of Chicago Press, 1990), 187–93.

17. Joyce Carol Oates, introduction to *American Gothic Tales* (New York: Plume, 1996), 7.

18. Torgovnick, *Gone Primitive*, 3–72.

19. Lovecraft, "Beyond the Wall of Sleep," in *Dagon and Other Macabre Tales*, 26.

20. Lovecraft, "The Dunwich Horror," in *The Dunwich Horror and Others*, ed. S. T. Joshi (Sauk City, WI: Arkham House, 1984), 157.

21. Lovecraft, "The Horror at Red Hook," in *Dagon and Other Macabre Tales*, 248.

22. Lovecraft, "The Horror at Red Hook," 260.

23. Lovecraft, "Facts concerning the Late Arthur Jermyn and His Family," in *Dagon and Other Macabre Tales*, 73. Hereafter cited in the text.

24. Lovecraft, *Selected Letters*, ed. August Derleth, Donald Wandrei, and James Turner (Sauk City, WI: Arkham House, 1965–76), 3.31.

25. But Lovecraft, as well as nearly all others, is wrong about the first impressions of the landscape itself at the time of the first colonial incursions. Denevan provides evidence that "by 1492 Indian activity throughout the Americas had modified forest extent and composition, created and expanded grasslands, and rearranged microrelief via countless artificial earthworks. Agricultural fields were common, as were houses and towns and roads and trails." William M. Denevan, "The Pristine Myth: The Landscape of the Americas in 1492," *Annals of the Association of American Geographers* 82 (1992): 370. Bragdon and Mandell describe the New England landscape first found by Europeans as nearly akin to an English garden, with sweeping meadows and deep woods cleared of much underbrush and with clear sightlines, all to support Native agriculture and hunting: Kathleen J. Bragdon, *Native People of Southern New England, 1500–1650* (Norman: University of Oklahoma Press, 1996), and Daniel R. Mandell, *Behind the Frontier: Indians in Eighteenth-Century Eastern Massachusetts* (Lincoln: University of Nebraska Press, 1996). However, the European colonists did dramatically alter the New England ecology to suit their agriculture and industry, as shown by William Cronon, *Changes in the Land: Indians, Colonists and the Ecology of New England* (New York: Hill & Wang, 1983).

26. The non-white skin of American Indians has always been a focus of racist words. In *In Cold Blood*, Truman Capote writes of Perry Edward Smith that "His mother had been a full-blooded Cherokee; it was from her that he had inherited his coloring—the iodine skin." Truman Capote, *In Cold Blood* (New York: Vintage, 1994), 16. It is as if the flesh of Indians is infected and must be treated to stop contagion.

27. Lovecraft, *The Annotated Supernatural Horror in Literature*, rev. ed., ed. S. T. Joshi (New York: Hippocampus Press, 2012), 60–61.

28. Cotton Mather, *The Wonders of the Invisible World* (London: John Russell Smith, 1962), 74.

29. John Smith, *The General Historie of Virginia, New England and the Summer Isles* (Bedford, MA: Applewood Books, 2006 [1629]), 1.72.

30. Charles Brockden Brown, *Edgar Huntly* (New Haven, CT: College & University Press, 1973), 29.

31. Nathaniel Hawthorne, "Young Goodman Brown," in *American Gothic Tales*, ed. Joyce Carol Oates (New York: Plume, 1996), 53.

32. Hawthorne, "Young Goodman Brown," 59.

33. Teresa A. Goddu, *Gothic America: Narrative, History, and Nation* (New York: Columbia University Press, 1997), 57. The Declaration of Independence refers to "merciless Indian savages."

34. Herman Melville, *The Confidence Man: His Masquerade* (Oxford: Oxford University Press, 2008 [1857]), 187.

35. This is an offensive, obscene, and demeaning racist word.

36. Edgar Allan Poe, *The Narrative of Arthur Gordon Pym of Nantucket* (New York: Penguin, 1980), 84.

37. There is another perspective of the American Indian as emblematic of the noble savage, a sentimental image but no longer alive or only on display on reservations similar to zoos for exotic animals. This other image is just another way of removing Indians from the real landscape, leaving graves to be looted. The confrontation in the wilderness, at the frontier, between the white settler and the indigenous people is a continuing story element. The story has variations. In many, the American Indians are eliminated, opening up the land for the use of colonists. In others, a white person goes native, so to speak, and joins the aboriginal either by being captured or by identifying as native. In the film *Avatar*, directed by James Cameron (2009, 20th Century Fox), the disabled marine goes native and saves the people of blue color, as if they are incapable themselves.

38. Leslie Fielder, *The Return of the Vanishing American* (New York: Stein & Day, 1968), 377.

39. Leslie Fielder, *Love and Death in the American Novel* (New York: Criterion, 1960), 129.

40. Lovecraft, *The Case of Charles Dexter Ward*, in *At the Mountains of Madness and Other Novels*, ed. S. T. Joshi (Sauk City, WI: Arkham House, 1985), 119.

41. The progeny of mixed races seems to have been a particular bugaboo in the fiction of Lovecraft. Of course, this is another perennial theme in American literature. The secret theme of the Leatherstocking Tales of James Fenimore Cooper, as Fiedler argues, is miscegenation. Natty Bumppo is for racial purity. In *The Last of the Mohicans* (Cambridge, MA: Harvard University Press, 2011), he says he is "a white man without cross," and has "no taint of Indian blood" (162, 82). In *The Deerslayer* (Teddington, UK: Echo Library, 2006), he has "a white heart and can't in reason, love a red-skinned maiden" (82). Lovecraft drags this theme into the open. In *Tom Sawyer*, evil is personified in Injun Joe, who is half American Indian.

42. Lovecraft, "He," in *Dagon and Other Macabre Tales*, 271. Hereafter cited in the text.

43. P. D. Mail and S. Johnson argue that the spreading of alcohol to the indigenous people was for colonist advantage and was an early form of chemical warfare. P. D. Mail and S. Johnson, "Boozing, Sniffing, and Toking: An Overview of the Past, Present, and Future of Substance Use by American Indians," *American Indian & Alaska Native Mental Health Research* 5, no. 2 (1993): 1–33.

44. Lovecraft, "The Call of Cthulhu," in *The Dunwich Horror and Others*, 135. Hereafter cited in the text.

45. Lovecraft, "The Transition of Juan Romero," in *Dagon and Other Macabre Tales*, 338. Hereafter cited in the text.

46. Lovecraft, "The Whisperer in Darkness," in *The Dunwich Horror and Others*, 212.

47. Lovecraft and Zealia Bishop, "The Curse of Yig," in *The Horror in the Museum and Other Revisions*, ed. S. T. Joshi (Sauk City, WI: Arkham House, 1989), 84. Hereafter cited in the text.

48. Lovecraft and Zealia Bishop, "The Mound," in *The Horror in the Museum*, 99. Hereafter cited in the text.

49. Zamacona is told about the underground world by Charging Buffalo, who is nearly parental in his concern and caring for the Spaniard and gives him a talisman for protection. But Zamacona disrespects him by paying him off with "trinkets." Lovecraft, "The Mound," 120.

50. This world turns out to be the cities of gold searched for by Coronado, a nice twist by Lovecraft.

51. Joseph Conrad, *The Heart of Darkness* (London: Folio Society, 1997), evokes this when he has Marlow think of "the heavy, mute spell of the wilderness—that seemed to draw him [Kurtz] to its pitiless breast by the awakening of forgotten and brutal instincts, by the memory of gratified and monstrous passions. This alone, I was convinced, had driven him out to the edge of the forest, to the bush, towards the gleam of fires, the throb of drums, the drone of weird incantations" (144).

52. Leigh Blackmore, "Some Notes on Lovecraft's 'The Transition of Juan Romero,'" *Lovecraft Annual* 3 (2009): 158.

53. Lovecraft, "Herbert West—Reanimator," in *Dagon and Other Macabre Tales*, 146.

54. Lovecraft, *The Dream-Quest of Unknown Kadath*, in *At the Mountain of Madness and Other Novels*, 308.

55. Lovecraft, *The Ancient Track: Complete Poetical Works of H. P. Lovecraft*, ed. S. T. Joshi (San Francisco: Night Shade, 2001), 75.

56. Douglas Edward Leach, *Flintlock and Tomahawk* (Woodstock, VT: Countryman Press, 1958), 1.

57. Joel Pace, "Queer Tales? Sexuality, Race and Architecture in 'The Thing on the Doorstep,'" *Lovecraft Annual* 2 (2008): 117. Jean O'Brien, *Firstings and Lastings: Writing Indians Out of Existence in New England* (Minneapolis: University of Minnesota Press, 2010), writes of the concerted work of New England local narratives from 1820 to 1880 to write away the indigenous population and instill the myth of the extinction of the American Indian. The New Englanders claimed former Indian places as Euro-American. This was in part to solidify the superiority of the white population and to justify the appropriation of Indian land, as well as to provide a foundation for the continuing Indian wars in the West. Even the graves of Indians were obliterated, either by looting or by such actions as planting trees on the grounds. But the extinction is false in New England and elsewhere. O'Brien, *Dispossession by Degrees: Indian Land and Identity in Natick, Massachusetts, 1650–1790* (Cambridge: Cambridge University Press, 1997), documents the survival of the Mashpee and Gay Head Wampanoag and the Nipmuck in Massachusetts; the Mashantucket, Pequot, and Mohegan in Conneticut; the Narrangansett in Rhode Island; the Abenaki in Vermont and western Maine; and the Passamaquoddy and Penobscot in Maine, and others. Wright, *Stolen Continents*, 121, suggests that in New York the history of Iroquoia is overwritten with an alien history with names like Syracuse, Ithaca, Homer, Rome, and Ovid.

58. Philip Freneau, "The Indian Burying-Ground," in *The Little Book of American Poets: 1787–1900*, ed. Jessie B. Rittenhouse (Boston: Houghton Mifflin, 1915), 3.

59. Freneau, "The Indian Burying-Ground," 4.

60. Freneau, "The Indian Burying-Ground," 4.

61. Lovecraft, "The Colour Out of Space," in *The Dunwich Horror and Others*, 57.

62. Lovecraft, "The Thing on the Doorstep," in *The Dunwich Horror and Others*, 291.

63. Lovecraft, "The Thing on the Doorstep," 285.

64. Marc A. Beherec, "The Racist and La Raze: H. P. Lovecraft's Aztec Mythos," in *The Intersection of Fantasy and Native America from H. P. Lovecraft to Leslie Marmon Silko*, ed. Amy H. Sturgis and David D. Oberhelman (Altadena, CA: Mythopoeic Press, 2009), 29.

65. Lovecraft and Adolphe de Castro, "The Electric Executioner," in *The Horror in the Museum and Other Revisions*," 68.

66. Beherec, "The Racist and La Raze," 29.

67. Lovecraft and de Castro, "The Electric Executioner," 74.

68. Beherec, "The Racist and La Raze," 33–34.

69. George R. Milner, *The Moundbuilders* (London: Thames & Hudson, 2004), documents how from 3000 BC to the sixteenth century American Indians quarried tons of earth to form thousands of mounds in the Eastern Woodlands. Some were burial sites, some effigies in the form of snakes and sacred totems, others platforms for dwellings. Much was looted but much also remained in the form of copper-engraved stone palettes, shells, masks, stone figures, and elaborately designed pottery. Stephen Plog, *Ancient Peoples of the American Southwest* (London: Thames & Hudson, 1997), itemizes the impact of the Hohokam and Anasazi on the American Southwest landscape with roads, irrigation canals, and towns.

70. William Romain, *Mysteries of the Hopewell* (Akron, OH: University of Akron Press, 2000), argues the Hopewell built their massive earthworks using a standard unit of measure and aligned many to cycles of the moon and sun, providing evidence of sophistication in geometry, mathematics, and astronomy.

71. Lovecraft, *At the Mountains of Madness and Other Novels*, 106.

72. Richard Slotkin, *Regeneration through Violence: The Mythology of the American Frontier, 1600–1860* (Middletown, CT: Wesleyan University Press, 1973).

Chapter Nine

From Salem to Eastwick

Witchcraft in the American Gothic

American Gothic fiction grows out of the early American colonial experience. The seeds are in early narratives of Indian warfare and tales of the dangerous but alluring power of the wilderness. Slavery also casts a dark shadow on American fiction. Another early source is the Salem witchcraft trials, which seem to reflect the dark, brooding side of Puritanism. American Gothic literature is set within what Poe phrases "the terror . . . of the soul."[1] A recurring image of this terror is the witch. H. P. Lovecraft finds Gothic horror grounded, partly, in the harsh and stern Puritan religious beliefs of the first colonists, and the unhealing wounds of the witchcraft craze.[2] In a 1923 letter, Lovecraft recounted exploring the Salem countryside, where the "atmosphere of witchcraft days broods heavily."[3] The landscape seemed alive with an old evil.

Here the exploration of the theme of witchcraft in American Gothic fiction will focus on some key narratives. The literature started with Cotton Mather (1663–1728) and is darkened by Nathaniel Hawthorne, novelized by John W. De Forest and others, and manipulated brilliantly by Edgar Allan Poe. Lovecraft revitalized the witchcraft story by adding a science fiction touch. Fritz Leiber's *Conjure Wife* (1943) brings the witch onto college campuses, and *The Witches of Eastwick*, in both the novel (1984) and film (1987), takes them back into small towns with a twist. The American Gothic archetype of the witch is long lived.[4] It is as if those wronged women were never properly mourned or atoned for, and so the land and the villages and the cities continue to suffer under the evil of those deeds. American Gothic literature resounds with this theme originating from the New England witch trials. Here "witch" will be taken to mean simply, a "person alleged to do harm by magic."[5]

Today, the figure of the witch is seen across the length and breadth of American literature and popular culture. There is even an app, "Bubble Witch Saga." Writers continue to use the Salem events or the witch theme in their work, for example, Robin Cook with *Acceptable Risk* (1995). The novel begins in 1692 during the Salem witch madness. Elizabeth Stewart is charged as a witch. She refuses to confess to witchcraft and is hanged. Cotton Mather makes a cameo appearance "behind the crowd and still mounted."[6] At the end of the silly film *Practical Magic* (1995),[7] the black-robed witches seem like Mary Poppinses floating down under black umbrellas, as the townsfolk cheer, not a pitchfork or noose in sight. The town seems to be celebrating their coming out finally as witches. *The Craft* (1996)[8] tries to be a darker film but ends up moralistic and cliché-ridden. It is about a coven of four misfit Catholic high school girls who are called the "bitches of Eastwick." Each of the four has psychological and physical scarring. They are shunned, lonely, and angry as most teenagers probably feel. In the film, mean girls get meaner, as if they are normal teenagers who happen to practice the dark arts. They use their powers to get back at their high school bullies, but bad deeds by teenagers, especially teenage witches, do not go unprosecuted. In a way, *The Craft* is about teenage anxiety that ends as a warning to be good or else. *Wicked* (2003), adapted by Winnie Holzman from the novel by Gregory Maguire, is a cheery musical of Glinda, the white, blonde, Good Witch of the North, and Elphaba, the alien, green Witch of the West.[9] This musical is a follow-up to *The Wizard of Oz* (1939), the iconic American film of Dorothy, the wizard, and the witches.[10] The film *The Witches of Eastwick* (1987) is cheeky more than scary, but *The Blair Witch Project* (1999) is scary and *Rosemary's Baby* (1968) even more so.

In 1692, witch hysteria engulfed Salem, Massachusetts. The community erupted with witch accusations, forced confessions, denials, trials, and death. Nearly two hundred people were accused, fifty-five tried, and nineteen executed. By far the most were women.[11] In addition, Giles Corey was pressed to death.[12] Inmates also died in prison: Francis Hill identifies three females, one male, and an unnamed infant of Sarah Good.[13] Women were the focus of the witchcraft accusations, trials, and executions. But men were the most frequent accusers of supposed witches.[14] Innocents were imprisoned in foul and stinking cells. Some were chained to walls; others were tied neck to heels.[15] Dorcas Good, a four-year-old girl, was put in iron manacles and chained to the wall of a cold, dark cell, where she went mad.[16] During the outbreak, authorities were cruel and unjust. Carol F. Karlsen shows how the bias was toward women.[17] "Witch-hunt" is now part of our lexicon for the malicious and unwarranted pursuit of innocents, usually a minority, often by people in power positions, socially, politically, or ecclesiastically. Jacqueline

Simpson references the evidence that "in most periods and regions at least eighty percent of the accused persons were women."[18]

Part of the background to the Salem horror may be found in the Puritan religious ideology defined by Cotton Mather. He is an imposing figure in American history: a Puritan divine, a prolific writer with nearly 400 titles to his credit,[19] and a politically powerful person in the early colony. Dorothy Z. Baker claims that book 6 of Mather's *Magnalia Christi Americana* (1702) was the beginning of the American short narrative.[20] Mather envisioned America as a contest between the forces of light (Puritans true to and graced by the Almighty) and the forces of darkness, epitomized by the loss of faith or possession by the devil (the witches in Salem and the indigenous peoples generally). This was truth for Puritans. Evil, as Mather seems to characterize it, is the devil reified in a diseased landscape. Puritans needed to cleanse the new world, which meant killing the indigenous people, in part, but also to protect the faith.[21] For Mather the New World held real evil. Furthermore, Mather contributed directly to the Salem witch trials as a publicist,[22] authoring *The Wonders of the Invisible World* (1693). The book was written to justify the Salem witch trials. It contains many Salem testimonies about purported witch sorcery and witch congregations.[23] In the book, Mather declares America was once the "Devil's Territories"[24] and witches were "An Army of Devils" (15) to take it back. He claimed witches call the devil the "Black Man" (102), who resembles "an Indian" (71), linking indigenous people with demonic forces. Mather's shadow seems to darken the New England landscape.

The Salem witches were accused of casting spells, or attacking others in the village in spectral form, or consorting with the devil, which was the darkest deed. The murdered witches were left unburied by the authorities, as they could not be interred in consecrated ground. Perhaps family members found places to lay the dead quietly to rest. Down through the years, the land, the villages, and the people suffered from the evil in those deeds. At least it seems so in the American Gothic. There was a Puritan thrall over the early New England settlers. It was a religion of fire and brimstone that seemed to feed a morbid despair and fear. The colonists may have believed they were surrounded by demons because that is what their religion told them.

Nathaniel Hawthorne (1804–1864) was born in Salem. One of his ancestors was John Hathorne, a presiding judge at the Salem witch trials. Hawthorne seems haunted by the Salem trials. His literary work focuses on a dark New England heritage. He penned classic American Gothic novels, such as *The Scarlet Letter* (1850) and *The House of the Seven Gables* (1851), along with numerous short stories. His writings seem soaked in evil and sin. Cotton Mather appears in Hawthorne's "Alice Doane's Appeal" (1835). Part of the story takes place on Salem's Gallows Hill, where "a physical curse may be said to have blasted the spot."[25] The narrator speaks of martyrs in the ground, "who died so wrongfully" (412). The tale ends with a re-created procession of the condemned up Gallows Hill, followed by their accusers. In the rear rides a horseman, Cotton Mather, like a dark avenger high on his horse. "Alice Doane's Appeal" arose from the Salem witch trials, and it "comes from the summons of the shadowy past" (412). Hawthorne's fiction is haunted by that past. It seems ancestors keep a deathwatch. In his works, sometimes you sense that the past and the people of the past still control all things, and his characters are bound and doomed by the past.

Another tale of witchcraft by Hawthorne is "Young Goodman Brown" (1835). Goodman Brown goes deep into the "haunted forest,"[26] on an "evil purpose" (194). On his dark journey, an elder, who very much resembles Brown, accosts him. The man bears a staff, which seems a great black snake. The two encounter Goody Cloyse, Brown's spiritual mentor, but who seems a witch in the woods. Deep in the forest Brown comes upon the whole village congregated at a "witch-meeting" (205), where he and his wife, Faith, are the new converts. Is this tale really about a tryst in the woods that haunts Brown with guilt and shame so much that he fantasizes an elaborate cover for himself? The next morning he returns to Salem village and wonders if he has only dreamed the witches' Sabbat. This is a tale of duplicity. It is told through the doubling of characters (Brown and the man he meets in the forest), spaces (the village and the woods), and beliefs (the stern Puritan religion and the wild witch service). In the forest, the demonic congregation seems to propagate "out of the darkness" (202). Hawthorne contrasts the pious conventions in the village to the wild declarations and acts in the woods. It is a complex tale stained by the lingering guilt over the Salem hangings.

The backstory to Hawthorne's *The House of the Seven Gables* is that Colonel Pyncheon was part of the mob that clamored "to purge the land of witchcraft"[27] in Salem. He especially accused Matthew Maule, whose land he coveted. The Pyncheon house now stands on that land. The novel is set in the late 1840s, distancing it from the Salem trials. As Maule was on the Gallows Hill scaffold, the colonel looked on from horseback, perhaps akin to Cotton Mather. Maule shouted as he died, "God will give him blood to drink,"[28] staring at the man on horseback. The Pyncheons live and die under that ancient Maule curse.

Hawthorne's *The Scarlet Letter* is set in seventeenth-century Puritan Boston. It tells of Hester Prynne, who was imprisoned for adultery, yet struggles for a life of dignity and strength for herself and her daughter, Pearl. Hester seems a woman of dignity, power, and courage, while her lover, Reverend Dimmesdale, seems weak and sickly as he hides his guilt. Over the novel hangs the dark cloud of Puritan repression and conformism. Boston is oppressive, dark, and forbidding, but the wood here seems liberating for Hester and Pearl, who are outcasts.[29] Charles L. Crow sees the wood as an escape from the Puritan fetters of Boston. Out in the forest, Pearl asks for a story about the "Black Man,"[30] as Cotton Mather said the witches called the devil. In the novel, Mistress Hibbins is the witch. In a way, the cruel and stern Puritan society imagined witches or caused people to be witches, that is, to be outcasts (those who act differently, are assertive, or reject the Puritan religion). Members of that oppressive and unforgiving community saw such people as threats, as American Indians were threats—threats that must be eliminated. Mistress Hibbins is subsequently "executed as a witch."[31] Hester does not conform; she is shunned, but she resists and survives.

During the nineteenth century, many other writers used the Salem witch trials as a source for their work. Marta María Gutiérrez Rodríguez identifies twenty-two works of fiction.[32] G. Harrison Orians also reviews the impact of New England witchcraft on fiction.[33] Both identify the earliest prose tale as an anonymous piece in the *New-York Literary Journal and Belles-Lettres Repository*, in the fall of 1820. Cotton Mather is referenced in the piece.[34] Only a few of the many books and stories will be discussed briefly here.

John Neal (1793–1876) mixes history with fiction in *Rachel Dyer* (1828). Donald A. Ringe calls this John Neal's "main contribution to the American Gothic."[35] Neal uses a nearly seventeenth-century language to evoke the horror of the experience in Salem. In the novel, there are characters from the actual Salem, for example, Martha Cory [Corey], who was hanged, and Reverend George Burroughs, who also was executed. There are also fictional characters, such as Rachel Dyer, who is a Quaker. Rachel refuses to confess to being a witch and dies in her cell. She loses hope and, in a prescient voice, says to Burroughs:

> "there may be some hope on earth for a beautiful witch . . . with golden hair . . . with large blue eyes . . . and a sweet mouth . . . but for a . . . for a freckled witch . . . with red hair and a hump on her back—what hope is there, what hope this side of the grave?"[36]

This gets at the truth of what happened at Salem and its continuing dark legacy. In Salem, the attacks were directed mostly at women and outsiders from the ruling society. In the novel, it seems Neal is attacking the abuses of the legal system, abetted by authorities, such as the acceptance of "spectral evidence," that is, people's dreams and visions as evidence that could lead to persecution and death for an accused witch.

Neither Orians nor Gutiérrez Rodríguez mentions Edgar Allan Poe (1809–1849) in their overviews of literature related to witchcraft. Poe is the American grandmaster of the Gothic form. His best work in the psychological and supernatural Gothic is unsurpassed. He dispensed with the old trappings of the Gothic and focused on individual terror, decadence, and the psychology of deranged and terrified minds. His greatest stories are landmarks in Gothic literature. They are models of precision, unity, and beauty in prose. He saw art as a way to break free from ordinary consciousness into a domain of beauty and wonder—a domain that was also haunted, but with a sublime terror.

In "The Black Cat" (1843), the nameless narrator devolves with increasingly brutal violent acts. First he carves out an eye of his black cat, Pluto. Then he hangs the maimed cat. Next he splits his wife's head open with an axe. The narrator claims it is all driven by "PERVERSNESS"[37] (the word is in upper case, as if a headline, to allay his guilt). The story reads as if it is a police statement. The narrator is trying a jailhouse confession to elicit sympathy for himself. His addiction to alcohol is one of his alibis. It also seems he is making a case for an insanity plea. Yet, as Joyce Carol Oates remarks, the story is like a study in "congenital evil."[38] Moreover, the story transforms the witch archetype. Pluto (the god of the underworld) turns out to have a double. He is another one-eyed cat, a black cat, except for a white mark on his chest, which turns out to be in the shape of a gallows. This is a supernatural cat. After killing his wife, the narrator calmly assesses his options for disposing of the body. He walls her up in the cellar and is very proud of his workmanship. He taps on the spot while the police are searching his house. Not a good move. His tap is answered by a cry, a scream, and a wailing shriek, as the voices of his crimes return. On his wife's head, he exclaims, is the "hideous beast whose craft had seduced me into murder" (859). He is still hoping for an out.

But mostly, he tells the true nature of the black cat, who returns from the dead. Now there is a second body, unburied. Early in the story, he writes that his wife, "who at heart was not a little tinctured with superstition, made frequent allusion to the ancient popular notion, which regarded all black cats as witches in disguise" (850). Throughout the tale the wife seems a shadowy figure. In this story it is the image of the witches' familiar that has the ultimate power. The familiar is the real emissary of the devil, perhaps the "Arch-Fiend!" (858). This story is the witch archetype reborn. It displays with horrid force the dominance and brutality of some men. It is a distorted mirror of Poe's Southern society. It illustrates in grotesque form the control and power of white men over women, and over everything that they owned. Lesley Ginsberg argues that the story is a microcosm of the master/slave relationship, where the drunken husband is the tyrant overlord and the cat and wife the abused dependents.[39] The story also illustrates the fear that those in power experience. They fear that all their crimes, their lynchings, and their domestic abuse will be unearthed. In this story a witch in the form of a black cat brings retribution. This is a great story with many layers and interpretations.

After this tale, it may be hard to find anything better. But writers kept at the tradition. John W. De Forest (1826–1906) writes of the Salem trials in

Witching Times (1856–57). One scene in the novel depicts Martha Carrier riding in the execution cart. Earlier Carrier had been dragged in chains to church and fitted with a paper cap that read, "A WITCH,"[40] as if a brand, similar to Hester's scarlet letter A. Women are to be marked for punishment, as if bruises from a beating. There on Gallows Hill is Cotton Mather on his horse, "austere and unpitying,"[41] during the hangings. Orians contends that the novel follows in many details the actual events at Salem: the examinations, imprisonments, trials, and hangings.[42] There is a fictitious hero, Henry More, and a heroine, his daughter Rachel More. Their attempts to bring fairness, justice, and caring are contrasted with the brutality and single-mindedness of the judges. Their caution is contrasted with the hysteria of the populace and their belief that there are witches attacking them and their children.

In "Lois the Witch" (1859), Elizabeth Gaskell (1810–1865) re-creates the time and atmosphere of the Salem witch epidemic. Gaskell is not an American writer (she is English), but her novella is of interest to illustrate the influence of the Salem horror. Gaskell published three stories under the pen name Cotton Mather Mills, Esq.,[43] and Cotton Mather appears in the novella. She merges fact with fiction in the story, as if to blur the distinction, or perhaps to allow her to expand on the theme of the oppression of women. She also speaks to the divide between the well-off and the poor, and the divide between the colonists and the indigenous people. Generally she uses the events in Salem to contrast the established order and people to an outsider such as Lois Barclay. In the tale, Lois is orphaned as a young woman. She is forced to travel to the New World where her uncle lives; he dies shortly after she arrives. Death is all around her. She is a stranger in a new land and a stranger to her uncle's family and the other townsfolk. She becomes a target as the frenzy escalates in Salem.

Witchcraft appears early in the story. Lois recollects the waterboarding, stoning, and drowning of a woman in England. This woman places a curse on Lois for the failure of her father to stop the persecution and death. It seems the only power the woman has lies in her words, as Laura Kranzler suggests.[44] All else has been taken from her. In this story, women, especially outsiders, are portrayed as oppressed by the power structure of society and controlled by men through many means, including religion.

Puritanism is like a disease in Salem. It seems to darken the minds of villagers. The village is full of tales of the savage indigenous people infesting the woods. Nattee is an indigenous slave in the home of Lois's uncle. She is separated from her people. She tells stories about the woods and magic; seemingly her only freedom is in stories and they represent her only tie to her people. But her stories frighten Lois. Lois tells her own tales of witchcraft back in England that shock the village. Both Nattee and Lois are outsiders and their stories separate them from the other villagers. Laura Kranzler argues that Lois and Nattee's stories are used as evidence against them "to condemn them as demonic manifestations of the Other."[45] Lois finds only jealousy, spite, and despair in the village. All Salem seems beset by fear of the supernatural. Lois is not safe in her new home, where she seems alone, and where a cousin calls her a "wicked English witch."[46]

They end up being accused and hanged for witchcraft. Both Lois and Nattee are easy prey for the Salem inquisition. They are powerless in a male and religious fanatical society. Lois's beauty arouses the desire of her cousin, and it seems to warp into religious accusations against her as a projection of guilt and shame. Nattee is the personification of the devil because she is indigenous. As they are driven to the gallows, the crowd hoots and throws mud and stones at them. Nattee is taken first. Lois, in despair, cries "Mother," and then "the body of Lois the Witch swung in the air."[47] It is a dreadful image.

Mary Eleanor Wilkins-Freeman wrote the witchcraft play *Giles Corey, Yeoman* (1893), featuring Corey, who was pressed to death in Salem. Esther Forbes published *A Mirror of Witches* in 1928. It is a strange historical novel of Doll Bilby possessed by the witchcraft mania in seventeenth-century Massachusetts. She is accused in the town of Cowan Corners, near Salem, where she is seen as an outcast, as different. She is depicted at times in a scarlet riding coat, and she "stared out of round cat's eyes."[48]

Another witchcraft tale is by Edith Wharton (1862–1937), who was primarily an American author of mainstream novels and short stories. Her *The Age of Innocence* (1920) won the Pulitzer Prize in 1921. Wharton also wrote a number of Gothic short stories, and one of these, "Bewitched" (1925), reworks the witch theme. The story appeared in Wharton's 1926 collection, *Here and Beyond*. It is set in an isolated New England farming community during a cold, dark winter. The bleak setting adds to the haunting aspects of the tale. It is reminiscent of the work of Hawthorne and is a complex story with several characters, full of ambiguities. The story could have been written in the distant past. At the start, three men, Sylvester Brand, Deacon Hibben, and Orrin Bosworth, are called to the Rutledges' farm to hear the tale of Saul Rutledge's enchantment. He is a shrunken man, as if drained of his soul. Saul looks "like a drowned man fished out from under the ice."[49] His wife, Prudence, claims Saul has been trysting with Ora Brand, his former sweetheart. Ora is dead, but calls for him to come to a haunted shack near Lamar pond. While the men listen to Saul tell his story, Bosworth feels "as if a winding sheet were descending from the sky to envelop them all in a common grave" (154). Prudence says Ora is a witch and must have a stake driven through her chest. Sylvester Brand, Ora's father, bristles at the notion and thinks it is all bunk. Bosworth, a younger man and a capitalist farmer, is wary of what he hears. Yet he feels "on the edge of a forbidden mystery" (152).

Traveling to the site of the phantom trysts, the three men find naked, spectral footprints in the snow and follow them to the shack. They enter the darkness. Saul shoots something, or is it nothing, or is it Sylvester's other daughter, Venny Brand, or is it the already dead Ora? Is it the gun that banishes the witch? Is it Brand's sin of marrying a cousin that leads to the death of his two daughters? Do the Brands carry an ancestral curse, as a Brand relative had been convicted of witchcraft and burned? Bosworth seems a distant narrator, almost bewitched himself by the train of events, and too bewildered to understand. A reader may feel the same way. Things return to normal at the end with Prudence Rutledge going to buy some soap, as if something needed to be cleansed. This is a fine story with a different image of a wintry, lonely, broken-hearted witch, who is exorcised from even a ghostly life by her father. As in many witch stories, the women die.

In his survey of witchcraft in American literature, Orians, in 1930, concluded that "witchcraft has been frequently enough handled in fiction to render unlikely the appearance of new and uncharted treatments."[50] But there was H. P. Lovecraft. S. T. Joshi says Lovecraft salvaged the witch archetype in "The Dreams in the Witch House" (1932). He "brought the witchcraft tale up to date . . . by incorporating Einsteinian physics."[51] In the story, Walter Gilman lives in Lovecraft's imaginary city of Arkham and is a student at Miskatonic University. He has a room in the "old Witch House."[52] The house had once been home to Keziah Mason, a witch who had escaped from a Salem jail in 1692, and "not even Cotton Mather could explain the curve and angles" (263) on her cell walls. Of the house it is said, "She had told Judge Hathorne of lines and curves that could be made to point out directions leading through the walls of space to other spaces beyond" (263). She has also spoken to the "Black Man" (264), the devil. In the first couple of pages, Lovecraft virtually exhausts the old archetype; later comes Brown Jenkin, who is Keziah's familiar, and a strange one—a rat-like creature with claws akin to human hands and a hairy humanoid face set with sharp teeth. Gilman begins to understand hyperspace and is drawn into other dimensions or is able to travel through other dimensions because of the house's architectural peculiarities. He thinks he is dreaming all his adventures in hyperspace travel. These travels seem paralleled by sleepwalking through Arkham. Fritz Leiber calls this Lovecraft's "most carefully worked out story of hyperspace-travel."[53] In the story the travel is akin to time and space teleportation through mathematics alone.

Fritz Leiber himself enlivens the witch archetype in "The Automatic Pistol" (1940). Inky Kovacs is a sort of witch. Well, he has a familiar, his automatic, which he fondles as if it is alive. No Nose is the narrator, a corrupt cop. He, Glasses, and Inky run bootleg liquor for Larsen, a burly hard crook. Larsen takes a liking to Inky's gun, but Inky keeps it away from him. Well, for a time. Most of the story takes place in a hideout with Larsen, No Nose, and Glasses, after Inky is found dead. Larsen has Inky's gun. The gun begins to act funny. No Nose empties the chambers because the gun keeps sweeping toward him. Then the gun keeps clicking, as if trying to shoot from its empty chambers. Glasses guesses the gun was "Inky's familiar."[54] Michael E. Stamm says the gun was "no ordinary weapon, but . . . the 20th-Century's equivalent of a witch's familiar."[55] Leiber has a twist in the tale, as it seems the familiar is the kingpin here. No Nose checks the gun out and is entranced by its feel, as everything about it seemed "unfamiliar."[56] No Nose is sick when Larsen feels up the gun. The three play poker with the gun shut up in a suitcase, loaded. As they play, Larsen tells them he killed Inky. They keep dealing cards. No Nose hears the gun struggling in the suitcase, as if alive. After Larsen shows his "black bullets" (the dead man's hand in poker: the black aces and black eights), the familiar puts eight slugs into him. There's nothing left but for No Nose and Glasses to clean up the mess and remove the evidence. The story is a fun take on the witch tale, written with a satiric nod to Dashiell Hammett and James M. Cain.

Leiber's *Conjure Wife* was first serialized in *Unknown* (1943) and then published as a book in 1953. The novel is a witchcraft tale set in a cozy New England college town, where sociology professor Norman Saylor uncovers his wife Tansy's practice of sorcery. She uses it to advance his career. Discovering her craft, he dissuades her from its practice. He is the vision of reason, and she is the ground of superstition. But Norman finds his reason on shaky ground as the novel proceeds. The dark arts of witchcraft embodied by three other women gradually but powerfully overwhelm them. Mrs. Carr, who admires "Puritan Massachusetts" and "is planning to reestablish that witch-ridden, so-called theocratic community,"[57] leads the coven. It starts with the killing of Totem, their cat. After that, things get worse. Mrs. Carr is after Tansy's young body.

The book portrays witchcraft as rampant among all women. It seems in part that Leiber is ironically setting up men as bastions of unknowing reason and women as "guardians of mankind's ancient customs and traditions" (76), through a knowing superstition. But even Norman thinks there might be a use for superstition in the "rotten, hate-filled, half-doomed world" (26). Here Leiber suggests that in a search for meaning in a world of real terror and psychological dislocation or even derangement, superstition might be a rational response.

The novel is a long series of arguments by Norman against the actuality of witchcraft until the arguments are exhausted, as Norman is exhausted. Joshi says that Leiber uses the law of probability to lead to the acceptance of the reality of sorcery.[58] There is nothing else left to believe. Norman marvels that perhaps it is simpler to say there are "malign forces outside the individual" (118) rather than a labored psychiatric explanation. He appeals in a way to the principle of simplicity, sometimes called Occam's razor, as attributed to William of Occam (1287–1347).[59] He compares the innovations in witch-craft formulas to experimentation. Somehow he is able to use symbolic logic in his combat with the triad of witches, but in the end he uses witchcraft against them, as if he has been converted. After a fashion, witchcraft moves from superstition to science. Gerald W. Page praises Leiber's ability to evoke "horror in commonplace things," as illustrated in the novel, which he calls "a triumph."[60] Stefan Dziemianowicz contends that Leiber updated the witch-craft archetypes, "to give them life and relevance in the modern age."[61] The novel is linked to the witch theme in American literature: it displays the witch as an ordinary professor's wife in an ordinary small town, yet shows there is still power and horror in the image. This power is also displayed in a recent film.

When released, *The Blair Witch Project*[62] became a sensation. The pro-moters used guerrilla marketing to inflame interest in the film. Produced on a shoestring budget, it was a box office hit. Set near the small town of Burkitts-ville, Maryland, the film shows three young filmmakers hiking into the woods searching for a legendary witch. They vanish in the woods and a year later their footage is found, as if an artifact of a lost mission. The film is presented as a documentary in a deliberate blurring of reality and fiction. In the film, the witch is always off-screen. She is the Blair Witch, the ghost of Ely Kedward, a woman banished from Burkittsville (then Blair) for witch-craft in 1785. She is said to be bloodthirsty. Apparently, she is the evil force behind a number of grisly deaths and disappearances in the forest.

In that forest, Heather, Josh, and Mike eventually become disoriented, wander in circles, and get lost. It is a desolate, cold, rainy, and forbidding place. They have wandered off the normal world into an unknown space of horror. In that space, they encounter strange twig creations, stick figures, and crudely lashed-together branches. Are these warnings? They seem very simi-lar to the "bizarre lattice structures . . . of sticks and boards"[63] that Colin Leverett finds in the woods of upstate New York in Karl Edward Wagner's "Sticks" (1974). The stick structures have a sinister feel in the film. The forest in the American Gothic is a dangerous space: in the film it is a land-scape unearthed from the past. The woodland is a character itself. During the day the forest seems dull and ordinary, but confusing, as if its dull look is a ruse. To the filmmakers the forest becomes a maze. At night, the trees in the forest are tall and dark; there is no escape. It seems a place of death. Judith Wilt argues that place says Gothic more than anything else.[64] The spectral wood triggers anxiety, fear, and dread. This landscape is as important as the human characters in the unfolding of the tale. The personified haunted wood-land thralls Heather, Josh, and Mike. It seems to enter into their heads, as if their souls now mirror the dark forest. The witch is not hiding in the woods; she *is* the woods.

The film is effective in its depiction of panic taking hold of the trio. Heather is the leader of the expedition, but it seems her crew mutinies. Both Josh and Mike take turns ridiculing her, accusing her of getting them lost, driving her to despair. A marvelous scene in the film is Heather speaking into the shaking camera, as if it is the last log on her journey into the darkness of the woods.[65] She says they are "hungry, cold, and hunted." And she appeals to her mother, as Lois the Witch did before dying. On this, their last morning, after Josh had disappeared during the night, Heather finds a bundle of sticks outside their tent. Inside there seem to be blood-soaked scraps of Josh's shirt and a bloody tooth.[66] That night Heather and Mike hear Josh's screams and track them to a derelict house in the woods. They will not get out of that house, a house of death with an electrical cord, hanging like a noose, and with stair walls splotched with tiny handprints.

This film is in a long tradition of witch fiction. At its release time, the film was innovative with its hand-held camera and documentary style. It seems that the witch archetype has been burned into the American mind ever since the Salem witch hysteria. This film successfully fuses the fear of the forest with the witchcraft archetype.

The Witches of Eastwick is both a novel and a film, and they are different. Both are set in the fictional town of Eastwick in Rhode Island. Eastwick, a small town, is a prettied-up double for Salem, as are the witches and the townsfolk. In the book the witches are named Alexandra Spofford, Jane Smart, and Sukie Rougemont, while in the movie the last names are changed respectively to Medford, Spofford, and Ridgemont. They have all lost their husbands in one way or another, and may have gained their powers by doing so. A devil-like character, Darryl Van Horne, moves into Eastwick, and they are all attracted to him. In the book he seduces each in turn, then all together. But Darryl unexpectedly marries a younger woman, Jenny, and the witches kill her through spells that cause cancer. When she dies, Darryl skips town with Jenny's brother, Chris. The witches each find a husband and move away from Eastwick. The book must be a satire of a romance novel.[67] The women use their powers mostly in frivolous ways, with the exception of the killing of Jenny. The book seems a passage from one set of husbands, through a devil, who is not really very devil-like, to another set of husbands. Perhaps the book is a male fantasy of what a modern witch should be: beautiful, hot, and always ready to hop into bed, not something to fear. Back in Salem, the purported witches were feared as a threat to that small, insular society. Those women suffered in terror. They had no power at all. There is little of the real Gothic in the book. It seems that John Updike has no sense of the Gothic, and little, if any, appreciation for the power structures in society. One reviewer of the book commented, "the whole thing—forget the witchcraft—is ridiculous."[68]

In the film,[69] the women do not run off to be married right away after they banish the devil. No Jenny dies and Darryl Van Horne (Jack Nicholson) does not take off with a male friend. But each of the women delivers the devil's baby—there are three cherubic boy babies, who all coo at Darryl's face on a television screen. They seem like little angels, not at all like Rosemary Woodhouse's baby.

The real Gothic is now in cities. In Ira Levin's *Rosemary's Baby* (1967), a young couple moves into the Bramford, an elegant apartment building in New York City. A friend, Hutch, warns them about its dangers. The building houses an old evil; it is a place of witchcraft. Guy Woodhouse is a struggling actor who suddenly starts to get good roles and great reviews. Rosemary is happy but also disturbed by an elderly pair, Minnie and Roman Castevet. Then she is joyous when she becomes pregnant, but becomes even more upset with the meddling of the Castevets. Rosemary becomes isolated in the apartment building; she is sure the Castevets want her child. She is upset for good reason. Little does she know her husband has bargained her off to the devil as a mate. This is the dark betrayal in the novel. Guy does not sell his soul to the devil for wealth and fame; he gives his wife, Rosemary. In the close of the novel, Roman Castevet howls at her, "Satan is His Father and His name is Adrian."[70] The baby is the spawn of the devil. Rosemary is horrified, but at the end she "tickled the baby's tummy . . . poked the tip of his nose,"[71] pleading with him to smile. It seems she has accepted her fate, her witchhood, for her child. That will be her continuing punishment. In the novel, the Satanists appear to be ordinary people living in a nice building in an urban setting. Rosemary is part of a long tradition of women being abused to further the ends of society; here it is the group of ruling Satanists in the apartment microcosm of the city. The film, *Rosemary's Baby*, closely follows the novel, but in the end Rosemary accepts the baby by rocking, gently, its black-draped cradle.[72]

The Salem witch trials haunt American fiction not just in genre literature but also in the mainstream, for example, Arthur Miller's *The Crucible* (1953). The play is set in Salem but seems more like an indictment of McCarthyism, which was a witch-hunt for communists in the United States government. In America it goes back to those innocents in Salem, who were interrogated, humiliated, imprisoned, and in some cases killed in a Puritan religious mania that swept up a village.

What happened in Salem is a foundational source for the American Gothic. The archetype of the witch is embedded in American culture. There are so many strands in this great warp of Gothic horror in America that speaks of the suffering of women, the poor, and outsiders. It is weaved with the fates of American Indians and African Americans. Maryse Condé (1937–), who is from Guadeloupe, wrote *I, Tituba, Black Witch of Salem* (1992). The original is in French as *Moi, Tituba, sorcière . . . noire de Salem* (1986). The novel is a fictionalized account of Tituba, who was accused of witchcraft in Salem. In the novel, she is brought to Salem from Barbados, where the Puritan minister, Samuel Parris, bought Tituba and her husband John Indian. Tituba is charged with witchcraft and then cruelly and sexually tortured by four men. For the Puritans it seems that black is "the color of sin . . . and worthy of punishment."[73] The novel includes an appearance of Hester Prynne, the main character in *The Scarlet Letter*. She is imprisoned for a time with Tituba, and Hester wants to make her "a feminist,"[74] leaping ahead many years. With this novel, Condé creates a grand character, Tituba; she becomes a "heroic and triumphant figure,"[75] virtually a mythic being. There is debate about the ethnic background of the historic Tituba; some argue she was an American Indian,[76] others a black slave. She was an outsider.

Eric Savoy suggests that the American Gothic arises from dark American obsessions, including the past inhabiting the present and the omnipresence of a grotesque violence.[77] He could be writing about the Salem witch trials and their continuing effects. Lovecraft says the "tales of witchcraft . . . lingered long after the dread days of the Salem nightmare."[78] This is the New England heritage of guilt, oppression, and fear; all expressed in a grotesque violence against women. These dark threads are laced throughout American literature, but most explicitly in the Gothic. Those women suffered torment. The Gothic articulates their screams of anguish, their cries for mothers. The image of a witch is a continuing archetype because it still speaks to a primal fear. It is not the fear of a witch; rather, it is the fear of relentless and violent persecution.

NOTES

1. Edgar Allan Poe, "Preface for *Tales of the Grotesque and Arabesque*," in *Tales and Sketches*, ed. Thomas Ollive Mabbott (Cambridge, MA: Harvard University Press, 1978), 1.473. Gerald Kennedy sees Poe's fiction as Gothic in striving to express the "primal fear" in the human condition in an age of collapsing social, religious, and political order. "Phantasms of Death in Poe's Fiction," in *The Tales of Poe*, ed. Harold Bloom (New York: Chelsea House, 1987), 112.

2. H. P. Lovecraft, *The Annotated Supernatural Horror in Literature*, rev. ed., ed. S. T. Joshi (New York: Hippocampus Press, 2012), 60–61.

3. Lovecraft, *Selected Letters*, ed. August Derleth, Donald Wandrei, and James Turner (Sauk City, WI: Arkham House, 1965–76), 1.223.

4. Of course, the witch as archetype and as a reality, at least in the minds of prosecutors, has an even longer history in Europe. Jacqueline Simpson, "Witches and Witchbusters," *Folklore* 107 (1996): 5, rightly argues that the subject is so large and vast that no book or article alone could capture it all. She identifies and summarizes some of the recent academic literature primarily as it applied to Europe. The most notorious text related to witchcraft is the *Malleus Maleficarum* (1486–87). It describes the purported evil acts of witches, outlines inquisitorial techniques, and prescribes punishments. A modern English annotated edition is *The Hammer of Witches*, trans. and ed. Christopher S. MacKay (Cambridge: Cambridge University Press, 2009).

5. Simpson, "Witches and Witchbusters," 5. Marta María Gutiérrez Rodríguez provides two definitions. She says originally a witch was someone "who possesses a supernatural, occult, or mysterious power to cause misfortune or injury to others." But this changed in the sixteenth century. Then a witch was "a person who exercises maleficent magical power by virtue of having made a pact with the Devil." "Witches and Literary Justice: The Salem Witchcraft Trials in Nineteenth-Century Historical Fiction," *GRAAT* 14 (June 2013) http://www.graat.fr/2gutierrez.pdf (accessed July 2013), 35.

6. Robin Cook, *Acceptable Risk* (New York: Berkeley, 1996), 27.

7. *Practical Magic*, DVD, directed by Griffin Dunne (1998; Burbank, CA: Warner Home Video, 2009). The film is based on the novel *Practical Magic* (1995) by Alice Hoffman.

8. *The Craft*, DVD, directed by Andrew Fleming (1996; Culver City, CA: Columbia Pictures, 2000).

9. *Wicked*, by Winnie Holzman, directed by Joe Mantello, Oriental Theatre, Chicago, May 18, 2006.

10. Dorothy's house crushes the Wicked Witch of the East. Glinda, the Good Witch, dresses in white and is beautiful with blond hair. The Wicked Witch of the West has green skin and dresses in black; she is another evil witch. Dorothy douses her with water, causing her to melt and die. Even in the movies water works on witches. *The Wizard of Oz*, DVD, directed by Victor Fleming (1939; Burbank, CA: Warner Home Videos, 1999).

11. Carol F. Karlsen, *The Devil in the Shape of a Woman: Witchcraft in Colonial New England* (New York: W. W. Norton, 1987), 40 and 51. She documents that of the 185 accused people identifiable by name, 76 percent were female. About half of the accused men were related to the accused females. Eighty-eight percent of those tried were female, and of the 19 executed, nearly 74 percent were female.

12. Karlsen, *The Devil in the Shape of a Woman*, 41.

13. Francis Hill, *The Salem Witch Trials Reader* (New York: Da Capo Press, 2000), xv.

14. Karlsen, *The Devil in the Shape of a Woman*, 40. Nearly 75 percent of the primary non-possessed (that is, individuals who did not have convulsions or other purported signs of possession) and accusers were men.

15. Francis Hill, *A Delusion of Satan: The Full Story of the Salem Witch Trials* (New York: De Capo Press, 2002), 1.

16. Hill, *A Delusion*, 96.

17. Karlsen, *The Devil in the Shape of a Woman*, 50–60.

18. Simpson, "Witches and Witchbusters," 5.

19. Dorothy Z. Baker, *American Gothic Fiction: The Legacy of Magnalia Christi Americana* (Columbus: Ohio State University Press, 2007), 8.

20. Baker, *American Gothic Fiction*, 5.

21. Writing of the Puritans in "The Picture in the House," Lovecraft said they "cowered in an appalling slavery to the dismal phantasms of their own minds. Divorced from the enlightenment of civilization, the strength of these Puritans turned into singular channels; and in their isolation, morbid self-repression, and struggle for life with relentless Nature, there came to them dark furtive traits from the prehistoric depths of their cold Northern heritage." *The Dunwich Horror and Others*, ed. S. T. Joshi (Sauk City, WI: Arkham House, 1984), 117.

22. Richard Weisman, *Witchcraft, Magic, and Religion in 17th-Century Massachusetts* (Amherst: University of Massachusetts Press, 1984), 133. Mather did appear at the court, at least once, according to Weisman (243).

23. Benjamin C. Ray, "Satan's War against the Covenant in Salem Village, 1692," *New England Quarterly* 80, no. 1 (March 2007): 94.

24. Cotton Mather, *On Witchcraft* (Mineola, NY: Dover, 2005), 14. Hereafter cited in the text.

25. Nathaniel Hawthorne, "Alice Doane's Appeal," in *Hawthorne's Short Stories* (New York: Vintage Classics, 2011), 411. Hereafter cited in the text.

26. Hawthorne, "Young Goodman Brown," in *Hawthorne's Short Stories*, 201. Hereafter cited in the text.

27. Hawthorne, *The House of the Seven Gables* (New York: W. W. Norton, 2006), 7.

28. Hawthorne, *The House of the Seven Gables*, 7.

29. Charles L. Crow, *American Gothic* (Cardiff: University of Wales, 2009), 48.

30. Hawthorne, *The Scarlet Letter* (New York: Penguin, 2003), 161.

31. Hawthorne, *The Scarlet Letter*, 103.

32. Gutiérrez Rodríguez, "Witches and Literary Justice."

33. G. Harrison Orians, "New England Witchcraft in Fiction," *American Literature* 2, no. 1 (March 1930): 54–71.

34. Orians, "New England Witchcraft in Fiction," 55.

35. Donald A. Ringe, *American Gothic* (Lexington: University Press of Kentucky, 1982), 119.

36. John Neal, *Rachel Dyer* (Amherst, NY: Prometheus, 1996), 262.

37. Edgar Allan Poe, "The Black Cat," in *Tales and Sketches*, vol. 2, 2.852. Hereafter cited in the text.

38. Joyce Carol Oates, introduction to *American Gothic Tales*, ed. Joyce Carol Oates (New York: Plume, 1996), 4.

39. Lesley Ginsberg, "Slavery and the Gothic Horror of Poe's 'The Black Cat,'" in *American Gothic: New Interventions in a National Narrative*, ed. Robert K. Martin and Eric Savoy (Iowa City: University of Iowa Press, 1998), 99–128.

40. John W. De Forest, *Witching Times* (New Haven, CT: College & University Press, 1967), 174.

41. Neal, *Witching Times*, 176.

42. Orians, "New England Witchcraft in Fiction," 68.

43. Laura Kranzler, introduction to Elizabeth Gaskell, *Gothic Tales*, ed. Laura Kranzler (New York: Penguin, 2000).

44. Kranzler, introduction, xxvi.

45. Kranzler, introduction, xxviii.

46. Gaskell, "Lois the Witch," in *Gothic Tales*, 166.

47. Gaskell, "Lois the Witch," 223.

48. Esther Forbes, *A Mirror for Witches* (Chicago: Academy Chicago, 1985), 197.

49. Edith Wharton, "Bewitched," in *The Ghost Stories of Edith Wharton* (New York: Scribner's, 1973), 151. Hereafter cited in the text.

50. Orians, "New England Witchcraft in Fiction," 70.

51. S. T. Joshi, *The Evolution of the Weird Tale* (New York: Hippocampus Press, 2004), 131.

52. H. P. Lovecraft, "The Dreams in the Witch House," in *At the Mountains of Madness and Other Novels*, ed. S. T. Joshi (Sauk City, WI: Arkham House, 1985), 263. Hereafter cited in the text.

53. Fritz Leiber, "Through Hyperspace with Brown Jenkin," in *The Second Book of Fritz Leiber* (New York: DAW, 1975), 190.

54. Fritz Leiber, "The Automatic Pistol," in *Night's Black Agents* (New York: Berkeley, 1978), 133.

55. Michael E Stamm, "Poetry of Darkness: The Horror Fiction of Fritz Leiber," in *Discovering Modern Horror Fiction II*, ed. Darrell Schweitzer (Mercer Island, WA: Starmont House, 1988), 19.

56. Leiber, "The Automatic Pistol," 134.

57. Leiber, *Conjure Wife* (New York: Orb, 1991), 212. Hereafter cited in the text.

58. S. T. Joshi, "Science and Superstition: Fritz Leiber's Modernization of Gothic," in *Fritz Leiber: Critical Essays*, ed. Benjamin Szumskyj (Jefferson, NC: McFarland, 2008), 126.

59. Ludwig Wittgenstein says: "The procedure of induction consists in accepting as true the simplest law that can be reconciled with our experiences." *Tractatus Logico-Philosophicus* (London: Routledge Classics, 2001), 84. Moreover, "Occam's razor is, of course, not an arbitrary rule. . . . It simply says that unnecessary elements in a symbolism mean nothing" (57).

60. Gerald W. Page, "Fritz Leiber, *Conjure Wife*," in *Horror: 100 Best Books*, ed. Stephen Jones and Kim Newman (New York: Carroll & Graf, 1998), 104.

61. Stefan Dziemianowicz, "Contemporary Horror Fiction, 1950–1998," in *Fantasy and Horror*, ed. Neil Barron (Lanham, MD: Scarecrow Press, 1999), 203.

62. *The Blair Witch Project*, DVD, directed by Daniel Myrick and Eduardo Sànchez (1999; Montreal, QC: Alliance Films, 2007).

63. Karl Edward Wagner, "Sticks," in *Where the Summer Ends*, ed. Stephen Jones (Lakewood, CO: Centipede Press, 2012), 59.

64. Judith Wilt, *Ghosts of the Gothic: Austen, Eliot, and Lawrence* (Princeton, NJ: Princeton University Press, 1980), 276.

65. Roger Ebert, *Roger Ebert's Four-Star Reviews* (Kansas City, MO: Andrews McMeel, 2008), 86, lauded the film and writes that this scene reminded him of explorer Robert Scott's notebook entries as he froze to death in Antarctica.

66. This may be a nod to Washington Irving's "The Devil and Tom Walker" (1824), in *The Legend of Sleepy Hollow and Other Stories* (Mineola, NY: Dover, 2008). Tom's wife goes hunting for Satan in the New England woods near their home. She never returns. Searching for her, Tom finds his wife's apron, but there is "nothing but a heart and liver tied up in it" (166). Tom is really looking for his valuables. The film has other nods to the history of the witch. When Heather and Mike are deciding which direction to take, Mike does not want to go west, because there was a Wicked Witch of the West, so they go east, forgetting there was a Wicked Witch of the East.

67. John Updike, *The Witches of Eastwick* (New York: Knopf, 1984).

68. Nina Baym, "Review of *The Witches of Eastwick* by John Updike; *Sex and Destiny* by Germaine Greer," *Iowa Review* 14, no. 3 (Fall 1984): 166.

69. *The Witches of Eastwick*, directed by George Miller (1987; Burbank, CA: Warner Home Videos, 2006).

70. Ira Levin, *Rosemary's Baby* (New York: Random House, 1967), 236.

71. Levin, *Rosemary's Baby*, 245.

72. *Rosemary's Baby*, DVD, directed by Roman Polanski (1968; Hollywood, CA: Paramount Pictures, 2006).

73. Maryse Condé, *I, Tituba, Black Witch of Salem*, trans. Richard Philcox (Charlottesville: University of Virginia Press, 2009), 95.

74. Condé, *I, Tituba*, 101.

75. Bernard Rosenthal, "Tituba," *OAH Magazine of History* 17, no. 4 (July 2003): 50.

76. See Elaine G. Breslaw, *Tituba, Reluctant Witch of Salem: Devilish Indians and Puritan Fantasies* (New York: New York University Press, 1996), for a case that Tituba was a South American Indian.

77. Eric Savoy, "The Rise of the American Gothic," in *The Cambridge Companion to Gothic Fiction*, ed. Jerrold E. Hogle (Cambridge: Cambridge University Press, 2002), 167–68.

78. Lovecraft, *The Annotated Supernatural Horror in Literature*, 61.

Chapter Ten

The City of Darkness

Fritz Leiber and the Beginning of Modern Urban Horror

Fritz Leiber (1910–1992) created the modern urban Gothic. He reanimated supernatural fiction with such stories as "Smoke Ghost" (1941) and "The Hound" (1942), and the novel *Our Lady of Darkness* (1977). In Leiber's stories, the ghosts seem to arise from the urban environment itself. It is a dangerous space of grime and waste and soot, which seep into and foul the hearts and minds of people. In the early story "Smoke Ghost," Leiber portrays the anonymity and loneliness of the city inmate on a bus, riding alongside, but alienated from "wooden-faced people."[1] In the same story Leiber describes the face of a ghost as reflecting "the hungry anxiety of the unemployed, the neurotic restlessness of a person without purpose, the jerky tension of the high-pressure metropolitan worker, the sullen resentment of the striker, the callous viciousness of the strike breaker, the aggressive whine of the panhandler, the inhibited terror of the bomb victim" (109), as if unfolding the origin of his urban Gothic narratives. Leiber depicts the city's power sources as malevolent sentient things out to harm humans. In "The Black Gondolier" (1964), it is oil, while in "The Man Who Made Friends with Electricity" (1962), Mr. Leverett finds out the real danger of living near a high-tension electricity tower. Everyday technology works against his characters—for example, an elevator in "Horrible Imaginings" (1982), and trains and buses in "Belsen Express" (1975). Leiber is also a social critic through his urban fiction. It is a fiction that depicts urban spaces as violent and dense but yet lonely. A hectic anxiety plagues the inhabitants of cities, as in "The Girl with the Hungry Eyes" (1949) and "I'm Looking for Jeff" (1952). Leiber also unearths a deeper unease, a fear beyond the technological, a fear of an ultimate nothingness in such stories as "Black Glass" (1978) and "A Bit of the Dark World" (1962).

Fritz Leiber was born on December 24, 1910, in Chicago. His earliest days were nomadic, traveling with his actor parents. During his youth he lived mostly with relatives. He studied psychology and philosophy at the University of Chicago. During 1936–1937, Leiber corresponded with H. P. Lovecraft, but, as S. T. Joshi argues, Leiber did not imitate Lovecraft but rather learned from him the crafts of style, plotting, and narrative.[2] Joel Lane suggests Leiber realized from Lovecraft "that weird fiction could undermine the reader's sense of the order of things."[3] It is the disturbance of reality, or a reader's sense of an orderly reality, that informs Leiber's work. Lane claims that Leiber "changed what it meant to write supernatural horror stories in an urban context."[4]

Leiber was a man of many talents: he was an actor, a chess expert, and an author in different genres. He excelled in Gothic horror as well as in science fiction and heroic fantasy stories featuring Fafhrd and the Gray Mouser. He won multiple awards in the three fields and achieved lifetime recognition from the Horror Writers Association and the World Fantasy Convention. The Science Fiction Writers of America named him a grand master, and the Science Fiction and Fantasy Hall of Fame inducted him in 2001.

Here, Leiber's urban Gothic horror is the focus. Leiber writes about the grimness of urban life and the social and economic realities of city life: the isolation, the poverty, and the conformity. Underneath it all is an ontological terror—a deep and unexplainable dread. His work influenced the direction of modern Gothic horror, perhaps especially found in the modern master of the urban Gothic, Ramsey Campbell.

THE GOTHIC

David Punter states, "Gothic writing is a contested site."[5] There are many viewpoints. Here, three aspects of the Gothic, or ways of understanding or appreciating Gothic narrative, will be briefly outlined. First there are the topographies and archetypes of the Gothic. These are the scenes or settings of the Gothic, such as castles and dungeons, and the recurring themes, such as the double and the haunted house. The early Gothic was sensational and outlandish, and it portrayed cruelty, for example, in the works of Monk Lewis and Charles Maturin. The novels stressed the iron fist of the past, constriction in space, along with settings away from the everyday. The European Gothic can also be thought of as an expression of rebellion against the obscenities of perverse power. This is the second aspect of the Gothic: it illuminated the decadent social edifice for what it really was—violent in enforcing a rigid social and religious order.

Charles Brockden Brown developed the American Gothic as a counterpoint to the European. In his novels we find a dangerous American wilderness and the indigenous people transformed into Gothic monsters, although he still used such themes as the double and the haunted house. Edgar Allan Poe emphasized decadence and the psychology of often deranged or disoriented individuals in the short story form. He mined real dread and with a grand artistry of language expressed the horror of a dark despair. H. P. Lovecraft saw profound dread as the core of the Gothic. This is the third aspect of the Gothic. Judith Wilt also contends that dread is the core of the Gothic. "Dread is the father and mother of the Gothic."[6]

These three aspects of the Gothic continue to be echoed today, but there are differences. Now the Gothic is multiform, from aliens to zombies spreading terror in forests and in cities. A key topographic image is the city and the Gothic experience of ordinary folks in a mazelike, disordered, and chaotic city. In a distorted manner it gives a voice to the underclass, releasing taboos and speaking out on societal ills, dislocations, and disparities. At its best, the Gothic releases the repressed or the suppressed within society. Although not universally accepted, the Gothic as literature arose as a response to the experienced evil within society and within us. Modern Gothic horror is a literature jabbing a flashlight into the darkness; that is, it continues to articulate our experience of dread in the face of the unknown.

THE EVOLUTION OF URBAN GOTHIC

The American urban Gothic begins with Charles Brockden Brown's *Arthur Mervyn* (1799–1800). Yellow fever transforms Philadelphia into a city of chaos, near barbarity, and revulsion. Alan Lloyd-Smith concludes, "Brown invented the American urban Gothic."[7] But in that novel, it is not a mechanized city that is the source of horror; rather, the city is infested by yellow fever. Cities did harbor disease as their density and poor sanitation allowed diseases to spread. In "The Man of the Crowd" (1840), Edgar Allan Poe depicts the frenzy, chaos, and grime of London streets. This tale seems to speak about the loss of identity in the city and perhaps the rule of crime within a faceless crowd. George Lippard's *The Quaker City; or, The Monks of Monk Hall* (1845) is another early dark novel of the underside of a city, Philadelphia again.

In the English Gothic, Robert Mighall suggests G. W. M. Reynolds's *Mysteries of London* (1844–48) and the novels of Charles Dickens as starting the urban Gothic. Mighall argues that Dickens's London, made into a "fog-bound labyrinth, holding secrets at every turn,"[8] built the foundation for other urban Gothic works. Robert Louis Stevenson's novella *The Strange Case of Dr. Jekyll and Mr. Hyde* (1886) sites terror in the streets and houses of Victorian London. Arthur Machen in "The Great God Pan" (1890) paints London as a "city of nightmares."[9]

H. P. Lovecraft in "He" (1926) portrays New York City as "quite dead, its sprawling body imperfectly embalmed."[10] The narrator in that story seeks out the old city—the past—in his nightly haunts and finds it. Jeffrey Andrew Weinstock argues that American *noir* crime fiction and movies of the 1930s and 1940s were a significant impulse in urban Gothic.[11] James M. Cain and Cornell Woolrich set their fatalistic tales of crime in gritty, dark urban settings. The *noir* films adapted from these stories depict the city as dark, riddled with crime. The characters seem caught in a dreadful march toward doom. But these are generally focused on the horrid acts of people played out in a city.

Joshi says Leiber modernized the weird tale by "placing it in the frenetic urban milieu."[12] Chris Baldick characterizes the traditional Gothic as expressing a "fearful sense of inheritance in time with a claustrophobic sense of enclosure in space."[13] But that is the old Gothic. The modern Gothic goes beyond mere hauntings from the past and constricted spaces. Leiber writes tales of terror out of the modern, bustling, dirty, and dangerous city. A city that breeds new forms of horror, as in "The Hound," another early tale. In *Our Lady of Darkness*, a much later novel, San Francisco is a "great predatory beast of night."[14] In this novel, Leiber makes San Francisco a Gothic city. Stephen King says *Our Lady of Darkness* explores the "idea that when a city becomes complex enough, it may take on a tenebrous life of its own . . . an evil sentience."[15]

FRITZ LEIBER'S SENTIENT CITYSCAPES

In Fritz Leiber's fictional universe, the city is the font of horror. He uses many of the old Gothic archetypes, but transforms them. His characters are troubled by an overwhelming sense of loss and despair. The city is crowded, but individuals seem so alone. It is a grim world in a city that is sentient and malevolent. In Leiber's stories, the fates of the characters are driven by the cityscape; horror comes from the city. Leiber's urban Gothic is not about cities per se, but about the mechanized city of the twentieth century. Humans are aliens in their own built environment. Fred Botting writes of a "grotesque, irrational and menacing presence pervading the everyday, causing its decomposing."[16] Leiber's city is decaying, grotesque, and menacing. He exposes the underlying violence in our environment and the fundamental disconnect between our ideals and reality. He takes the traditional motifs of the Gothic and reinvents them in an urban setting. Sam Moskowitz concludes that Leiber is a pioneer in working "to modernize the ancient symbols of terror."[17]

In "Smoke Ghost," Mr. Wran, thinking about modern ghosts, says to Miss Millick, "I mean a ghost from the World today, with the soot of the factories in its face and the pounding of machinery in its soul" (104). This is an industrial-age ghost, dragged out of crumbling castles and dark forests into the streets of the city. And the ghost itself emerges first as "a shapeless black sack" (112), as if the trash of the city comes alive to menace people. The ghost in the story seems an amalgam of the debris on city rooftops, the grime on factory windows, the steel and concrete of city buildings, and the loneliness and fear of Wran. It is not something coming back from the dead, or a haunting presence from the past. The city is not merely a setting for an invasion of some otherworldly monster. In the story, the city ghost bears a resemblance to a gang leader who exhorts homage through supernatural brutality. At the end Wran pays homage to the sooty thing, "the brute" (123), as if it is a common city thug, not a thin wraith, but a goon with steel in its fists and a furnace behind its eyes.

Bruce Byfield sees "Smoke Ghost" as the beginning of Leiber honing his literary techniques for supernatural stories within an ordinary, everyday background, places that we all experience.[18] The human condition of the twentieth century is defined by the city. This story is praised for its new images and new take on horror as an experience within the modern city. Stefan Dziemianowicz calls "Smoke Ghost" a "groundbreaking urban horror story."[19] Michael E. Stamm says the story illustrates the modern city that can "take on or create certain non-human powers or forces."[20]

Another story where the city creates an unknown force is "The Hound" (1942). It is a thing that stalks David Lashley. The thing haunts his room, leaving a stench. He is beset by terror and seized by the "fear-ridden helplessness of childhood."[21] The thing seems like a wolf, as he tries to understand it with an old image. But at the end, as David is pulled to safety, a man says, "Hound? Wolf? . . . It was nothing like that. It was—" (199), as if he cannot describe the horror and live. In this story, it is the city itself that is the horror. It is a ravenous entity. The people in the city are its prey. It seems humans have constructed their own demise. That is part of Leiber's genius. Why is David Lashley the prey? Because he is weak, a sort of wuss, and an easy quarry? The city feeds on the weakest first. The thing pursuing Lashley is "part and parcel of the great sprawling cities and chaotic peoples of the Twentieth Century" (187). The city is portrayed as mechanically alive: a radiator "whined dismally," and from the railroad yards there came the "hoarse panting of a locomotive" (185). There are the "howls and growls of traffic and industry—sounds at once animal and mechanical" (187). Leiber takes the werewolf theme and transforms it into the city itself becoming a beast. The thing has eyes like "molten metal" and its jaws are "slavered with thick black oil" (187).

Even Lashley's girlfriend, Gertrude Rees, is changed by the city. She seems to transform into an oily, icy beast in his arms. There is no real beauty in the city; it is all a camouflage over the ugliness. Sounds and the stench grow stronger throughout the story, as if the beast is always drawing nearer. Lashley tries to reason through his experience, as happens often in Leiber's stories. But throwing open his window, he hears the howl of the city as if from "one cavernous throat" (194). Joshi contends that in "The Hound" the beast is a "symbol for the horrors of urbanism."[22] Yes, that and more, it is an amalgam of city horrors and the growing anxiety, despair, and fear of those living in the city into an image of supernatural force and destruction.

This story is set in wartime during the blitz. One can interpret the story as the reification of Lashley's fear of the bombings. The howl of the beast is really the warning siren. The "solid edge of darkness" (198) that knocks Lashley down is the blackout. It is the war that Lashley fears, and perhaps he is only a "sleep-walker" (195). The story is a tale of delirium in the midst of bombing. It is a masterwork by Leiber, who conjures supernatural horror from an ordinary cityscape. The hound seems to be evolving throughout the story, becoming more real as David's fears grow, as his insecurity in the shop and with his girlfriend grows. Perhaps his fears are creating the hound out of the debris of the city, out of the machines and noise and smells. It is David's way of making sense of the madness of the city and the horror of war.

Beware of an inheritance from an unknown relative who lives in the city. There you may lose your identity. In Leiber's "The Inheritance" (1942), the narrator is asked to give more than he will ever get back. There is a slow accumulation of details, as the nephew is slowly possessed by his uncle, David Rhode, a former lieutenant of police. The nephew inherits his uncle's room for a few months and his few possessions. He is on the skids, with only forty-seven cents in his pocket. So he moves in, despite the landlord's discolored eyes, as if the apartment building is the house of the dead. He is alone in the city and a sad case, a victim of economic decline. The nephew finds his uncle's uniform "lifelike in the shadows,"[23] his service revolver, and a box of old files and clippings, many on a serial killer.

In the big city, the nephew is lonesome and feels closest to his dead uncle, perhaps "inheriting his loneliness" (143). He feels the city unleashes forces to "make people lonely" (142), to separate them, to disconnect community, and to make them easier prey. He hears neighbors moving and talking, but he does not know them. The nephew experiences the city as full of "lonely unfriendly sounds" (143). Surrounding his dreary room, there is the city of "dingy buildings . . . great looming masses of warehouses and factories . . . the dismal expanse of track and cinders in the railroad yards . . . lightless alleys, and the nervous surge of traffic" (147). The only people the nephew imagines are "forms that . . . never walked upright, but slunk through the shadows close to the walls" (147). It is a grim city, a city itself that hungers for killings. It wants the nephew to continue its murders, as if it needs to be satiated by suffering and death.

Throughout the tale the nephew has twinges of fear, a sense of something wrong, a growing uneasiness. But he reasons it all away. He has a sequence of grotesque dreams, all bringing "a sick horror" (150). This sense of terror is focused on a slip of paper with an address, which seems to stare at him "like some sentence of doom, like some secret too terrible for a man to know" (150). His panic grows, and he feels someone or something trying to get him. In his last dream, he soars across the city to the address on the slip of paper. He confronts a figure crouching in the shadows as a little girl approaches. The figure is in a police uniform. As the nephew nears it, he sees the face, contorted into an animalistic snarl, but then realizes it is his face. This character is a hero of sorts, as he throws himself through "waves of darkness" (153) into the distorted face and finds himself in the body. This is a fine tale reinventing the Gothic archetype of the double and possession into a modern horror tale of serial killing in a city. In the city, even when a serial killer dies, his killings may continue.

The power sources of the city share in its sentience and malevolence. In "The Man Who Made Friends with Electricity," Mr. Leverett rents Peak House in Pacific Knolls from Mr. Scott, a real estate agent. It is near a high-voltage electricity transmission tower. The crackling wires speak with different voices: with a "frying sound," and a continuous "buzz."[24] Leverett likes the sounds, but not for long. Not when the tower becomes webbed with "dark muttering wires" (145). Leverett has a mounting sense of dread as the transmission tower gets inside his head.

The story is told through a sequence of conversations between Leverett and Scott. Leverett tells Scott of hearing the wires; he says electricity is a "live thing" (142). But electricity has it out for him because he knows its secrets. Leverett is worried it will call down its savage brother from the thunderclouds. Scott thinks it is all crazy. One night a thunderstorm rages in Pacific Knolls. The next day Leverett is found dead, entangled in phone and high-tension lines. This story is part of Leiber's mythology of malevolent cities as part of a sinister plot against humanity.

Oil is the terrible power in "The Black Gondolier." The narrator is a friend of Daloway, who lives in Venice, California. It is a desolate replica of the Italian city, a fake city, with canals and squares, but now decrepit with the concrete chunking off the arched bridges. The canal banks are lined with oil wells and oil pumps. The city is a grim image of the destructive force of our need for energy to power our cities.

Daloway is a loner, a drifter, and a mechanic of sorts, a person outside the march of progress and success. He keeps to his shabby trailer. The narrator visits Daloway in his trailer and listens to his tales while outside there are the "ceaseless, ponderous low throbs of oil wells." They are surrounded by the "stench of petroleum."[25] Oil is everywhere. It has its "dark agents" (16) and "black ghosts" (19) out in the world of humans. "Sentient, seeking, secretive oil" (18) has engineered modern technology, transportation, and cities to further its purpose. In part, the story is a caricature of corporate oil barons in cahoots with carmakers and service stations to stifle innovation and maintain oil as the only power source. It seems a takeoff on corporate espionage and ruthless business tactics to control markets.

In the story, oil lives and conspires to rule, to reach beyond the planet. All across the country "oil towers [are] thick as an army's spears" (14), as if oil is preparing for battle. Leiber provides a deep history of oil in the story, which adds to its surreal feel. Oil is derived from a fossil, as is coal. Barbara Freese in *Coal: A Human History* mentions that people once thought that coal was alive, like a plant, like oil in Leiber's story.[26]

The last pages of the story feature a ferocious storm as in "The Man Who Made Friends with Electricity." Perhaps the savage brother of electricity comes with the "fist of the rain and the lightning's shining spear" (29) (akin to oil's spears) to smite Venice. It ends up as "a battered city of the dead" (30), as if Leiber is predicting the future of cities. The narrator goes to check on Daloway. At the end there are only oily footprints (perhaps similar to those foreboding ones in Algernon Blackwood's "The Wendigo," 1910) from the trailer to a spot where a thin boat had been dragged back into the canal. The canal surges with oil, dark and foreboding. Yet the real menace in the story is the "utter black inhumanity" (10) that pervades it. Oil is a symbol for self-destructive human avarice. The story projects an all-pervading sense of death and dread. The black gondolier on a black gondola, gleaming black as if coated with black oil, is a modern figure of the grim reaper.

Even small towns are dangerous, as in *The Dealings of Daniel Kesserich: A Study of the Mass Insanity at Smithville*. The novella was published in 1997 but was written in the 1930s, and there are faint echoes of Lovecraft in it. The story is presented in a near-documentary style with George Kramer as commentator. What happened at Smithville was "inexplicable in terms of mankind's present knowledge,"[27] according to Kramer. He writes to "bring order into a black chaos of events in the real world and a threatening chaos of hypotheses in my own mind" (9). Set in a small town, it is a tale of time shifts and mystery. The town itself may be the source of hysteria, as Kramer thinks, "to my jangled nerves, it seemed that Smithville, in a gesture of menace, drew back from me, crouching in the darkness" (64).

Kramer travels to Smithville to hook up with old college chums, Kesserich, an amateur scientist, and John Ellis, a physician. But there is sadness and anxiety in the town as Ellis's wife Mary has eaten a poisoned orange and died; this story may be a twisted fairy tale. Kramer cannot seem to find either Kesserich or Ellis. At Kesserich's house, Kramer notices fragments of red sandstone appearing out of thin air. They form a trail that ends at an orange grove. Later Kesserich's house blows up and Kramer finds a notebook in the ruins, which is included in the novella as an authenticating document. There are signs of a disturbance at Mary's grave. The townsfolk react with a spreading hysteria. They dig up the grave and Mary's body is gone. The guilty ones must be Kesserich and Ellis.

Kramer finds Ellis at his home, where Ellis gives the backstory. He outlines Kesserich's notion that all time is real at the same time. Kesserich has invented some mechanism that allows him to shift between times. However, Ellis's story is interrupted. Police and townsfolk, virtually carrying pitchforks, besiege Ellis's house. It seems very much like the attack on Dr. Frankenstein's castle. Ellis is accused of robbing the grave. He escapes the mob in his touring car. Did Kramer see someone else in the car, a woman? This is a Frankenstein story of reanimation. Smithville is every town and the tale owes a little to the deep mystery surrounding us in the universe that Lovecraft evokes so well. You can sense that the source of the Gothic for Leiber is moving to the built environment along with a merging of horror with science fiction in this early story.

THE DANGEROUS ALLURE OF TECHNOLOGY

In "Smoke Ghost," Wran says, "It's a rotten world. . . . It's time the ghosts . . . took over and began a rule of fear" (111). That is what happens in Leiber's urban Gothic. The city rules through a pathological paranoia engineered by its manufactured spaces, its industrial violence, and its unnatural crowds. It is the mechanization of our space. His characters are reacting to living in spaces designed seemingly for machines rather than humans. Leiber's core theme is the impact of the mechanized city on its inhabitants. The city is dangerous in part due to the technology that supports and maintains it.

In "Horrible Imaginings" (1982), one's dreams and fantasies go sour in the city while aging in an old apartment building that hides a thirteenth floor. This is a story of a lonely old man who seems trapped in the endless hallways, the stairwells, and the odd elevator of an old apartment building. The elevator is the technology here that seems a source of allure and fear. In addition, Leiber takes an old superstition about the number thirteen and gives it life in this story. The building is a microcosm of the larger city outside its walls, where people are afraid of one another, or ignore one another, or attack one another. The building may be a projection of the old man's decaying mind. Ramsey Ryker is a widower and is sadly alone. He hungers for sex and suffers from inexplicable dreams of being sexually attacked by little men, smoking cigars. The reek of cigars is a signal of impending terror.

Ryker wanders mournfully through the hallways of the strange apartment building. During his wanderings, he catches sight of a young woman, who is there, then not there. They engage in a sort of tango of brief glimpses and failed encounters, until at last Ryker and the dark lady are in the slow-moving elevator that alights at the non-existent thirteenth floor. He is in ecstasy; the woman is naked under her coat. His fantasy of kissing and fondling her comes true. But every dream is really a nightmare. Into the elevator swarm a hoard of miniature men, smoking cigars, as if a new form of Machen's Little People. They seem the cronies of the apartment demigod. They drag Ryker away, and the young woman takes the cocaine and dreams again her dreamy little dreams to escape the awful city. There is much in this story of frustrated sex, the sinister charm of drugs, and the hidden things in old apartment buildings clearly more odious than an old castle. One wonders if Ryker's longing for the young woman is a longing for death, of release from life, and his sexual nightmares are an expression of despair and dread.

The city seems a hard place for all, but perhaps mostly for the elderly.

"The Button Molder" (1979) takes place in San Francisco. An older man has recently moved to a four-room apartment with easy access to the roof so he can gaze at the stars. Astronomy is an essential escape from the "age of mechanized hive-dwelling and . . . conformist artificial media,"[28] as if every-one has already been recycled in the melting ladle and lost their authentic identity. The protagonist is trying to resist the allure of technology and be himself, alone. Leiber's story title comes from Henrik Ibsen's *Peer Gynt* (1867). The Button-Moulder is a chilling figure in the play. He is after Peer Gynt's soul to merge it with the mass of souls in his ladle, where Gynt will lose his sense of self.

This story makes the familiar world distressingly unknown territory, as is the world experienced by Peer Gynt. It is narrated as if a friend is relating a strange story to the reader with asides and nearly whispered secrets. The man lives alone and likes it. He is a writer and wants to be separate from the "swarming people" (244), as if city dwellers are just drones. In his new apartment, the man is disturbed at first by "the swinish grunting and chomp-ing of the huge garbage trucks that came rooting," like "mechanical giant hogs" (245). Perhaps they are collectors of human identities. He is trying to write his philosophy of life but succumbs to writer's block, which also in-fects his fiction writing. The narrator has a sequence of odd experiences on the roof. But he conjures up an explanation for all but one, the violet light. Moreover, in his apartment, a thin dark figure seems to flit across his line of sight as he enters, but it can be explained. He wonders what would happen if reason failed. What you see or hear or feel can be reasoned away, he thinks. Except perhaps what he sees at the end of the story. Is it an alien thing that visits him? Or is it all an illusion? Is it a product of loneliness and fantasy, his writing taking real form in the world to frighten him? In the closing para-graphs, he is on the roof and spies a violet light that persists. He is unable to explain the apparition. Back in his apartment something—apparently a woman—is approaching. He sees the unknown and struggles to describe it, noting its color, size, and features. Seemingly he does this to distance the terror, as if in describing it he can overcome his fear. It is science for him. He is frozen in awe at this thing that is utterly alien to him and his world. She moves closer, her dark hair rising as a web and her arms encircling, but he also leans closer, the better to observe her "violet eye-points . . . [and] lead-colored skin" (274). Improbably she moves away, as if she has what she wanted from him or has given him what he needed—maybe she is his muse. Then the spell cracks and he is alone. He questions the reader at the end to solve the mystery for him, as we as readers have taken part in his adventure.

Death is at the core of "Belsen Express." Here the city is transformed into a Nazi death camp for a Mr. George Simister. Modern trains and buses become vehicles for the Gothic in the story. Simister's horrible imaginings are going to come true in the city. He is a racist, complaining about Slavs and Jews, but with a morbid fear of the Gestapo stretching back to before World War II. He feels they have an "evil tyranny over his imagination," and they could reach across "the dark Atlantic"[29] and through time to snare him. Every morning, he takes the commuter rail to his office with a colleague, Holstrom. One day, jostled by the crowd, Simister is driven, like an animal, toward a wrong exit. The guard there appears to be Aryan, blond with cold blue eyes. The panic grows. Rushing aboard his train a later morning, it seems crazy, but he thinks the destination sign reads Belsen. Exiting, he is herded onto a bus, where the riders are "all jammed together like cattle" (114). It leaves an odor of "obnoxious exhaust fumes" (114). In the last scene in the story, Simister is in his office, where he seems jolly, but suddenly he screams, grabs his chest, and falls dead. One doctor says it is a heart attack, another, carbon monoxide poisoning. It is paranoia coming true in the city.

The city also harbors dangerous mechanical artifacts in hidden-away places or shops that appear out of nowhere. "Midnight by the Morphy Watch" (1974) centers around one of Leiber's keen interests, chess. Stirf Ritter-Rebil, a writer and chess player, discovers and buys a marvelous watch, given supposedly to Paul Morphy on May 25, 1859, by his adoring fans. Does the watch contain Morphy's spirit or at least his chess genius, which seemingly had been passed down through Alekhine, Steinitz, and Nimzovich? Stirf becomes adept at chess, bettering others he could not before. In his head there is a glowing chessboard as a guide, as if Morphy's hand suggests the right piece to move. Stirf ends up dogged by four shadows, the four dead chess champions. The watch not only brings chess genius but also delirium, or death, or disappearance. In the city anything can be found, and it is likely to be dangerous. Inanimate things take on life in the city. Especially for a loner like Morphy, ensconced "in solitude . . . in the same room"[30] for twenty-five years in New Orleans. This story is set in the city environs as if it is a museum of the dead.

THE SOCIOLOGY OF THE GOTHIC

Leiber's stories are set within an urban maze of political, social, and sexual traumas of the middle and later twentieth century. Joshi argues that Leiber updated the Gothic to speak to societal issues, one being hurried urbanization and its effects on people.[31] Leiber's characters are struggling to understand themselves, their fears and cravings. But their environment seems to be conspiring against their happiness and their lives. The city in Leiber's fictional world is a place of the "isolation of the individual in society where all communal systems of value have collapsed,"[32] as Leslie Fiedler writes.

Moreover, his stories seem responsive to the current events of his time, such as World War II, the atomic bomb, the Holocaust, militarism in the United States, and the Cold War. The stories are fashioned in part from the twentieth century: "the frustrated, frightened century . . . the jangled century of hate and heavy industry and total wars" (112), as Catesby Wran thinks in "Smoke Ghost." Albert Camus expresses it this way: "the blood-stained face history has taken on."[33] Ours is a world of mass killings, genocide, and organized terror.

A double murder is told in "I'm Looking for Jeff" (1952). Martin Bellows, a drinker, is in for a harrowing night on the town. It is a town of bars. He starts off in the TomTom bar, where a barkeep, Pops, talks about a beautiful young woman who keeps asking for Jeff. Her name is Bobby. Pops's son Sol has never seen the woman. He thinks his dad is off his rocker. Martin barely listens to Pops's tale but likes the woman's description. He is a loner, and the empty stools along the bar seem to reflect the empty lives of city dwellers. Is it only drinking that conjures up the joyous noise and light? Otherwise all is "dark corners" and "noiseless gloom."[34] Bobby is an apparition for Pops. She does not reveal herself to all, only to the select, those from whom she wants something, like Martin Bellows. She trails after him. Martin and Bobby go bar hopping, falling deeper into drink. She is a beauty with a fine spider line scar across her face. They fall through the descending steps of drink and end up back at the TomTom. Now she seems "no longer a thing of smoke but strong with the night and night's secret powers" (146). Martin catches the "cool flame of savagery" (147) that burns in the city. And then there is Jeff next to Martin, and Bobby claims Martin's promise to do whatever she asks. So Martin breaks a beer bottle and shoves it into Jeff's face. Bobby and Martin flee to her house, where he "followed her into darkness" (149). It is the darkness of death and decomposition, as if the city is composed of the dead. Bobby, an avenging ghost, comes back for Jeff, who had killed her, beaten her to death with a beer bottle. Martin is her tool. Even the dead are incited to violence in the modern city.

Martin Bellows was searching for love. But in a city of loners, love is dangerous. Leiber explores this idea further in "Dark Wings" (1976). The young women, Rose and Vi (Violet), have just discovered they are twins. It is a story suffused with Carl Jung. It is a strange, distorted erotic tale, focused on the terror of Rose about men, or the fear of the Animus, her male half buried in her unconscious. It turns out to be Vi. And the raven at the window and the attacker on the bed seem to be symbols of the Shadow, that dark thing representing all that is beyond consciousness. Perhaps it is also a nod to Edgar Allan Poe.

The twins enjoy drinking and talking. They touch and laugh. As the evening lengthens they reveal themselves to each other as if they are one. Vi tells of being raped by her foster father. Rose is horrified. But in the end, as seems to be true in all Leiber's stories of the city, there is only terror to be found in an apartment. There is no real love here, but bondage and rape. There is no real caring in the modern city, just deception and terror and pain to enliven sex. A "brimstone stench" is the perfume of love and "devouring kisses" the touch of love in an apartment soundproofed to keep in the screams. But, as Groener remarks in "Scream Wolf" (1960), "people in a big city never seem to bother about a scream next door."[35]

Pinioned and raped on the bed, Rose sees Vi as a great raven and the night as "great dark wings beating rhythmically,"[36] as if the shadow had arisen from the unknowable. The story ends with "There, there; there, there; there, *there!*"[37] Perhaps at first the soft sounds of a cooing mother, the soft voice of a love, but then they become the booming force of sadomasochistic sex, like a hammer. There are many questions about this tale. Is this all a hysterical fantasy of Rose, who is trying to be a writer? Has her imagination taken flight and is she really alone in the apartment that becomes a refuge for a bird of the night? Or is it a ruse by, not Vi, but Vic, who has tricked Rose into letting him into her apartment, her great fear now realized? Leiber's tales of the city sometimes are like mazes where readers get lost, as if he is re-creating the city in his texts.

Not all the inhabitants of the city are human. "The Girl with the Hungry Eyes" is an advertiser's dream, a beauty who allures all. But it is a nightmare. The "Girl" turns out to be "the quintessence of the horror behind the bright billboard."[38] She sucks the dreams and life out of people. Advertising drains away choice and life; it "gets everybody's mind set in the same direction" (236). It happens through her eyes, deep with a hunger "that's all sex and something more than sex" (230). This is marketing capturing the hearts and spirits of people. One reading of the story is that it tells of a supernatural takeover of the prime technology of marketing: photography. It is usurped by a vampire-like being to feed her needs. She needs the emotions and experiences of others. She feeds off their fears and loves; she sucks away their lives.

Marshall McLuhan, the Canadian media guru, extols the story. He says the girl's eyes, "abstracted from her body," become "a metaphysical enticement, a cerebral itch, an abstract torment."[39] McLuhan says Leiber shows "an intuitive grasp of mysterious links between sex, technology and death."[40] John Langan interprets the story through the standpoint of Freud's *Beyond the Pleasure Principle* (1920), linking the longing for sex with a death wish.[41] Indeed, the "Girl" sees deep into men's hunger, sees "the hatred and the wish for death behind the lust" (236). She is a commodified beauty with the magical allure of sex and death. Langan argues that the "Girl" is the thing that links sex, death, and greed.

She drives all to spend and spend, caught in the sexual mystery of her eyes, willingly spinning in a death spiral. She knows that hunger and feeds off it. Her hunger for the experiences of people is also the agency of advertising in emptying people of their individualism; it is all done through our love and fear of sex, death, and technology. For Leiber, advertising seems the dead heart of consumerism. No stake will kill this thing. Leiber wonderfully transforms the vampire archetype in this tale. The "Girl" is inescapable and so sexually alluring through technology that death becomes alluring. She is an embodiment of the city as a ravenous, killing beauty.

Leiber explores the spirit of violence in the United States in "Coming Attraction" (1950) and "America the Beautiful" (1970), where an Englishman visits the United States of the future. Both of these stories blend science fiction and horror, and are dystopian views of the future.

"Coming Attraction" depicts a vicious sexual brutality. A nuked New York City is the stage for sex and violence. Women are abused and men take pleasure in causing them pain. The city is ruined and the leftovers of radioactivity seem to eat away any morality. The women wear masks. It is a symbol of helplessness and disfigurement. Masks in that future keep women under control. The cops are males. It is a world of male weaknesses being used to beat up on women, who are physically and psychologically scarred and scared. New York City is portrayed as a ruin with its Inferno and Heaven districts. It is a nuclear-created hell with the Empire State Building a mangled stump. The Englishman travels through a city of bomb-scarred beggars, or fakers, babies with "webbed fingers and toes," religious fanatics singing anti-sex songs, and walls of billboards hawking wrestling instruction and "predigested foods."[42] These are the attractions of a new world after an apocalypse. The city continues, damaged, but still a hulking beast transforming its inhabitants into grotesque beings attacking each other.

An English poet visits Texas in "America the Beautiful" (1970) to deliver a set of lectures. The story is set in a future of endless, brutal wars across the world. He stays with a genteel American family, the Grissims. It is a nice family, but haunted by shadows. The "shadows are everywhere in America," even in the "Grissims' serene and lovely home."[43] It seems these shadows are all the dead from the long history of violence in America. In the story it seems that the American spirit needs continuing jolts of violence, like shock therapy, to live contentedly. The country is, however, utopian after a fashion, with clean energy, and clean air and water, and refined buildings and electric cars. There is bounty everywhere. But it is a utopia with darkness at its core. And most utopian of all, Americans are now all moderates.

However, utopias seem false, and this one is no different. The life of the Grissims is described as idyllic in their house and grounds; everything seems so nice and relaxed. But there is darkness in the house. The shadows seem darkest around Emily Grissim. When the Englishman and Emily are about to make love, she wants to show a live battle in Bolivia on the view window. The story seems to be saying that violence and war and death are part of the American spirit. Leiber evokes a great golden apple with a "great scaly black dragon"[44] as his metaphor for America. It is similar to Ursula K. Le Guin's parable "The Ones Who Walk Away from Omelas" (1973). Omelas is a utopian city of sorts, but it exists because a child is kept locked away in everlasting, conscious misery, filth, and terror.[45] It is an obscenity. Some people leave the glorious city. In Leiber's story, the Englishman leaves that future image of America.

THE DARKNESS OF THE CITY

The city is the center of the modern dark chaos. The "fearful recognition" of the nearness of chaos and the latent horror in this recognition is a basis of the "urban Gothic mode,"[46] according to Robert Mighall. Leiber's characters experience this dark underside of urban life. City dwellers are trapped in a city that seems infected and infecting. Leiber depicts this infection in many stories as a sort of spreading blackness, sometimes all-consuming as in "Black Glass" (1978). Leslie Fiedler contends that the Gothic "is committed to portraying the power of darkness."[47] It is a "metaphysical anxiety" of an "ultimate nothingness,"[48] according to Mario Praz.

The pivotal scene of Leiber's "Black Glass" takes place on the observation deck of the South Tower of the former World Trade Center in New York City. This is a foreboding locale and now one of anguish.[49] The city is clogged with "grime, the smog, the general filth and pollution," and there is "crime in the growling, snarling streets."[50] The city blocks display sex shops emphasizing torture, stores brandishing knives, seedy smoke shops, and junk food restaurants. It is a city hawking sickness; a city with "violence seething just below the surface"; a city where the skyscrapers are alive as they "had reason to foresee doom and robe themselves in black" (106). They seem modern idols or monuments to dread. In the story, crowds seem to trap "solitary movers" (119) into their anonymous and relentless movement. The narrator is an older man. He spies an enchanting young woman in green whom he follows, and loses, and finds again as if their fates are mated. The city grows darker, like "an inky infection" (108). In "The Hound" the city is "ripe for infection" (191). This infection is akin to that evil Hannah Arendt says is like a fungus or an infection, which may work according to some unknown law of nature.[51] The darkness grows throughout the story.

The man follows the young woman's clues to the World Trade Center. The elevator to the deck may be a time machine, or it distorts reality. It is dark inside—a darkness almost palpable. When he exits there is a stench like coal and "an insect wailing wind" (122). It is symbolic of the long-term effects of burning coal and the triumph of insects in the end. On the roof the sky has a "furnace glow" (124), as if the sky itself is consumed. The view of the city is one of desolation, a great ecological disaster. The dark ocean has risen halfway up the Empire State Building. The fungus is now everywhere. Has the narrator been transported to the "age the darkness has almost buried New York" (129)? Or is it all a dream as he is brought back to consciousness on the roof by other observers? There are questions at the end: was it real or hallucinatory for the protagonist? Ramsey Campbell calls "Black Glass" one of Leiber's "most evocative transformations of an urban landscape into a vista of fantastic menace."[52]

The city seems to be taking this menace out into the high desert in "A Bit of the Dark World" (1962). There are three main characters: Viki Quinn, Franz Kinzman, and Glenn Seabury, the narrator. A Mr. M. drives the car early in the story but is not at Rim House, the center of the tale. The characters are trying to leave the city behind, but "it's hard to get out of the city even in the wilderness."[53] They have now internalized the horror of the city. Or is the city spreading its evil influence out into the wilderness?

On the drive, they talk of supernatural tales, and Mr. M. is reminded of the real horrors of the twentieth century. But Glenn means supernatural horror and, as if quoting Lovecraft, says: "Hauntings, the suspension of scientific law, the intrusion of the utterly alien, the sense of something listening at the rim of the cosmos or scratching faintly at the other side of the sky" (245). The rim in the story is Kinzman's Rim House perched on a mountain ledge. There is an undertow of combat between reason and fear, or rather reason and the unknown, in the story.

At Rim House, a sort of outpost in the unknown, all Glenn's senses intimate strangeness. There is a "nasty smell of burnt linen" and an "odd bitter taste." He feels touched by "threads, cobwebs" and hears "an occasional whistling . . . a soft rumbling . . . [and] the hissing rattle of fine gravel." He sees the "upper rim of the sun peering back down" (254). It seems they have all ventured far into the supernatural zone.

There is that pervasive blackness. What they saw back on a mountain peak, during the drive, was "a black shape—black with the queer churning blackness" (258). They talk about the fear of black, of the fear of night, of the black between the stars. Viki speaks of the fear of "inky black cracks appearing in things" (259), as if the world is easily broken. Kinzman says it is the "breaking-up we feel in the modern world" or "the fragmentation of knowledge" (260). As a reader, you feel they are nearing the horror that society works to keep at bay. This is ultimate dread that cannot be escaped. A presence looms over and around Rim House. In a terrifying transformation, the characters' lamps give off darkness, not light. Outside the house they are in "a dead inkier blackness—*blacker than black*" (273) spreading a chill of death. Their car's headlights sweep out bands of a deep dark. This is very like Herman Melville's comment on Nathaniel Hawthorne that part of his soul was "shrouded in a blackness, ten times black."[54] And in Edgar Allan Poe's "The Pit and the Pendulum" the unnamed narrator trembles in the pit as "the tall candles sank into nothingness; their flames went out utterly; the blackness of darkness supervened."[55] This is the all-consuming, cosmic horror beyond our ken. This horror is located mostly in the city for Leiber, but also out there, where the city has ranged.

The darkness is everywhere in *Our Lady of Darkness*. From Corona Heights, Franz Westen's apartment window is "full of darkness" (106). In the city, his apartment "was as dangerous as—perhaps more dangerous than—Corona Heights" (109). Even the roofs of the city "were a whole dark alien world of their own, unsuspected by the myriad dwellers below" (42). The streets are dark. The buildings are ominously dark. And late in the novel, Westen in his room "saw only darkness" (207). The world is "blackly cancerous" (202) and now "the stars were infected" (202).

Our Lady of Darkness is about the city as alive, as a menacing being. It is a terrible myth of the modern city as a Gothic breeding ground. A city crammed with lonely people who fear the dark as it creeps ever nearer, who feel trapped in a maze of cement and steel. As Westen peers at Corona Heights through his binoculars, his peering draws forth the horror. Or did he see what had been hidden? This is similar to "A View from a Hill" (1925) by M. R. James, where Fanshawe borrows old, odd field glasses to view the English countryside. Without the binoculars the countryside is bucolic. A distant pleasant green hill is thick with wood on top. With the binoculars, there is a "gibbet and a man hanging on it."[56] Leiber mentions this story in the novel, a very self-conscious novel about the Gothic tradition. Roger B. Salomon argues that the binoculars are the lens of death; it is not just a matter of perspective, but "horror actually exists."[57] In Ramsey Campbell's story "The Other Side" (1986), Bowring lives in a flat on the better side of the river. He is a voyeur with binoculars, which he uses to spy into the sordid territory across the river as if into his own sordid obsessions.[58] In Leiber's novel the binoculars seem a way to see beyond the façades of steel and concrete, to see the paramentals. Throughout the novel there are brief glimpses of these things, as if they are too awful to describe. They are midway between "hepatitis viruses and incubi" (157), like a supernatural infection. The paramentals are one way Leiber reifies the city's sentience.

There are several mysteries in the book, which at times seems like a treasure map of clues and portents. Leiber creates an occult science elaborated by the character Thibaut De Castries, a mysterious person, perhaps a phony, but the systematizer of *Megapolisomancy: A New Science of Cities*— a pseudoscience. There are false books in the novel that provide a sense of history to the narrative. There is a journal of Clark Ashton Smith. There is the *Fifty Book, the Grand Cipher* of De Castries, found at the end but burned, like a witch, as if it were diabolical, but not before it is microfilmed for future scientific study. Real people join created characters in the streets of San Francisco, for example, George Sterling and Jack London.

The novel has its mysterious texts, but these are not ancient, worm-eaten manuscripts with spells and curses. Modern texts can be just as rare, just as evil, and just as powerful as ancient texts. *Megapolisomancy*, the pseudoscience of the city, is purported to be a way to manipulate big cities. De Castries carries out a series of field experiments but with unruly subjects, such as Jack London, who disturb his protocols. He is trying to observe, predict, and then control living things, cities. But cities are powerful, and the power of cities is long lived: "big buildings had been threatening to crush man ever since the first megacity" (167).

The novel is a bit of an autobiography. Franz Westen is somewhat like Fritz Leiber, later in his life. Both reside in a small room and are recovering alcoholics, each lost his wife, and each is a writer and chess player. Leiber deploys the Gothic double archetype to write himself into the novel. This contributes to the blurring and distorting of reality and fantasy, horror and awe, science and superstition in the novel. It is a modern novel and is a sort of web or maze. Westen eventually succumbs to superstition, as the sense of peril scratches ever closer to him. He scrawls five-pointed stars on his walls. One of his friends in the apartment building, the young woman Cal, saves him at the end by chanting a sort of formula calling on the gods of music and science and philosophy to exorcise the thing taking over his Scholar Mistress, which is attacking him. His Scholar Mistress is a shape he has made on his bed from Gothic books and magazines. The magazines and books come alive on the bed and attack him in a way similar to the ghost in M. R. James's "'Oh, Whistle, and I'll Come to You, My Lad'" (1904).

Our Lady of Darkness sums up Gothic horror. It is homage to the long tradition.[59] But it also takes horror into the soul of a city. In the novel, the city is not a fortress against the dark; rather, it is the dark. The sheer mass of the city is a tipping point for the animation of steel and concrete. And it is malevolent and bent on augmenting its power and strength. "Big cities . . . become . . . such perilous places" (35).

The novel is also about the conflict of reason and senses. Here "the human mind would cast doubt on itself in order to explain away unusual and unconventional things" (103). But "deny your mind, deny your sensations, and you deny reality" (106). Rationality at all costs is a form of denial. It is a way of avoiding the disorder or shift in order caused by the city itself, which is hostile to its inhabitants. In *Our Lady of Darkness*, Leiber creates a mythology and a pseudoscience of cities; he merges science and superstition.

FRITZ LEIBER'S LEGACY

Leiber set the stage and the standard for modern urban Gothic. He broke new ground for Gothic horror in cities. It is not just the same old themes played out. The touch of the supernatural is different in the city, and is so because it is the city itself that is the source of the Gothic. It is our built environment that is dangerous and threatening, and the source of the supernatural. The city is no protection against the dark forest of panic. As Franz Westen broods in *Our Lady of Darkness*, "We can't even trust the walls that guard us" (186). There is no time storm from the past havocking the city. If anything, the city threatens the future.

This radical break continues to affect the direction of Gothic horror, for example, in T. E. D. Klein's urban horror. Klein centers this often in New York City. "The Children of the Kingdom" (1980) paints a dark image of the city. Right off, there is a harrowing bus ride through one "shabby, nameless city"[60] after another. Strikingly, the narrator is horrified by his own neighborhood, at first unrecognized. In addition, Klein depicts Manhattan in a blackout that releases all the horrors. The dark raging streets and the sluglike things in the sewers seem to be a reification of all the fears of white New Yorkers.

The prime example of Leiber's heritage is found in the current master of the urban Gothic, Ramsey Campbell. He commends Leiber as "the father of the urban tale of supernatural terror, and one of the last century's great masters of the weird."[61] He says that Leiber wrote "stories in which the supernatural arose from the everyday setting."[62] Campbell notes Leiber's stories became his models, as he "wanted to achieve that sense of the supernatural terror which arises from the everyday urban landscape."[63] Many of Campbell's tales are set in a Gothic Liverpool.

Leiber illuminates the experience of modern sordid urban life told through the lens of the Gothic. The movie *Seven* (1995), directed by David Fincher, is in the urban horror mode started by Leiber. It is a brooding thriller about a grisly serial killer, played by Kevin Spacey, whose murders mirror the seven deadly sins. What is noteworthy about the film is its depiction of a grim, hellish city. The decaying city itself seems to incite rage and terror. The streets are always thick with swarms of angry people under perpetually dark, cloudy, rainy skies. There is palpable rawness to the city as though it is a beast itself.[64]

Leiber's stories are nested within the real world. For example, "Belsen Express" speaks to the horrors of the Nazis and the death trains and death camps. "The Black Ewe" (1950) plays off the fear of being spied on and government conspiracies. There is someone who knows more about you than you do. It also riffs off the fear that the government is hiding something from us. In "Horrible Imaginings," does the elderly Ryker get punished for his erotic thoughts? In "Coming Attraction," Leiber explores the fear of atomic war during the Cold War and the anxiety it caused and the violence it impelled. "I'm Looking for Jeff" articulates the loneliness and sexual hunger that sweeps through bars. And in "America the Beautiful" Leiber brilliantly portrays the violence underneath the veneer of polite civilization. That is the violence that the sentient skyscrapers and towers in his tales symbolize.

Although resonating with reality, Leiber builds a mythology of the city. In "Smoke Ghost" it is an old dark sack forgotten on a roof that becomes a kingpin of mental extortion. In "The Hound" the city spawns a mechanical/animalist thing to run down the weak. In "The Inheritance" the city takes progressive possession of uncle and then nephew to carry out a killing spree of the innocent. The neon ads and billboards and magazine and TV screens are all media for the city to control the wants, needs, and desires of people. Oil and electricity, the energy of cities, are sentient and hostile things with humans as mere pawns in their grand plans for galactic horror. In *Our Lady of Darkness*, Westen worries that there is "some universal disease or cosmic pollution . . . spiraling from Corona Heights to the whole cityscape and so up to the stars, infecting even Orion and the Shield" (185), as if the horror of the city longs to reach out of the planet. The city is "interfering with the rule of number and order in the universe" (185). Science is overthrown. And in the magnificent *Our Lady of Darkness*, he satirizes human hubris in trying to control the world. This is a humorous book but also deadly.

Eric Savoy suggests that the Gothic in America is "an innovative and experimental literature."[65] This description fits Leiber. In some of his later works, Leiber is a character in his own urban stories, as if he is working out the diabolical intent of the modern city with himself as a single-subject field experiment. He paints a grim darkness that will submerge us, as in "Black Glass." In that tale he captures our unease in big cities. Crowds seem to have evolved into another species. We are alone in a horde that moves of its own collective intent.

In Leiber's fictional world, there is an ongoing debate between reason and terror. There is a blurring of reality and fantasy in his stories. Leiber always portrays the city environment as alive and dangerous, and a space of darkness. The distortion of reality is a condition of modern life in the city.

Dreams are found throughout his short fiction, signaling the challenge of recognizing reality and fantasy. Yet his fiction is rooted in the realism of city life. But in this Gothic space, his characters experience a "destructive contact with some mysterious, terrible forces,"[66] arising from the city itself.

Leiber's characters often search for a rational explanation that fails. They have moved from the ordered world, or the hope of an ordered world, to a world of chaos and disorder. It makes no sense that the modern city is sentient; yet it is immense and inescapable. Leiber also gives voice to social anxieties and spotlights the disparities in cities. Moreover, he triggers our fundamental fear of the dark, that is, the great unknown. Perhaps, as said in "The Black Gondolier," mankind is just a "whim of that darkness" (33). *Our Lady of Darkness* is many things; one is a tribute to the Gothic tradition and the authors who sustained that tradition. We all owe tribute to Fritz Leiber for reanimating the Gothic tradition, for giving it new life in our modern city-scapes.

NOTES

1. Fritz Leiber, "Smoke Ghost," in *Night's Black Agents* (New York: Berkeley, 1978), 114. Hereafter cited in the text. The title of this book is taken from Shakespeare's *Macbeth* 3.2.53.

2. S. T. Joshi, "Passing the Torch: H. P. Lovecraft and Fritz Leiber," in *The Evolution of the Weird Tale* (New York: Hippocampus Press, 2004), 124.

3. Joel Lane, "No Secret Place: The Haunted Cities of Fritz Leiber," *Wormwood* no. 10 (Spring 2008): 18.

4. Lane, "No Secret Place," 32.

5. David Punter, introduction to *A Companion to the Gothic*, ed. David Punter (Oxford: Blackwell, 2000), viii.

6. Judith Wilt, *Ghosts of the Gothic: Austen, Eliot, and Lawrence* (Princeton, NJ: Princeton University Press, 1980), 5.

7. Alan Lloyd-Smith, *American Gothic Fiction: An Introduction* (New York: Continuum, 2004), 30.

8. Robert Mighall, "Gothic Cities," in *The Routledge Companion to Gothic*, ed. C. Spooner and E. McEvoy (London: Routledge, 2007), 56.

9. Arthur Machen, "The Great God Pan," in *The House of Souls* (New York: Knopf, 1922), 22.

10. H. P. Lovecraft, "He," in *Dagon and Other Macabre Tales*, ed. S. T. Joshi (Sauk City, WI: Arkham House, 1986), 267.

11. Jeffrey Andrew Weinstock, *Charles Brockden Brown* (Cardiff: University of Wales Press, 2001), 54.

12. Joshi, "Passing the Torch," 131.

13. Chris Baldick, introduction to *The Oxford Book of Gothic Stories*, ed. Chris Baldick (Oxford: Oxford University Press, 1992), xix.

14. Leiber, *Our Lady of Darkness* (New York: Orb, 2010), 9. Hereafter cited in the text.

15. Stephen King, *Danse Macabre* (New York: Gallery, 2010), 383.

16. Fred Botting, *Gothic* (London: Routledge, 1996), 160.

17. Sam Moskowitz, *Seekers of Tomorrow: Masters of Modern Science Fiction* (Westport, CT: Hyperion Press, 1974), 302.

18. Bruce Byfield, "Divination and Self-Therapy: Archetype and Stereotype in the Fantasies of Fritz Leiber" (M.A. thesis, Simon Fraser University, 1989), 27.

19. Stefan Dziemianowicz, "Contemporary Horror Fiction, 1950–1998," in *Fantasy and Horror*, ed. Neil Barron (Lanham, MD: Scarecrow Press, 1999), 203.

20. Michael E. Stamm, "Poetry of Darkness: The Horror Fiction of Fritz Leiber," in *Discovering Modern Horror Fiction II*, ed. Darrell Schweitzer (Mercer Island, WA: Starmont House, 1988), 20.

21. Leiber, "The Hound," in *Night's Black Agents*, 185. Hereafter cited in the text.

22. Joshi, "Passing the Torch," 131.

23. Leiber, "The Inheritance," in *Night's Black Agents*, 145. Hereafter cited in the text.

24. Leiber, "The Man Who Made Friends with Electricity," in *The Black Gondolier* (New York: E-Reads, 2003), 139. Hereafter cited in the text.

25. Leiber, "The Black Gondolier," 10. Hereafter cited in the text.

26. Barbara Freese, *Coal: A Human History* (Cambridge, MA: Perseus, 2003), 57.

27. Leiber, *The Dealings of Daniel Kesserich: A Study of the Mass Insanity at Smithville* (New York: Tor, 1997), 8. Hereafter cited in the text.

28. Leiber, "The Button Molder," in *Smoke Ghost and Other Apparitions* (Seattle: Midnight House, 2002), 243. Hereafter cited in the text.

29. Leiber, "Belsen Express," in *Heroes and Horror* (New York: Pocket, 1980), 104. Hereafter cited in the text.

30. Leiber, "Midnight by the Morphy Watch," in *Heroes and Horrors*, 156.

31. S. T. Joshi, "Science and Superstition: Fritz Leiber's Modernization of Gothic," in *Fritz Leiber: Critical Essays*, ed. Benjamin Szumskyj (Jefferson, NC: McFarland, 2008), 117.

32. Leslie Fiedler, *Love and Death in the American Novel*, rev. ed. (New York: Dell, 1966), 117.

33. Albert Camus, *Resistance, Rebellion and Death* (New York: Vintage, 1995), 67.

34. Leiber, "I'm Looking for Jeff," in *Smoke Ghost*, 138. Hereafter cited in the text.

35. Leiber, "Scream Wolf," in *The Second Book of Fritz Leiber* (New York: DAW, 1975), 137.

36. Leiber, "Dark Wings," in *Smoke Ghost*, 336.

37. Leiber, "Dark Wings," 336.

38. Leiber, "The Girl with the Hungry Eyes," in *Night's Black Agents*, 241. Hereafter cited in the text.

39. Marshall McLuhan, *The Mechanical Bride: Folklore of Industrial Man* (Corte Madera, CA: Gingko Press, 2002), 101. Leiber knew of this commentary, noting it in his foreword to *The Second Book of Fritz Leiber*, 9.

40. McLuhan, *The Mechanical Bride*, 101.

41. John Langan, "'Feed Me, Baby, Feed Me': Beyond the Pleasure Principle in Fritz Leiber's 'Girl with the Hungry Eyes,'" in *Fritz Leiber: Critical Essays*, 101–15.

42. Leiber, "Coming Attraction," in *Selected Stories*, ed. Jonathan Strahan and Charles N. Brown (San Francisco: Night Shade, 2010), 36.

43. Leiber, "America the Beautiful," in *Selected Stories*, 193.

44. Leiber, "America the Beautiful," 200.

45. Ursula K. Le Guin, "The Ones Who Walk Away from Omelas," in *The Wind's Twelve Quarters* (New York: Harper & Row, 1975), 275–84.

46. Robert Mighall, *A Geography of Victorian Gothic Fiction: Mapping History's Nightmares* (Oxford: Oxford University Press, 2003), 40.

47. Fiedler, *Love and Death*, 114.

48. Mario Praz, "Introductory Essay," in *Three Gothic Novels*, ed. Peter Fairclough (London: Penguin, 1986), 9.

49. Years past, I took photos of my son on the top of the South Tower observation deck with the smoggy city stretched out behind and below. He was squinting from the sun. There was no darkness. The day after the fall of the towers, I was teaching an early morning class. I went just in case. The students looked stunned and afraid. Some were missing. I do not remember what I said, but the students did not want to talk—they were like stone or rather glass ready to break, so I dismissed all. They left in groups holding one another. This was in Canada.

50. Leiber, "Black Glass," in *Smoke Ghost*, 105. Hereafter cited in the text.

51. Hannah Arendt, *The Jew as Pariah: Jewish Identity and Politics in the Modern Age* (New York: Grove Press, 1978), 251.

52. Campbell, introduction, *Smoke Ghost*, 2.

53. Leiber, "A Bit of the Dark World," in *Night's Black Agents*, 245. Hereafter cited in the text.

54. Herman Melville, "Hawthorne and His Mosses," in *Moby Dick: An Authoritative Text; Reviews and Letters by Melville, Analogues and Sources Criticism*, ed. Harrison Hayford and Hershel Parker (New York: W. W. Norton, 1967), 540.

55. Edgar Allan Poe, *Tales and Sketches*, ed. Thomas Ollive Mabbott (Cambridge, MA: Harvard University Press, 2000), 1.682.

56. M. R. James, *The Ghost Stories of M. R. James*, ed. Michael Cox (Oxford: Oxford University Press, 1986), 193.

57. Roger B. Salomon, *Mazes of the Serpent: An Anatomy of Horror Narrative* (Ithaca, NY: Cornell University Press, 2002), 104.

58. Campbell, "The Other Side," in *Waking Nightmares* (New York: Tor, 1991), 185–99.

59. See Rosemary Pardoe and John Howard, "Fritz Leiber's *Our Lady of Darkness*: Annotations," *Ghosts and Scholars* 21 (1996), http://www.waldeneast.fsnet.co.uk/annotations.htm (accessed July 23, 2013), for insightful notes on the many Gothic writers who appear in the novel.

60. T. E. D. Klein, "Children of the Kingdom," in *Dark Gods* (New York: Bantam, 1986), 3.

61. Ramsey Campbell, "Fritz Leiber," *Irish Gothic Horror Journal*, http://irishGothichorrorjournal.homestead.com/lostsouls.html#anchor_148 (accessed June 21, 2013).

62. Campbell, "All the Ghosts That Made Me," in *Ramsey Campbell, Probably*, ed. S. T. Joshi (Harrogate, UK: PS Publishing, 2002), 432.

63. Campbell. "Introduction: So Far," in *Alone with the Horrors* (New York: Tor, 2004), 13.

64. *Seven*, directed by David Fincher (September 22, 1995, New Line Cinema).

65. Eric Savoy, "The Rise of American Gothic," in *The Cambridge Companion to Gothic Literature*, ed. Jerrold E. Hogle (Cambridge: Cambridge University Press, 2002), 168.

66. Salomon, *Mazes*, 29.

Selected Bibliography

Aaron, Daniel. *The Unwritten War: American Writers and the Civil War*. New York: Knopf, 1973.

Armstrong, Karen. *A Short History of Myth*. London: Cannongate, 2005.

Ashley, Mike. *Algernon Blackwood: A Bio-Bibliography*. New York: Greenwood Press, 1987.

———. *Algernon Blackwood: An Extraordinary Life*. New York: Carroll & Graf, 2001.

Atwood, Margaret. *Strange Things: The Malevolent North in Canadian Literature*. Oxford: Oxford University Press, 1995.

Baker, Dorothy Z. *American Gothic Fiction: The Legacy of* Magnalia Christi Americana. Columbus: Ohio State University Press, 2007.

Bellin, Joshua David. *The Demon of the Continent*. Philadelphia: University of Pennsylvania Press, 2001.

Bergland, Reneé. *The National Uncanny: Indian Ghosts and American Subjects*. Hanover, NH: University Press of New England, 2000.

Berkove, Lawrence I. *A Prescription for Adversity: The Moral Art of Ambrose Bierce*. Columbus: Ohio State University Press, 2002.

Bierce, Ambrose. *A Much Misunderstood Man: Selected Letters of Ambrose Bierce*. Edited by S. T. Joshi and David E. Schultz. Columbus: Ohio State University Press, 2003.

———. *The Short Fiction of Ambrose Bierce*. Edited by S. T. Joshi, Lawrence I. Berkove, and David E. Schultz. 3 vols. Knoxville: University of Tennessee Press, 2006.

———. *A Sole Survivor: Bits of Autobiography*. Edited by S. T. Joshi and David E. Schultz. Knoxville: University of Tennessee Press, 1998.

Blackwood, Algernon. *Ancient Sorceries and Other Weird Stories*. Edited by S. T. Joshi. New York: Penguin, 2002.

———. *Best Ghost Stories of Algernon Blackwood*. Edited by E. F. Bleiler. New York: Dover, 1973.

———. *The Centaur*. London: Macmillan, 1911.

———. *The Complete John Silence Stories*. Edited by S. T. Joshi. Mineola, NY: Dover, 1997.

———. *Day and Night Stories*. New York: E. P. Dutton, 1917.

———. *The Empty House and Other Ghost Stories*. 1906. Kelly Bray, UK: House of Stratus, 2008.

———. *Episodes before Thirty*. New York: Dutton, 1923.

———. *The Wolves of God and Other Fey Stories*. London: Cassell, 1921.

Blight, David W. *Race and Reunion: The Civil War in American Memory*. Cambridge, MA: Harvard University Press, 2001.

Bloom, Clive. *Gothic Histories: The Taste for Terror, 1764 to the Present*. London: Continuum, 2010.

Botting, Fred. *Gothic*. London: Routledge, 1996.

Brown, Charles Brockden. *Edgar Huntly, or Memoirs of a Sleepwalker*. Edited by Philip Barnard and Stephen Shapiro. Indianapolis, IN: Hackett, 2006.

———. *Ormond; or, The Secret Witness*. Edited by Mary Chapman. Peterborough, ON: Broadview Press, 1999.

———. *Three Gothic Novels*. New York: Library of America, 1998.

———. *Wieland, or, The Transformation*. Edited by Philip Barnard and Stephen Shapiro. Indianapolis, IN: Hackett, 2009.

Camus, Albert. *The Myth of Sisyphus and Other Essays*. Translated by Justin O'Brien. New York: Vintage, 1995.

———. *The Rebel: An Essay on Man in Revolt*. Translated by Anthony Bower. New York: Vintage, 1956.

Cannon, Peter. *H. P. Lovecraft*. Boston: Twayne, 1989.

Chase, Richard. *The American Novel and Its Tradition*. Baltimore: John Hopkins University Press, 1980.

Colombo, John Robert. *Blackwood's Books: A Bibliography Devoted to Algernon Blackwood*. Toronto: Hounslow Press, 1981.

Condé, Maryse. *I, Tituba, Black Witch of Salem*. Translated by Richard Philcox. Charlottesville: University of Virginia Press, 2009.

Crow, Charles L. *American Gothic*. Cardiff: University of Wales Press, 2009.

Davidson, Cathy N. *The Experimental Fictions of Ambrose Bierce*. Lincoln: University of Nebraska Press, 1984.

Davidson, Cathy N., ed. *Critical Essays on Ambrose Bierce*. Boston: G. K. Hall, 1982.

De Forest, John W. *Witching Times*. New Haven, CT: College & University Press, 1967.

Dodds, Eric R. *The Greeks and the Irrational*. Berkeley: University of California Press, 1951.

Faust, Drew Gilpin. *This Republic of Suffering: Death and the American Civil War*. New York: Vintage, 2008.

Fiedler, Leslie. *Love and Death in the American Novel*. New York: Criterion, 1960.

———. *The Return of the Vanishing American*. New York: Stein & Day, 1968.

Forbes, Esther. *A Mirror for Witches*. Chicago: Academy Chicago Publishers, 1985.

Freud, Sigmund. "The 'Uncanny.'" In *Collected Papers*, vol. 4, edited by Ernest Jones and translated by Alix Strachey, 368–407. London: Hogarth Press, 1950.

Gaskell, Elizabeth. *Gothic Tales*. Edited by Laura Kranzler. New York: Penguin, 2000.

Ginsberg, Lesley. "Slavery and the Gothic Horror of Poe's 'The Black Cat.'" In *American Gothic: New Interventions in a National Narrative*, edited by Robert K. Martin and Eric Savoy, 99–128. Iowa City: University of Iowa Press, 1998.

Goddu, Teresa. *Gothic America: Narrative, History, and Nation*. New York: Columbia University Press, 1997.

Graves, Robert. *The White Goddess*. London: Faber & Faber, 1961.

Grenander, Mary E. *Ambrose Bierce*. New York: Twayne, 1971.

Halberstam, Judith. *Skin Shows: Gothic Horror and the Technology of Monsters*. Durham, NC: Duke University Press, 2000.

Hawthorne, Nathaniel. *Hawthorne's Short Stories*. New York: Vintage Classics, 2011.

———. *The House of the Seven Gables*. New York: W. W. Norton, 2006.

———. *The Scarlet Letter*. New York: Penguin, 2003.

Hill, Francis. *The Salem Witch Trials Reader*. New York: Da Capo Press, 2000.

Hurley, Kelly. *The Gothic Body: Sexuality, Materialism, and Degeneration at the Fin de Siècle*. Cambridge: Cambridge University Press, 2004.

Joshi, S. T. *The Evolution of the Weird Tale*. New York: Hippocampus Press, 2004.

———. *H. P. Lovecraft: A Life*. West Warwick, RI: Necronomicon Press, 1996.

———. *H. P. Lovecraft: The Decline of the West*. Mercer Island, WA: Starmont House, 1990.

———. *Lovecraft's Library: A Catalogue*. 3rd ed. New York: Hippocampus Press, 2012.

———. *A Subtler Magick: The Writings and Philosophy of H. P. Lovecraft*. Mercer Island, WA: Starmont House, 1996.

———. *The Weird Tale*. Austin: University of Texas Press, 1990.

Kafer, Peter. *Charles Brockden Brown's Revolution and the Birth of American Gothic*. Philadelphia: University of Philadelphia Press, 2004.

Karlsen, Carol F. *The Devil in the Shape of a Woman: Witchcraft in Colonial New England*. New York: W. W. Norton, 1987.

Kierkegaard, Søren. *Fear and Trembling and The Sickness unto Death*. Edited and translated by Walter Lowrie. Garden City, NY: Anchor, 1954.

King, Stephen. *Danse Macabre*. New York: Gallery, 2010.

Kneale, James. "From Beyond: H. P. Lovecraft and the Place of Horror." *Cultural Geographies* 13 (2006): 106–26.

Kristeva, Julia. *Powers of Horror: An Essay on Abjection*. New York: Columbia University Press, 1982.

Lawrence, D. H. *Studies in Classic American Literature*. London: Martin Secker, 1933.

Leiber, Fritz. *The Black Gondolier and Other Stories*. Edited by John Pelan and Steve Savile. New York: E-Reads, 2003.

———. *Conjure Wife*. New York: Tor, 1991.

———. *The Dealings of Daniel Kesserich: A Study of the Mass Insanity at Smithville*. New York: Tor, 1997.

———. *Heroes and Horror*. New York: Pocket, 1980.

———. *Night's Black Agents*. New York: Berkeley, 1978.

———. *Our Lady of Darkness*. New York: Orb, 2010.

———. *The Second Book of Fritz Leiber*. New York: DAW, 1975.

———. *Selected Stories*. Edited by Jonathan Strahan and Charles N. Brown. San Francisco: Night Shade, 2010.

———. *Smoke Ghosts and Other Apparitions*. Edited by John Pelan and Steve Savile. New York: E-Reads, 2001.

Levin, Ira. *Rosemary's Baby*. New York: Random House, 1967.

Lévy, Maurice. *Lovecraft: A Study in the Fantastic*. Translated by S. T. Joshi. Detroit, MI: Wayne State University, 1988.

Lloyd-Smith, Alan. *American Gothic Fiction: An Introduction*. London: Continuum, 2004.

Lovecraft, H. P. *The Ancient Track: The Complete Poetical Works of H. P. Lovecraft*. Edited by S. T. Joshi. San Francisco: Night Shade, 2001.

———. *The Annotated Supernatural Horror in Literature*. Edited by S. T. Joshi. Rev. ed. New York: Hippocampus Press, 2012.

———. *At the Mountains of Madness and Other Novels*. Edited by S. T. Joshi. Sauk City, WI: Arkham House, 1985.

———. *Collected Essays*. Edited by S. T. Joshi. 5 vols. New York: Hippocampus Press, 2004–6.

———. *Dagon and Other Macabre Tales*. Edited by S. T. Joshi. Sauk City, WI: Arkham House, 1986.

———. *The Dunwich Horror and Others*. Edited by S. T. Joshi. Sauk City, WI: Arkham House, 1984.

———. *The Horror in the Museum and Other Revisions*. Edited by S. T. Joshi. Sauk City, WI: Arkham House, 1989.

———. *Miscellaneous Writings*. Edited by S. T. Joshi. Sauk City, WI: Arkham House, 1995.

———. *Selected Letters*. Edited by August Derleth, Donald Wandrei, and James Turner. 5 vols. Sauk City, WI: Arkham House, 1965–76.

Machen, Arthur. *The House of Souls*. New York: Knopf, 1922.

———. *Selected Letters*. Edited by Roger Dobson, Godfrey Brangham, and R. A. Gilbert. Wellingbourough, UK: Aquarian Press, 1988.

———. *The Shining Pyramid*. New York: Knopf, 1925.

———. *Tales of Horror and the Supernatural*. New York: Pinnacle, 1983.

———. *The Three Impostors and Other Stories*. Edited by S. T. Joshi. Oakland, CA: Chaosium, 2001.

———. *The White People and Other Stories*. Edited by S. T. Joshi. Oakland, CA: Chaosium, 2003.

Mather, Cotton. *On Witchcraft*. Mineola, NY: Dover, 2005.

Midgley, Mary. *Wickedness: A Philosophical Essay.* London: Routledge Classics, 2001.

Morris Jr., Roy. *Ambrose Bierce: Alone in Bad Company.* New York: Crown, 1995.

Morrison, Toni. *Playing in the Dark: Whiteness and the Literary Imagination.* Cambridge, MA: Harvard University Press, 1992.

Moskowitz, Sam. *Seekers of Tomorrow: Masters of Modern Science Fiction.* Westport, CT: Hyperion Press, 1974.

Murdoch, Iris. *The Sovereignty of Good.* London: Routledge Classics, 2001.

Neal, John. *Rachel Dyer.* Amherst, NY: Prometheus, 1996.

Neiman, Susan. *Evil in Modern Thought: An Alternative History of Philosophy.* Princeton, NJ: Princeton University Press, 2002.

Northey, Margot. *The Haunted Wilderness: The Gothic and Grotesque in Canadian Fiction.* Toronto: University of Toronto Press, 1976.

Orians, G. Harrison. "New England Witchcraft in Fiction." *American Literature* 2 (March 1930).

Penzoldt, Peter. *The Supernatural in Fiction.* London: Peter Nevill, 1952.

Poe, Edgar Allan. *Essays and Reviews.* New York: Library of America, 1984.

———. *The Narrative of Arthur Gordon Pym of Nantucket.* New York: Penguin, 1980.

———. *Poe: The Complete Poems.* Edited by Richard Wilbur. New York: Dell, 1959.

———. *Tales and Sketches.* Edited by Thomas Ollive Mabbott. 2 vols. Urbana: University of Illinois Press, 2000.

———. *The Unknown Poe.* Edited by Raymond Foye. San Francisco: City Light Publishing, 1980.

Ringe, Donald A. *American Gothic: Imagination and Reason in Nineteenth-Century Fiction.* Lexington: University Press of Kentucky, 1982.

———. *Charles Brockden Brown.* Rev. ed. Boston: Twayne, 1991.

Salomon, Roger B. *Mazes of the Serpent: An Anatomy of Horror Narrative.* Ithaca, NY: Cornell University Press, 2002.

Savoy, Eric. "The Rise of American Gothic." In *The Cambridge Guide to Gothic Fiction,* edited by Jerrold E. Hogle, 167–88. Cambridge: Cambridge University Press, 2002.

Scarborough, Dorothy. *The Supernatural in Modern English Literature.* New York: G. P. Putnam's Sons, 1917.

Schaefer, Michael W. *Just What War Is: The Civil Writings of De Forest and Bierce.* Knoxville: University of Tennessee Press, 1997.

Starrett, Vincent. *Arthur Machen: A Novelist of Ecstasy and Sin.* Chicago: Walter M. Hill, 1918.

Sullivan, Jack. *Elegant Nightmares: The English Ghost Story from LeFanu to Blackwood.* Athens: Ohio University Press, 1978.

———, ed. *Lost Souls.* Athens: Ohio University Press, 1983.

Sweeney, Gerard M. "Beauty and Truth: Poe's 'A Descent into the Maelstrom.'" *Poe Studies* 4, no. 1 (June 1973): 22–25.

Thornton, Russell. *American Indian Holocaust and Survival.* Norman: University of Oklahoma Press, 1990.

Updike, John. *The Witches of Eastwick.* New York: Knopf, 1984.

Valentine, Mark. *Arthur Machen.* Bridgend, Wales: Seren, 1995.

Vuckovic, Jovanka. *Zombies: An Illustrated History of the Undead.* New York: St. Martin's Griffin, 2011.

Wagner, Karl Edward. "Sticks." In *Where the Summer Ends,* edited by Stephen Jones, 57–79. Lakewood, CO: Centipede Press, 2012.

Waugh, Robert H. *The Monster in the Mirror: Looking for H. P. Lovecraft.* New York: Hippocampus Press, 2006.

Weinstock, Jeffrey Andrew. *Charles Brockden Brown.* Cardiff: University of Wales Press, 2011.

Weisman, Richard. *Witchcraft, Magic, and Religion in 17th-Century Massachusetts.* Amherst: University of Massachusetts Press, 1984.

Wharton, Edith. *The Ghost Stories of Edith Wharton.* New York: Scribners, 1973.

Wilbur, Richard. "The House of Poe." In *The Recognition of Edgar Allan Poe: Selected Criticism since 1829*, edited by Eric W. Carlson, 255–77. Ann Arbor: University of Michigan Press, 1966.

———. Introduction to *Poe: The Complete Poems*, edited by Richard Wilbur, 7–40. New York: Dell, 1959.

Wilt, Judith. *Ghosts of the Gothic: Austen, Eliot, and Lawrence*. Princeton, NJ: Princeton University Press, 1980.

Wittgenstein, Ludwig. *Tractatus Logico-Philosophicus*. Translated by D. F. Pears and B. F. McGuiness. London: Routledge Classics, 2001.

Žižek, Slavoj. *Looking Awry: An Introduction to Jacques Lacan through Popular Culture*. Cambridge, MA: MIT Press, 1992.

Filmography

28 Days Later. DVD. Directed by Danny Boyle. 2003 (USA); Century City, CA: 20th Century Fox Home Entertainment, 2004.

Avatar. Film. Directed by James Cameron. Century City, CA: 20th Century Fox, 2009.

The Blair Witch Project. DVD. Directed by Daniel Myrick and Eduardo Sànchez. 1999: Montreal, QC: Alliance Films, 2007.

The Craft. DVD. Directed by Andrew Fleming. 1996; Culver City, CA: Columbia Pictures, 2000.

Forbidden Planet. DVD. Directed by Fred M. Wilcox. 1956; Burbank, CA: Warner Home Video, 2010.

Practical Magic. DVD. Directed by Griffin Dunne. 1998; Burbank, CA: Warner Home Video, 2009.

Rosemary's Baby. DVD. Directed by Roman Polanski. 1968; Hollywood, CA: Paramount Pictures, 2006.

Seven. DVD. Directed by David Fincher. 1995; Los Angeles, CA: New Line Home Video, Cinema, 2004.

The Village. DVD. Directed by M. Night Shyamalan. 2004; Burbank, CA: Buena Vista, 2005.

The Witches of Eastwick. DVD. Directed by George Miller. 1987; Burbank, CA: Warner Home Videos, 2006.

The Wizard of Oz. DVD. Directed by Victor Fleming. 1939; Burbank, CA: Warner Home Videos, 1999.

World War Z. Film. Directed by Marc Foster. Hollywood, CA: Paramount, 2013.

Index

Aaron, Daniel, 42, 52
abjection, 26 27
Abraham, Nicolas, 10
Acceptable Risk (Cook), 164
"The Affair at Coulter's Notch" (Bierce),
    36, 39, 42
"An Affair of Outposts" (Bierce), 39
African Americans, 143n115, 175
Algernon Blackwood: A Bio-Bibliography
    (Ashley), 94n1, 94n11
*Algernon Blackwood: An Extraordinary
    Life* (Ashley), 95n41
*Algernon Blackwood's Canadian Tales of
    Terror* (Colombo), 81, 96n59
"Alice Doane's Appeal" (Hawthorne), 165
"Alone" (Poe), 118
Ambrose Bierce: Alone in Bad Company
    (Morris Jr.), 54n2
"America the Beautiful" (Leiber), 194,
    194–195, 200
American Civil War, 17; Ambrose Bierce
    in, 35, 36, 37, 41, 53; Ambrose Bierce's
    non-fiction on, 36, 37–38; Ambrose
    Bierce's stories of, 2, 37, 38, 48, 51–52;
    deaths in, 36, 43; impact on the United
    States, 40, 53
American Holocaust (Stannard), 157n4
American Indian Holocaust and Survival
    (Thornton), 157n4
American Indians, 148, 159n37, 163;
    Apache, 145; colonizing Europeans'
views of, 145, 149, 165, 166; conflict
    with Europeans, 12, 159n37, 163;
    devastation of, 15, 18n13, 141n51, 145,
    146, 153, 155, 157n4, 159n43, 160n57,
    166; as Gothic image, 6, 13, 14,
    146–147, 149, 150–152, 153–154, 156;
    Lenni Lenape, 12; racist attitudes
    toward, 13, 96n59, 145, 146, 149, 150,
    152, 158n26, 159n35, 159n41; Tituba
    as, 175, 179n76; and white women's
    captivity stories, 13, 14. *See also*
    indigenous peoples
Ancient Peoples of the American Southwest
    (Plog), 161n69
Arendt, Hannah, 131, 135, 195
Armstrong, Karen, 81, 121
Arthur Mervyn (Brown), 2, 5–6, 6, 8,
    10–12, 16; begins the American urban
    gothic, 5, 15–16, 183; premature burial
    motif, 10; yellow fever in, 5, 10, 11, 16,
    183
Ashley, Mike, 79, 81, 83, 85, 87, 94n1,
    95n27
At the Mountains of Madness (Lovecraft),
    114, 117, 121, 126, 129, 131, 147, 156;
    and abomination, 135–136, 140n33;
    and existential loneliness, 108n24;
    setting as Ultima Thule, 136
Atwood, Margaret: on the Canadian
    wilderness, 82; on the Wendigo, 84
Auden, W. H., 103

About the Author

James Goho is an independent scholar and researcher with publications on the Gothic, social science studies in academic journals, and short stories in mainstream literary magazines. His interest in Gothic centers on its socio-historic context and its arousing of human dread. He earned a B.A. from the University at Buffalo and an M.A. from the University of Manitoba. He has published a number of essays on Gothic horror writers, including Edgar Allan Poe, H. P. Lovecraft, and Ramsey Campbell. The results of his social science research are found in such academic journals as *Medical Teacher* and *Journal of Distance Education*, and the book *Assessment and Evaluation in Higher Education* (2005), while his short fiction has appeared in *Descant*, *Grain*, and elsewhere. Goho has been a sessional instructor at the University of Manitoba, where he taught research methods, and was the director of research and planning at Red River College.